Here, There and Everywhere

A GEOGRAPHY SOURCE-BOOK

Compiled and edited by

John H. Beeston, B. A. (Hons. Geography) London

*Sometime Senior Geography Master at the Grammar School,
Ilkley, Yorkshire*

GEORGE G. HARRAP & CO. LTD

London   Toronto   Wellington   Sydney

First published in Great Britain 1972
by George G. Harrap & Co. Ltd
182-184 High Holborn, London WC1V 7AX

ISBN 0 245 50626 8

Composed in 11/12pt *Plantin type and printed
by Willmer Brothers Limited, Birkenhead
Made in Great Britain*

Preface

There have been many Travel Anthologies, but very few comprehensive selections from travel literature which have been specially designed for school use. This has been particularly the case since geography became more "scientific" in character.

Yet vivid description, full of life and colour and movement, comprising intimate studies of human life and endeavour, remains the basis on which school geography is built. A publication of the (former) London County Council affirmed, "Whatever method is adopted, descriptive teaching should predominate," while the Ministry of Education Pamphlet No. 39 (1960) declared that geography in school should be both descriptive and explanatory. The phrase "description explicative des paysages" recurs in the text.

Every teacher of geography has his or her own favourite portions of travel books and articles, but experience has shown that it is not always easy to have such extracts immediately available when required. The present writer, during his long teaching career (and since), accumulated a large number of suitable excerpts, and here he presents an edited selection from these, in the hope that they may be useful to those still engaged in the work. Emphasis has been placed throughout on those factors which seem likely to be of permanent significance, though notes have been added where desirable.

These extracts are of such a length and character that they may be used by the scholars themselves. Each portion could, it is believed, form the basis of a lesson or series of lessons, a piece of research, or a project. The collection could be used in any type of post-primary school, with any syllabus, scheme of work or text book, with all types of visual aids and with radio lessons. It is therefore felt that all such schools would find it an advantage to have at least one set.

It may be assumed that all books, periodicals, and newspapers quoted are, or were, published in London, unless otherwise stated.

JOHN H. BEESTON

Acknowledgments

In the preparation of this anthology, every effort has been made to ascertain which extracts are protected by copyright, and to trace the holders of such copyright. In those cases where no reply has been received permission to reproduce has been assumed.

If any rights have inadvertently been infringed, apology is offered and pardon requested.

Grateful acknowledgments are made to the following for permission to reproduce copyright material:

ALDUS BOOKS, Ltd (acting for Adprint, Ltd) and Miss Elspeth Huxley for extract 260.

GEORGE ALLEN and UNWIN, Ltd, and the respective authors for extracts 147, 305c, 309, 311b.

EDWARD ARNOLD (Publishers) Ltd and the respective authors for extracts 160 and 334a.

BBC PUBLICATIONS and the respective authors for eleven extracts from *Radio Times*, and twenty-three from *The Listener*.

ERNEST BENN, Ltd, and the respective authors for extracts 113 and 169 (both from books originally published by Fisher Unwin).

A. and C. BLACK, Ltd, and the respective authors for extracts 84b, 269a, 380b.

BLACKIE and SON, Ltd, and the respective authors for extracts 189 and 194.

THE BODLEY HEAD, Ltd, and the respective authors for extracts 66 and 313.

THE BRITISH and FOREIGN BIBLE SOCIETY and the respective authors for seventeen extracts from their magazine *The Bible in the World*.

THE BRITISH TOURIST AUTHORITY and the respective authors for nine extracts from their monthly magazine *In Britain*.

JONATHAN CAPE, Ltd, and the respective authors for extracts 151 and 285.

CASSELL and Co., Ltd, and the respective authors for extracts 206, 377c, 393.

W. and R. CHAMBERS, Ltd, and the respective authors for twenty-seven extracts from their former magazine *Chambers's Journal*.

CHRISTY and MOORE, Ltd (acting for Robert Hale, Ltd) and Bernard Newman, Esq., for extract 112.

THE CLARENDON PRESS and the respective authors and editors for extracts 6, 141, 182, 256a, 333.

CONSTABLE and Co., Ltd, and the respective authors for extracts 184, 235, 335b.

THE CONTEMPORARY REVIEW Co., Ltd, and the respective authors for extracts 200 and 226.

CURTIS BROWN, Ltd (acting for Michael Joseph, Ltd) and Herbert Hodge, Esq., for extract 316.

THE DAILY TELEGRAPH, Ltd, and the respective authors for extracts 58, 86, 108b, 140a, 241.

THE DALESMAN PUBLISHING Co., Ltd, Clapham, Lancashire, and William Langstaff, Esq., for extract 50.

SIR F. FRASER DARLING, for extract 262b.

PETER DAVIES, Ltd, and Bill Adams, Esq., for extract 18.

J. M. DENT and SONS, Ltd, and the respective authors for extracts 75, 78c, 79, 106, 120c, 135b.

GERALD DUCKWORTH and Co., Ltd, and the respective authors for extracts 111 and 358b.

E. P. DUTTON and Co., Inc., New York, for extracts 196, 201, 203, 205, 362, from the book *A Novelist's Tour of the World*, by Vicente Blasco Ibañez. Translated by Leo Ongley and Arthur Livingston. Copyright 1926, 1953 by E. P. Dutton & Co., Inc., publishers, and reproduced with their permission.

THE EAST ANGLIAN MAGAZINE, Ltd, and P. E. Evans, Esq., for extract 40.

FABER and FABER, Ltd, and the respective authors for extracts 60b, 156b, 170, 210.

THE GEOGRAPHICAL ASSOCIATION and the respective authors for extracts 38, 74, 173, 372.

STANLEY GIBBONS, Ltd, and A. N. Donaldson, Esq., for extract 215.

VICTOR GOLLANCZ, Ltd, and J. R. Ullman, Esq., for extract 385.

THE HAMLYN PUBLISHING GROUP, Ltd (acting for C. Arthur Pearson, Ltd) and the respective authors for extracts 150a and 157; acting for Odhams, Books Ltd, for extracts 102, 312, 321.

GEORGE G. HARRAP and Co., Ltd, and the respective authors for extracts 123, 137, 153, 172, 221, 314, 395a.

HARVARD UNIVERSITY PRESS and Douglas L. Oliver, Esq., for extract 284.

WILLIAM HEINEMANN, Ltd, and the respective authors for extracts 10 and 161.

HODDER and STOUGHTON, Ltd, and the respective authors for extracts 7, 85, 168, 227d, 327, 332, 339a, 354a.

HURST and BLACKETT, Ltd (Hutchinson Publishing Group) and Hans Helfritz, Esq., for extract 223.

HUTCHINSON and Co., Ltd (Hutchinson Publishing Group, Ltd) and the respective authors for extracts 150b, 175a, 298a, 339c.

JARROLDS PUBLISHERS (LONDON), Ltd (Hutchinson Publishing Group) and the respective authors for extracts 94b, 156a, 211.

JOHN JOHNSON and the executors of A. F. Tschiffely, Esq., for extracts 373a and 395b (from a book published by Heinemann, Ltd).

THE LUTTERWORTH PRESS and Gordon Cooper, Esq., for extract 19.

MACMILLAN and Co., Ltd, and the respective authors for extracts 16, 158b, 159, 208, 220, 222, 232b, 280a, 298b, 315, 323, 324, 339b, 344.

METHUEN and Co., Ltd, and the respective authors for extracts 28, 44, 71a, 78a, 103a, 120a, 134, 360, 373b, 376a, 383, 386.

JOHN MURRAY (Publishers), Ltd, and the respective authors for extracts 3, 117, 174b, 224, 374, 387b.

THE MUSEUM PRESS, Ltd (Sir Isaac Pitman and Sons, Ltd) and Rex W. Finn, Esq., for extract 22.

THE NATIONAL FEDERATION OF WOMEN'S INSTITUTES and the respective authors for the following extracts from their magazine *Home and Country* 2, 60a, 69, 188, 243, 250b, 343.

THE NEW STATESMAN and the respective authors for extracts 192 and 229.

THE NORTHERN IRELAND TOURIST BOARD for extract 26.

THE OBSERVER, Ltd, and the respective authors for extracts 78b, 145a, 254.

STANLEY PAUL and Co., Ltd (Hutchinson Publishing Group, Ltd) and the respective authors for extracts 237a, 305a, 356.

A. D. PETERS and Co. (acting for Chapman and Hall, Ltd) and Alec Waugh, Esq., for extract 294a.

RICH and COWAN, Ltd (Hutchinson Publishing Group, Ltd) and the respective authors for extracts 207, 227a, 240b.

ROUTLEDGE and KEGAN PAUL, Ltd, and the respective authors for extracts 162 and 311a.

THE ROYAL SCOTTISH GEOGRAPHICAL SOCIETY and H. M. Cadell, Esq., for extract 348 from the *Scottish Geographical Magazine*.

SAMPSON LOW, MARSTON and Co. (per B.P.C. Publishing, Ltd) and the respective authors for extracts 52, 255a, 335a.

THE SAVE THE CHILDREN FUND and the respective authors for the following extracts from their magazine *The World's Children:* 98, 101, 110, 178, 246 a and b.

THE SCOTSMAN and the respective authors for extracts 57 and 326.

CHARLES SCRIBNER'S SONS, New York, and A. J. Ruhl, Esq., for extract 359.
MARTIN SECKER and WARBURG, Ltd, and H. M. Vaughan, Esq., for extract 280b.
SEELEY, SERVICE and Co., Ltd, and the respective authors for extracts 155, 330, 378a, 380a.
SYNDICATION INTERNATIONAL (I.P.C. Services, Ltd) and the respective authors for twenty-eight extracts from their magazine *Homes and Gardens*.
WALKABOUT, Melbourne, Australia, and the respective authors for extracts 297, 302, 304, 307.
THE WHITETHORN PRESS, Ltd, Leeds, and the respective authors for extracts 49 and 268.
YORKSHIRE POST NEWSPAPERS, Ltd, and the respective authors for twenty-nine extracts from the *Yorkshire Post*.

Contents

The Oceans and their Islands

The Republic of Ireland and the United Kingdom

Continental Europe

Asia

Africa

Australia and New Zealand

North America, Central America and the West Indies

The Oceans and their Islands

1. Spitsbergen Background

Rising 1500 miles north-east of the Scottish coast is an archi-pelago of mountainous islands, the most northerly being within 600 miles of the North Pole. Of this group of islands the largest is West Spitsbergen, with an area of 15,000 square miles. It is generally supposed that there is a native population in Spitsbergen, but this is not so. In the archipelago are no Eskimos, Samoyedes, nor Lapps, and the population has con-sisted of recent years almost entirely of miners of various European countries, and (at one time) of an American mining settlement. . . .

These miners and more especially their wives and families must find the long Polar night trying. The period of darkness lasts 114 days; there are in addition forty days when the sun does not rise above the horizon, but when there is a brief period of twilight around noon. . . .

No tree, nor even bush, grows on Spitsbergen, but during the summer it is a land of great charm. . . . To those who have voyaged to the North Cape of Norway to view the midnight sun, low in the horizon, the midnight sun of Spitsbergen would be a revelation. It is high enough not only to shine but to impart heat. I recall more than one occasion when the warmest part of the twenty-four hours was at midnight. . . .

When I returned to the Scottish Highlands, I missed, even in the most beautiful places of the west, those breath-taking views of a land on which the sun never sets from March until August, and which Man, even now, enters at his peril.

SETON GORDON, in the *New English Review*

2. Vulcanism in Iceland

We started off on the main street of Reykjavik, past the English Book Shop and on past the National Theatre and the striking stone figure of the first settler, which, situated on a small hill, with Mount Esja in the background, dominate the city. Passing along by the harbour, packed with vessels from all over the world, we soon left the comparatively smooth, tarred roads of the city to join the rough, dusty road to Hveragerdi. For some way we followed the line of the insulated hot water pipes, bringing the famed hot water from the springs into the city. All the houses in Reykjavik are supplied with their resources; the water leaves the pumping station at 90 degrees Centigrade, and reaches the houses so hot that re-heating is unnecessary. . . .

We approached the vast Lava Desert, stretching as far as the eye can see and beyond, a grim reminder of past volcanic eruptions, now covered with a grey-green moss which softens the huge lumps of lava, with here and there clumps of bright flowering Thyme. We had been steadily climbing, and at last reached the top, leaving the grim lava behind. Below us, at the bottom of the steep hill, lay a beautiful green fertile valley; puffs of white steam popped up all over, and below we could see the small town of Hveragerdi, the centre of the glasshouse industry, heated by natural hot water. . . . Our friend drove us away up into the foothills, and we arrived at a geyser just bubbling to bursting point. They "blow up" with tremendous force, and this particular "display" lasted for about 10 minutes; it died away to gather up more energy and gush again after an interval of an hour.

LUCIE BISHOP, in *Home and Country*

3. The Polar Bear in Greenland Waters

It seems hardly right to call polar bears *land* animals; they abound here—110 geographical miles from the nearest land— upon very loose broken-up ice, which is steadily drifting into the Atlantic at the rate of 12 to 14 miles daily; to remain upon it would secure their destruction were they not nearly amphibious; they hunt by scent, and are constantly running across and against the wind, which prevails from the northward, so that the same instinct which directs their search for prey, also serves the important purpose of guiding them in the direction of the land and more solid ice. No instance is known of Greenland bears attacking men, except when wounded or provoked. A native of Upernivik, one dark winter's day, was out visiting his seal-nets. He found a seal entangled, and, whilst kneeling down over it upon the ice to get it clear, he received a slap on the back—from his companion as he supposed; but a second and heavier blow made him look smartly round. He was horror-stricken to see a peculiarly grim old bear instead of his comrade! Without deigning further notice of the man, Bruin tore the seal out of the net and commenced his supper. He was not interrupted; nor did the man wait to see the meal finished.

The Voyage of the "Fox" in Arctic Seas,
by F. L. M'LINTOCK

4. Shakespeare's "Still Vex'd Bermoothes"

Equidistant from the American ports of Charleston, Baltimore and New York, 700 miles out in the North Atlantic Ocean, lies the limestone island known as Great Bermuda, with its group of satellite islets, more than 300 in number but most of them no more than large-sized rocks. The total area of the Bermudas is only 29 square miles. Bermuda, as the group is collectively called ... features as the scene of Shakespeare's comedy "The Tempest"....

Sited sub-tropically, Bermuda possesses an almost perfect climate. It avoids the extreme of heat, but even in mid-winter it is never cold. It lies out of the paths of hurricanes and tornadoes. It is a green island, and tropic and temperate vegetation and flowers mingle in a profusion of colours. You can drive through long avenues of red hibiscus and pink and red oleanders, past fields that are white sheets of Easter lilies. The beaches are of palest sand flecked with red and amber coral. The island possesses neither snakes, scorpions nor wild beasts. The most you have to fear is an octopus while bathing....

Bermuda is highly prosperous, and yet manages to do without either industry or agriculture worth mentioning.... It is a colony of Britain and a tourist playground of the United States, yet its inhabitants, only 40,000[1] in all, maintain a sturdy independence of outlook. They are both pro-British and pro-American, but

[1]The estimated population in 1968 was 51,000.

above all pro-Bermudian.... The colony's domestic affairs are
controlled by a close-knit, local oligarchy, based on a narrow
property franchise and dominating every sphere of public and,
above all, commercial life.

DAVID FARRER, in the *English-Speaking World*

Note. Universal suffrage was introduced in 1966, and the Constitution
of June 1967 abolished all privileges attached to ownership of property.

5. The Gulf Stream

There are permanent currents in all the oceans but, perhaps
because of the large amount of shipping crossing it, the circulation of the North Atlantic is best known. "Circulation" is the
right word to use because the current system can be looked on as
a large circular eddy carrying water in a clockwise sense round
the ocean. In the southern part of the North Atlantic the current
flows from east to west (the North Equatorial Current). In the
west the Gulf Stream starts as a narrow, intense north-easterly
current slowly broadening but getting weaker until it becomes
the slow eastward motion known as the North Atlantic Drift.
Then some of the water flows north, to lose its identity in the
Barents Sea, but most of it trends gently southward in the east
to complete the circle. In the middle, the still centre, is the
Sargasso Sea.

The narrow, intense part of the Gulf Stream flows from west
of Cuba eastward through the Florida Straits. It is about 100
miles wide and about a mile deep, and it flows at about three
knots. This adds up to some thousands of millions of cubic feet
every second, but I am told that all the figures in the world do
not give as vivid an impression as does being at anchor in the
Stream, out of sight of land, with the water continually rushing
past like a strong tidal stream at the flood.

Three knots is a velocity to reckon with, even for liners like
the "Queens": in the days of sail it could be catastrophic.
Ponce de Léon, one of the first to describe the Florida Current,
as this part of the Gulf Stream is called, makes an understate-
ment when he records, in 1513: "We had great wind but could
not go forward but only backward."

HENRY CHARNOCK, in *The Listener*

6. The Azores

About 900 miles west of Portugal, on roughly the same latitude as Lisbon, lies a group of islands called the Azores. Rocky and of bold relief, they are of volcanic origin, and rest on a great ridge called the Dolphin Ridge, which rises from the bed of the Atlantic. The Azores belong to Portugal, and to that country most of their produce is sent. There are ten islands set out in three groups, the largest island being San Miguel, which is 41 miles long and 9½ miles wide. Ponta Delgada is the chief town of San Miguel. Ships call at Fayal Island, where there is a good harbour at Horta. Pico, in the central group, contains the highest mountain, Gran Pico, which rises to 7,600 feet above sea-level. This peak is composed of volcanic rocks, and small eruptions still disturb the area. Flores is the island where Sir Richard Grenville and his fleet took shelter before attacking the Spanish fleet. Tennyson, in his poem "The Revenge", gives an account of this sea-battle.

Over 30 inches of rain fall on the islands during the year, most of it in winter. Agricultural products are tobacco, apples, grain, oranges, pineapples and wine. Adequate rainfall nourishes grass for herds of dairy cattle, and good butter and cheese are produced. The population of the Azores is 232,000,[2] almost all of whom are engaged in farming or in dealing with the products of the land.

Vol. III of the *Oxford Junior Encyclopaedia*,
ed. LAURA E. SALT and GEOFFREY BOUMPHREY

Note. The number of islands in the Azores is usually given as nine, not ten.

7. Rolling Down to Rio

Day after burning day, and still the north-east trade held full and steady. On the sixth day after the snow-capped peak of Tenerife had fallen astern, we expected to see the outer islands of the Cape Verde group.

We knew that the atmosphere in the neighbourhood of the islands is often so thick with dust, carried across 500 miles of sea from the Sahara, that you may not see the land before

[2]The population in 1960 was stated to be 337,000.

you are almost upon it; so we kept a very sharp look-out.
About three o'clock, the long-awaited cry of "Land ho!"
was raised.... Yes, there was the land; and our anxiety was
almost justified, for the highest peaks of San Antonio seemed
to be almost overhead, while the lower part of the island
was still invisible. From the Cape Verde islands our course
lay nearly due south, and day after day "Cap Pilar" ambled
steadily through brilliant seas. She went as a saw through a
sheet of steel, with clouds of flying-fish scattering like sparks
from beneath her forefoot....

Two days later the wind failed. After weeks of the steady
drive of the north-easterlies—suddenly flat calm. She lay quite
still upon the sea, her canvas slatting as she rolled to the
long ocean swells. Then came the rain, with sudden puffs of
wind from every quarter, and clouds like boulders, rolling
upon us from all round the horizon; first on one tack, then
on the other.

Once again our whole outlook changed. Soon the north-
east trades were forgotten and the south-easterlies hardly
thought about. The crossing of this muggy strip of dead
air between the two trades—the notorious calms called the
Doldrums—became our only ambition; and day and night
we had to use every laborious artifice of sailing in a continual
struggle to gain even so much as a mile.

Night and day, with scarcely a pause, the rain fell out of a
sky with neither shape nor colour in it. Sometimes it rained
so hard that it was difficult for a man to breathe. Rain—
rain—rain! and hardly a murmur of wind to get us out of it.
In your bunk you lay sweating in the muggy heat. On deck
there was nothing to do but stand and look at the sails
hanging in ugly sodden bunches, like dirty dishcloths or a
scarecrow's overcoat....

After a day or two the clouds lifted, and the sun beat
upon us from a cloudless sky, till the pitch boiled and bubbled
from the seams in our decks. All day long the heat poured
down upon a helpless ship. She lay so lifeless that the fish
no longer came near her. All through the long day her idle
sails hung miserably till the dusk grew out of the sea to hide
their shame....

Then, after nearly fourteen days of calm, once more the
sky began to breathe. Softly from the south the wind came

in.... One moment it was a gentle whisper from due south, and the next it was at east-south-east and freshening. The ship burst into life. Sweetly the high sails filled and fell asleep. Gently the ship leaned over to the tiny wavelets, talking altogether, whispering of the south and the brave trade winds.... By dawn we were clear of every anxiety and bowling merrily into the South Atlantic.

The Voyage of the "Cap Pilar", by ADRIAN SELIGMAN

8. Life on Napoleon's Island

What is it like to live on St Helena, a small, remote island where history lies thick? It sounds idyllic, doesn't it? It's every escapist's dream, but dreams don't have to be lived in.

The remoteness is the first, the overwhelming fact to be faced. A great rock, towering from a vast and empty sea, St Helena lies in mid South Atlantic, over a thousand miles from any mainland. "Empty sea" is no exaggeration, for nowadays only about eight mail boats and about ten cargo boats call in a whole year. With no airport and the ships irregularly spaced, radio and cables are the only links with the outer world for weeks on end....

There are long stretches with no letters, no parcels, no coming and going, no change of scene, no new faces. Newspapers and magazines are far, far out of date, and orders from overseas take months to arrive. In such circumstances ... fresh meat is extremely scarce because of shortage of pasture, and usually appears only once a week; consequently fish, corned beef, rice, cheese, bread and vegetables are the staples for everyone....

Walking is fascinating, provided you don't mind hills, for the scenery is extraordinary and wildly varied. Dense woods, tilted pastures with rocky outcrops, flax fields with their clusters of wide ribbony leaves, farmland, valleys of striped rainbow sands, thorn-crusted cactus thickets and bare volcanic hills patch the island. What is more, everything is set at crazy angles, for the whole place is violently crumpled into steep hills and deep valleys. Except in the little port of Jamestown houses are widely scattered.

MEG HOYTE, in *Homes and Gardens*

9. Tristan da Cunha

Tristan's 230 inhabitants have only seven surnames among them—Green, Swain, Hagan, Rogers, Glass, Lavarello and Repetto. The founder of the settlement was William Glass, a Scots Corporal in the Royal Artillery, who, with his family and two other men, got permission to remain on the island in 1817 when the garrison was withdrawn.... Shipwrecked men, deserters and escapists gradually increased the population, and women were imported from St Helena and the Cape.... The island's only easily inhabitable and tillable land is a narrow plateau on the north side, some four miles long and half a mile wide.... In recent decades the islanders have allowed their pastoral and agricultural prospects to deteriorate steadily ... but the decline of the island's economy is not entirely due to wilful neglect. Basically, it has probably resulted from the change-over from sail to steam, which took the island out of the regular shipping lanes....

The only really outstanding virtue of the island men is their great skill as boatmen. They make their own rickety boats from odds and ends of wood, the frame being covered with canvas.... In addition to about ten of these canvas boats there is one lifeboat. In these frail but seaworthy craft the islanders make periodic visits to Inaccessible Island and Nightingale Island which lie some 20 miles south-west of Tristan and ten miles apart. These islands are visited for the purpose of collecting birds and eggs.... The fishing in Tristan waters is magnificent, many kinds of fish, including crayfish, being abundant. It is thus obvious that if any serious attempt is to be made to put Tristan life on a sounder basis it should come through fishing.

NORMAN HOWELL, in *Libertas*, Johannesburg

10. The Penguins of Antarctica

The penguins always excite fresh interest in everyone who sees them for the first time. Their resemblance to human beings is always noticed. This is partly due to the habit of walking erect, but there are truly a great many human traits about them. They are curious about any unusual object and will come a long way to see a man. When out on these excursions the leader of a party keeps them together by a long shrill squawk. Distant parties salute in this way and continue calling till they get pretty close. A party can be made to approach by imitating the call. Emperor penguins are very ceremonious in meeting other emperors or men or dogs. They come up to a party of strangers in a straggling procession, some big important aldermanic fellow leading. At a respectful distance from the man or dog they halt; the old male waddles close up and bows gravely till his beak is almost touching his breast. Keeping his head bowed he makes a long speech, in a muttering manner, short sounds following in groups of four or five. Having finished the speech, the head is kept bowed a few seconds for politeness' sake, then it is raised and he describes with his bill as large a circle as the joints of his neck will allow, looking in your face at last to see if you have understood. If you have not comprehended, as is usually the case, he tries again. By this time his followers are getting impatient. They are sure he is making a mess of it. Another male will waddle forward with dignity, elbow the first aside as if to say, "I will show you how it ought to be done", and goes through the whole business again.

JAMES MURRAY, in the Appendix to the book
Heart of the Antarctic, by SIR ERNEST SHACKLETON

11. Mauritius

The island of Mauritius ... is shaped like a pear and is of volcanic origin, ringed with reefs of white coral upon which the long, blue rollers of the Indian Ocean break with a thunderous roar.... The crown of the island is a volcanic mount, with a crater in the middle of it—a deep, round crater, known as Le Trou aux Cerfs, which once belched fire and brimstone but now is full of green undergrowth.... Looking down into its shadowy depths, we saw a group of Indian women washing their clothes in the still, dark pool which lies at the bottom of the crater.... They looked like a flock of brightly-coloured birds in their red and blue and yellow saris....

Not far from Port Louis, the only large town, is a very fine racecourse, a natural stadium, beautifully situated amongst

sloping hills. . . . The crowds who throng the course are of
every colour and are attired in every kind of fashion from the
Parisian gowns of the French ladies to the sarong of the
Malay.

Sugar is the staple industry of Mauritius. . . . Wherever
one goes there are forests of sugar-cane with purple stems,
dark-green leaves, and feathery pink flowers. The cane grows
from twelve to fifteen feet high and makes an impenetrable
jungle. Cyclones are the chief danger to the valuable crops,
but fortunately these are rare. . . . During French rule, slaves
were employed in the plantations, but when the slaves
were liberated it was necessary to import Indians to work in
the cane. . . . Now the Indians make up the majority of the
population. Their huts and villages can be seen in all parts
of the island, and each little village has its mosque or temple
with a coloured dome.

D. E. STEVENSON, in *Chambers's Journal*, Edinburgh

Note. Mauritius (about 800,000 people) became an independent member of the Commonwealth in 1968.

12. The Seychelles

This Crown Colony lies about 1,000 miles east of Zanzibar,
out in the blue wastes of the Indian Ocean. The group of
about a hundred islands is spread over an area several
hundreds of miles wide, and is a veritable wonderland of
beauty.

The Seychelles are not easy of access, for owing to the
rocky nature of the central islands it has not been practicable
up to the present to build an aerodrome. The only way to
reach them from East Africa is on the occasional steamer
which plies from Mombasa to Bombay. It is very easy, if one
does not plan the return voyage carefully, to be stranded on
the islands for a number of weeks.

One cannot easily forget the approach by sea to the central
island of Mahé. It is a view of rare and enchanting beauty.
Towering up behind the little harbour of Port Victoria are
mountains which reach a height of 3,000 feet. The huge granite
slabs near the summit were swathed in mist, but down below
the sun was glinting on the brilliant green of coconut planta-

tions, and the bright yellow of some of the most wonderful beaches in the world.

This was the same view seen by the old French buccaneers and privateers as they came in under sail so many years ago, and later by a succession of political exiles. . . . My companion in the Governor's launch pointed out to me Sans Souci, the Governor's country residence, tucked away up on the mountain side. . . . The islands were uninhabited until 1768, although the pirates of the Indian Ocean used them as a base for operations over a wide area, and even in these modern days men are still looking for hidden treasure.

REV. F. J. BEDFORD, in *The Bible in the World*

13. Using the Trade Winds Today

The dhows from Somalia, Oman, Kuwait, Persia, Pakistan and Cutch are sailing home on the south-west monsoon on the blue waters of the Indian Ocean—the only ocean in the world where there is a complete reversal of wind-direction during the year. The dhows, with their triangular lateen sails and in all their shapes and sizes, have been coming and going to and from Mombasa, Dar-es-Salaam and Zanzibar for 2,000 years. Their numbers, regrettably, are diminishing. Nearly 300 came to Zanzibar alone ten years ago; this year less than 100 have arrived and gone.

As always, the craft and their crews brought an added touch of colour to already colourful shores—the dhows with their Somali crews in multi-coloured turbans or in embroidered caps; Arab crews in orange turbans, with flowing beards, and wearing embroidered daggers; Persian crews in white robes bring carpets, dried fish, salt and ghee, and sail away with coconuts, cloves, coconut oil, and adventurous passengers who have no shelter but a piece of sail cloth to protect them from the winds and the rain.

In a bad year as many as ten dhows fail to arrive home and are lost to the sea without human witness. The dhows sail with the wind, and the largest is not more than 200 tons. Some of them nowadays have diesel engines which are used to bring the little ships in and out of port, and with a strong wind they can sail from Zanzibar to the Persian Gulf in twelve days. The crews are the inheritors of a Columbus tradition, but there is a fear that with prosperity from oil in Kuwait and throughout the Persian Gulf the ambition to sail south will diminish.

DOUGLAS WILLIS, in *The Listener*
(in June 1955)

14.   The Cocos-Keeling Islands[3]

Situated midway between Ceylon and Australia, and 600 miles south-west of Sumatra, the little group of coral atolls known as the Cocos-Keeling Islands suddenly sprang from obscurity to front-page news when, in 1945, it was announced that the R.A.F. had established an air base there. . . .

Dusk was falling as I left Perth, in West Australia, to fly to Ceylon in a "Skymaster" of R.A.F. Transport Command. Dawn came and through an opening in the clouds I saw a complete circle of breakers which quickly turned into an incomplete ring of green islands surrounding a placid lagoon of varying shades of blue. This was the Cocos, and soon we came in to land on the 2,000-yards-long steel mesh runway which is surely one of the airstrip wonders of the world.

The story of the link-up of the Cocos Islands with the British Commonwealth is the story of the Clunies-Ross family's connection with them since 1827. Here was no annexation of a piece of territory and the sending out of settlers to populate it. Rather it is the story of the achievements of one man, John Clunies-Ross, who built up a prosperous and happy little community on a deserted island and prevailed upon the British Government to accept it as part of a rapidly growing Empire. . . .

The social system founded by the first "King of the Cocos" was a scheme for social security existent long before social security in Great Britain. It is based upon six chief principles, namely: employment for all; optional retirement at the age of 65 on half-pay; free medical attention; care of the fatherless and of widows; a high standard of living; and a simple code of laws.

SYDNEY MOORHOUSE, in the
Canadian Geographical Journal, Ottawa

[3]The official title is now "The Cocos (Keeling) Islands".

15. The Coconut-Palm in the South Seas

What a boon to the South Sea Islander is the coconut-palm; in fact without it, the low coral atolls in the South Pacific would be uninhabitable to man. It furnishes him with drink and meat. The ripe nut, the copra of commerce, is food for man either raw or grated and mixed with other foods, as well as food for fowl and pigs and fish-bait. It provides oil for the hair and skin. The dried and polished shell makes water-bottles and oil flasks. The fibre which surrounds the nut in the husk is twisted into cord, used for every purpose where cord or rope is needed, such as binding together the rafters and posts of huts, and the timbers of canoes. The sheath at the base of the leaf resembles a coarse sacking. The leaf makes an outside layer for the thatch, a coarse basket, and mats for the floor. The midrib is used for fence palings and house walls. The dried leaves are bunched together and tied with green ones for torches. The trunk of the trees is used for posts and rafters of houses.

Summer Isles of Eden, by FRANK BURNETT

16. The Islands Around Tahiti

Whoever approaches Tahiti from the north passes between a crowd of coral islets, each of which is a ring, or sometimes a sort of horseshoe, of grass and low shrubs scarcely rising above high-water mark, and enclosing a smooth lagoon. Some are tiny, some a mile or more in circumference. Some have a surface only a few yards wide, others are broader and higher, with soil enough to support rows of coconut palms. Islands of this type are called Atolls ... and their shape has usually been explained by supposing them to have been built up along the edges of a submarine volcanic crater, the rest of which is filled by the lagoon.[4] Most of these atolls are un-inhabited, but those large enough to have plenty of coconuts and perhaps other fruit-bearing trees can support a certain population, who live off the fruit and the crustaceans they find on the reef, and the fish they catch in the lagoon; and by collecting the mother-of-pearl shells and selling the coco-

[4]There are other theories regarding the formation of atolls.

nuts for copra to any trading ship that comes their way. Strange and picturesque are these little specks of islands in the vast ocean.

Memories of Travel, by VISCOUNT BRYCE

17. Hawaiian Paradise

Hawaii is fabulous, incredible, colossal, and the whole thing is done in Technicolour. A professor friend who accompanied me on the trip looked back on the hills bedded in cloud, the rain clearly visible a few hundred feet away, the sun streaming down over us, the mixed Caucasian-Chinese-Japanese-Korean-Hawaiian-Filipino couples surfboarding as if they hadn't a care in the world. "Beautiful," he said, "but theoretically impossible."

Now Hawaii and its 500,000[5] people of a dozen races have proved to the American Congress that it is not only actually happening but that it is theoretically possible.... This island-cluster paradise was ... organized as a Territory of the United States in 1900 after a petition to Congress made by its Government[6].... It has a lower illiteracy rate than the average American State. It has had a constitutional government for more than 100 years. It exceeds three States in land area and four in population....

Hawaiians are proud that they have no race problem. In their restaurants, clubs, dance halls and homes I have seen a dozen races mingle with no sense of strangeness or inhibition. One-third of all marriages in Hawaii are between different racial types. The combination of Hawaiian, Caucasian and Oriental can produce most exquisite physical specimens, as a short walk in Honolulu or along Waikiki beach can confirm....

Pineapple, sugar and tuna fish are not the only exports from Hawaii.... Cane fibre insulation, honey, coffee, wearing apparel and hula dancers are all among Hawaii's contribution to the welfare and happiness of nations.... In the

[5]In 1968 the population of the Hawaiian Islands was stated to be 738,000.
[6]In 1959 it became the fiftieth state of the U.S.A.

middle of the Pacific, it is the crossroads of all air traffic from North and South America to the Far East.

S. L. SOLON, in the *News Chronicle*

18. Clipper Race off Pitcairn

It was mid-morning when we sighted Pitcairn Island. There was a piping wind and we were running fast. A little way astern another clipper followed. She'd been there yesterday, and all the starry night. She was so close that we could see the long lift and the pitch of her sharp cutwater, and almost hear the breaking music of her bow-wash. . . . There was not anywhere a patch of colour on her. She was a tall white bird, fast hovering at our heel. Our Old Man scowled at her. And we scowled, too, fearing what he would do. Just thirty days we'd been at sea. The hard-tack was all weevils. The pork was rancid. Oh, pineapples, oh, oranges! And then of course, the Old Man did just what we feared he'd do. We damned him mightily. And yet, we did not damn him in our hearts. A sailor may be hungry, but he's a sailor still.

The islanders had seen us and were coming off to meet us. Their boats were stacked with fruit. We saw their piles of golden oranges, and yellow bunches of bananas, and heaps of sweet green coconuts all full of luscious milk, and the green leaves of mellow pineapples. And our Old Man sailed on! . . . And on came that tall white clipper after us. You don't catch clipper captains halting in a race to let their crews munch fruit! . . . We raced her two more days, then lost her in a wet wind from the westerly. She'd never gained a foot.

Ships and Women, by BILL ADAMS

19. Easter Island

Easter Island, or Rapanui, is located in the eastern part of the South Pacific Ocean, about 1,400 miles east of Pitcairn and about 2,000 miles west of Chile. Its area is about fifty square miles, and it has been aptly described as a heap of stones and lava. Lonely and desolate, it belies its attractive name, given to it by its first European discoverer, the Dutch Admiral Roggeveen, because he came across it on Easter Day, 1722.

I would certainly not recommend Easter Island as an escapist haunt, even if the Chilean Government, to whom it belongs, would agree to the presence of a stranger there. This is unlikely, for the island is now used as a convict settlement. Apart from this, however, it offers no romantic South Sea environment. It has no harbours, no trees except a few fig trees, and no running water. Cisterns, wells, and a few springs of fresh water on the beach, uncovered at low tide and fed from the lakes in the extinct craters, furnish the water supply. Some of its volcanic peaks reach an altitude of 1,800 feet.

The climate certainly is almost ideal, being moist and temperate, the south-east trade wind blowing for the major part of the year. Bananas, sugar, cotton, tobacco, sweet potatoes, melons, pumpkins, pineapples, maize and tomatoes are grown in small quantities. More than three-fourths of the island is pasture land, the rest being covered with broken lava.

The redeeming feature of this otherwise most uninteresting spot is the vast collection of statues made of lava cut from the crater of a volcano. They number over five hundred and fifty.... These gaunt figures have puzzled investigators from the first day they were seen, and the secret of their erection remains a mystery.

Isles of Romance and Mystery, by GORDON COOPER

The Republic of Ireland
and the United Kingdom

20. Southern Ireland

You should linger in Ireland, walk, or better still ride the country roads, to receive what must be missed by the visitor who flies through in a high-speed car on the fine main roads. It is away from these that the hinterlands lie, where there are no strangers and faces are friendly and interested, and you must salute and be saluted.

The swift traveller, indeed, will see plenty of beauty—the greenest grass in the world in Meath and Kildare, where cattle fatten, and limestone soil makes bone for exquisite young horses; brown bog on the central plain of Ireland, lovely in May with white bog-cotton, sunlit, wind-blown, lovely in different ways at other seasons; the Curragh of Kildare, a natural training ground for men or horses and rarely failing to provide a beautiful picture of racehorses exercising. These roads lead to the spectacular beauty of Ireland, of lovely coastline and islands, mountains, lakes, rivers, green pastures. . . .

Irish winters are generally soft and mild—softer and milder the further south you go. Kerry, "facing America", with the softest light of all, is a gardener's paradise. There everything grows luxuriantly and wondrous tall. Great fuchsia hedges hang rich, blood-red drops against pale Atlantic bays. An odd rose, pansies, primulas, stocks and other flowers bloom in a winter garden; the birds sing the New Year in, the gorse is then already sheets of gold.

PAMELA HINKSON, in *Homes and Gardens*

21. The Lakes of Killarney

There are three lakes; the largest, Lough Leane (or, the Lower Lake), a sheet of water five miles in length by half as much in width, is dotted with some thirty islands and islets. The charm of these lakes is due to the blending of mountain and lake, wood and running water, and owes no small measure of its effect to the wealth and variety of the vegetation. The "Arbutus unedo" (Strawberry tree) is native here, and ferns grow in great profusion. The gleaming scars on the mountain sides peep out of a smother of greenery, and their feet trail it after them as they dip into the waters below; and where the woods fail, their place is taken by an emerald setting of soft green grass.

from the volume "Europe" in *Stanford's Compendium*
by G. G. CHISHOLM

22. The Western Coastlands of Ireland

The counties of Limerick and Clare comprise the lower basin of the Shannon, which divides them, and are on the flat side.... Limerick, where the Shannon becomes tidal, has long been a port. Fifteen miles away is Shannon Airport, but in Limerick one is ever conscious of the past, for the city has had a stormy history and has seen much war.... Like Rineanna (the site of the airport), Ardnacrusha, where the Shannon hydro-electric works were placed, is in Clare....

Galway is the gateway to the central west—a city which has a somewhat foreign look, and which certainly has a long history of trade with Spain. It lies at the seaward end of the twenty-seven miles of Loch Corrib, and the closely-packed salmon waiting to ascend the weir to the lakes is a local spectacle. Beyond Galway Bay lie the Aran Islands, which may be reached by steam-boat, and on which life is still entirely Gaelic in character. The road from Galway to the west runs close to Corrib through Iar Connacht to Oughterard ... westwards from here it aims at Connemara, passing Ballynahinch, to the south of which lies the much-pictured Roundstone harbour. Connemara is probably Ireland's second best-known tourist magnet; though properly it is no larger than the Isle of Anglesey, it contains a wealth of mountain and marine scenery, with the Twelve Bens dominating the landscape. The local capital is Clifden, near where the first transatlantic flight terminated....

North of Connemara is more mountain country, leading to

the holy hill, Croagh Patrick, overlooking Clew Bay with its thousand islets ... West Mayo has many of the characteristics of Connemara; North Mayo has grand cliff scenery; Sligo holds Yeats's Isle of Innisfree.

Introducing Ireland, by REX W. FINN

23. The Peaceful Shannon

There are over a hundred and twenty navigable miles of the Shannon, widely meandering through shamrock green meadows or flowing deeply between dark trees. There are only six locks and the Shannon must be the finest cruising area in the whole of the British Isles, with delightful rural lakes, strung like aquamarines along the silver thread of the river.

Two of them, Lough Ree, sixteen miles long by as much as six miles wide, and Lough Derg, which is fifty square miles, are really inland seas. In Lough Derg you could put the whole of the Broads, which are shared by over five thousand craft, whereas on the Shannon waterway there are not more than one hundred cruisers for hire and about fifty private yachts. The river no longer carries commercial traffic. The sad story is similar to that of the English inland waterways. Railways deliberately competed along the same lines of communication as the river and the canals, and the waterways gradually declined.... The Shannon is such a truly rural river, even the two power stations are fuelled with peat, and only two riverside communities have populations of over 1,200—Athlone, at the heart of Ireland, a centre of communications and a market town, and the city of Limerick at the head of the great Shannon estuary.

The most famous of the Shannon beauty spots is not on the Shannon (in this article I am sure an Irishism may be forgiven). It is Lough Key on the large tributary of the Shannon known locally as the Boyle Water. The lake is dotted with small islands covered with smooth domes of trees. It is said that if these are felled unwisely, winter winds will rip an opening and tear down these little woods.

ANNE BOLT, in *Homes and Gardens*

24. Wealth from Ireland's Bogs

Ireland's bogs, which for centuries have been a vehicle for ballad composers, poets and artists, are now humming with great industrial activity.... Thousands are employed every year in winning turf, as well as in transporting and distributing it, while numerous other industries are benefiting by the turf 'Rush'....

There are over 4,700 square miles of bogs in Ireland, representing one-eighth of its entire area. From these bogs are cut the peat, or turf as it is called in Ireland, which keep the nation's domestic and industrial fires burning. The Turf Development Board got the toughest assignment, namely to exploit the Bog of Allen, which occupies most of the midland counties.... The aim is to produce 1,000,000 tons of turf per year when mechanical cutting is in full operation. Nor is it intended that this machine-won turf shall interfere with the individual turf-cutters, who now produce 3,500,000 tons a year and sell in the open market what they do not consume themselves. More than half the machine-won turf will be used to generate electricity in power-plants built right on the bogs, for it is the opinion of competent engineers that good-quality turf is equal to coal for steam raising....

Already a thriving industry has been built up in peat-moss litter, which is obtained easily from the upper layers, or top-soil, of the bogland. The screened coarse litter is used for stabling, and has three times the absorptive power of straw. Medium moss, or mull, is used as a horticultural fertilizer, and the fine mull for packing purposes.

PATRICK DOYLE, in *Chambers's Journal*, Edinburgh

25. Dublin's Fair City

Dublin lies beautifully between the mountains and the sea. Her coast-line has an Italian air; laid out beside a bay blue as an Italian bay, under dove-grey skies or silver and golden mists, she is ever beautiful. The Irish air is soft as silk, and the whole feeling of Ireland as you come to her is gentle.... Yet Dublin is historically the least Irish of Ireland's cities. Her position in the centre of the country's east coast marks her out as the natural gateway as much for invasion as for trade, and century after century the sea "vomited floods of foreigners into Eireann" through her. Each successive wave of invasion has left its mark on the city and a legacy of alien posterity. . . .

Dublin, like Belfast, stands at the mouth of a river valley: the Liffey, although not such a useful river as the Lagan, is a fine stream, and its estuary in Dublin Bay makes a commodious harbour. Although it is true that Dublin Bay cannot be compared with Belfast Lough as a haven for ships, yet its sweep, which has often called forth comparisons with the Bay of Naples, is truly majestic, and protected as it is, by the promontory of Howth, from the north and north-east winds that blow down the Irish Sea, it affords secure anchorage. This natural harbour has been vastly improved by man. . . .

Dublin cannot be classed as a manufacturing city. Its largest industry is the world-famous Guinness's brewery which occupies a huge site on Victoria Quay in the north-west corner of the Liberties. . . . Dublin is also renowned for its poplin, an industry introduced by the Huguenots in 1693; but the greater part of the city's energies are devoted to the transit trade, livestock being the principal commodity.

Countries of the World, ed. SIR JOHN HAMMERTON

26. Belfast and its Docks

Belfast's name—BEL, an entrance or ford; FEARSAD, a sandbank—bespeaks its origin, and the opportune linking up of the present City Hall with Donegall Street and Chichester Street epitomizes its development past and present.

What Garden of Remembrance more fitting, then, than the City Hall Gardens, the old-time cherry garden of Belfast Castle only 160 years ago, to recast the apotheosis of an obscure hamlet into quadruple honours as (1) the Capital of Northern Ireland (2) the eighth city in the British Isles (3) the United Kingdom's sixth port, and (4) the world's great linen centre! All achieved within three much interrupted centuries.

In 1603 (when Belfast was presented to Arthur Chichester[1], a Devonian, then Governor of Carrickfergus) its only feature was the ford across the then shallow Lagan (near the present Queen's Bridge), communicating between the Antrim and

[1]His heir became Earl of Donegall.

C

Down counties. So shallow was the river for even two centuries later that only the smallest craft could reach the town at high tide. . . .

Belfast's city and its spacious docks have risen literally from the mud of its meandering shallow river. The rise and fall of the tide is pencilled in its subsoil only six feet down, and may be observed in the Blackstaff stream as far inland as Great Victoria Street, adjoining the Great Northern Railway terminus. Hence, all Belfast's magnificent modern edifices—in fact, any erections except cottages—have piles as foundations. So the central Belfast of today is essentially a city on stilts. To make their spacious harbour the Belfastians carved and channelled the silt as a child carves out castle and canals on the sands. So has been achieved access at all tides to great ships drawing over 30 feet to quayage extending seven miles, and with dock railways of 17 miles.

The Ulster Guide (in a chapter by ALFRED S. MOORE)

Note. In recent years, Belfast has been unable to maintain the ratings indicated in the second paragraph above.

27.   The Giant's Causeway

When I was a small boy at school, Ireland was for me a romantic green country lying beyond the Irish Sea, off the west coast of Britain. I always remembered its shape from its resemblance to a sheep-dog lying on its side, and this memory assisted me in my geography lesson, when required to draw a map of the British Isles. Beyond that I knew very little about the Emerald Isle, except that it rained there very frequently, and that Ireland was noted for its production of potatoes and flax. But two names did capture my imagination: one a lovely rolling name, MacGillycuddy's Reeks, which I learned were a range of mountains in the south-western corner, on one of the dog's hindlegs; the other was the Giant's Causeway. . . . Now the Giant's Causeway is for me no longer merely a picture in a book, a name on a map, for recently I paid it a visit. . . .

The Causeway is made up of three sections, the Grand, Middle, and Little Causeways, and from an elevation I could distinguish the curious geometrical formations that have puzzled geologists for centuries, each multi-sided segment sitting neatly among its fellows as the pieces in a child's box of bricks. It has been said that the Causeway contains more than 35,000 pentagonal, hexagonal, and polygonal columns, the product of volcanic eruption, and subsequent cooling, untold ages ago. But whether or not this is a fact, it is surely the surrounding scenery as much as the Causeway itself which makes this portion of the Antrim coast so delightful—the broad horizons of sea and sky, the mountains, and the towering cliffs rising sheer above the Atlantic.

GUY PRIEST, in *Chambers's Journal*, Edinburgh

28. The Isle of Man

Many people associate only three things with the Isle of Man: tailless cats, crowds of holiday-makers, and the T.T. Motor-Cycle Races. Only those who have visited the island—and by that is meant those who have explored its countryside and not merely stayed in Douglas—realize that within its narrow limits the Isle of Man has scenery comparable with the finest to be found in the British Isles, with a background of history and tradition as different from that of England as if it were a foreign country. . . .

Although the island reflects the scenery of the surrounding kingdoms, it is no mere soulless imitation it offers, but a countryside of mountains, hills, glens and moors, and a varied coastline ranging from a low-lying, sandy shore to precipitous cliffs 1,000 feet in height, invested with an individuality and charm which is wholly and unmistakably Manx. . . .

There are no medieval manor-houses, the majority of the larger houses being either modern or not earlier than the eighteenth century, but there are two splendid castles: one at Peel, which is roofless, but otherwise in a fine state of preservation, and one at Castletown, which is the most perfect example of medieval military architecture in the British Isles. Both were royal castles, for the Kings of Mann . . . did not encourage their followers to build castles and so store up trouble in the shape of rebellious barons. . . .

Many places in the British Isles have been likened to the Bay of Naples, but none with so much justice as Douglas Bay . . . Douglas is not only a holiday resort, but the seat of the

Insular Government, and the modern home of a Parliament
which is the oldest in the world.[2]

In Praise of Manxland, by MAXWELL FRASER

29.   The Attractions of Wales

Caernarvon was the most important of the six castles built
by King Edward I in North Wales. The others include Conway,
Harlech and Beaumaris, and all of them incorporate the latest
strategical devices of the closing years of the thirteenth century,
a period when the medieval science of fortification is generally
acknowledged to have reached its peak. These, together with
the fortresses of Pembroke and Caerphilly (which, with the
sole exception of Windsor, is the greatest in all Britain) have
earned for Wales the title of "the land of castles". But the
ancient Principality is famous for other things besides turrets
and battlements: the beauty of its hills, mountains and river
valleys, its glorious coastal scenery and sandy beaches, gardens
like those of Bodnant and Powis, the treasures of the National
Museum of Wales at Cardiff, and even the curious little railways which wind their way into the hills—indeed to the very
summit of Snowdon. Wales is also noted for its singers; it is the
land of song as much as it is the land of castles, as anyone can
testify who has attended the Royal National Eisteddfod or the
International Eisteddfod at Llangollen. And this very word
"eisteddfod" reminds us that the Principality has no more
precious heritage than the Welsh language itself. No wonder
these people are great singers—listen to them talking in the
market-place and you will realize that there is music in their
very speech.

In Britain

30.   From the Top of Snowdon

There we stood on the Wyddfa (the summit of Snowdon),
in a cold bracing atmosphere, though the day was almost
stiflingly hot in the regions from which we had ascended.
There we stood enjoying a scene inexpressibly grand, compre-

[2]Icelanders and others will dispute this statement.

hending a considerable part of the mainland of Wales, the whole of Anglesey, a faint glimpse of part of Cumberland, the Irish Channel, and what might be either a misty creation or the shadowy outline of the hills of Ireland. Peaks and pinnacles and huge moels (hills) stood up here and there, about us and below us, partly in glorious light, partly in deep shade. Manifold were the objects which we saw from the brow of Snowdon, but of all the objects which we saw, those which most filled us with delight and admiration, were numerous lakes and lagoons, which, like sheets of ice or polished silver, lay reflecting the rays of the sun in the deep valleys at his feet.

Wild Wales, by GEORGE BORROW

31. Cardiff: Capital of Wales

It was not until 1955 that formal recognition of Cardiff as the capital of the Principality was granted—though it must be admitted that many people already regarded it as such for a number of reasons, quite apart from the fact that it is by far the largest city in Wales.

This world-famous port is situated around the tidal estuary of the river Taff which flows into the Bristol Channel. . . . Although Cardiff has a colourful history stretching through the centuries, the modern city really began its growth as the 18th century merged into the 19th, bringing the age of steam, iron, coal, powered machinery, factories, railways, canals and ports through which the rapidly increasing trade of Britain led to commercial dominance. . . .

Cardiff became the greatest coal-exporting port in the world. There was an abundance of iron in the locality and coal was at hand to smelt it—rich seams of highest grade coal, later to bring a boom of coal-rush wealth to South Wales, but first found in convenient outcrops. . . . Since that time, many changes have occurred to reduce the once-paramount importance of coal, but the dock system at Cardiff, which grew steadily through the 19th century, now handles many and varied general cargoes, in addition to its traditional coal traffic. Its geographical position enables Cardiff to serve wide industrial areas, including those of South Wales itself but stretching right up to the Midlands. . . . Cardiff itself is not an industrial city, in the ordinary sense; one must go up into the Glamorgan valleys to find the region's main industrial areas ... [but Cardiff] is more than ever the commercial and cultural centre of this virile area; it more than ever justifies its selection as the capital of Wales.

DUDLEY EVANS, in *In Britain*

32. "Falmouth for Orders"

When I first descended upon the famous Cornish seaport and seaside resort of Falmouth, it was with a warm glow of anticipation, for a phrase rang like a bell in my memory—"Falmouth for Orders"—a phrase which at once brings back the old and romantic days of sail, the days of the wool clippers from Australia and the Falmouth Packet. It was in the 17th and 18th centuries that Falmouth grew in importance through the establishment of a packet station used by the boats which carried the Royal Mails across the seas. With its magnificent natural harbour it became the last port of call for outward-bound vessels sailing beyond the tip of the Cornish peninsula for the oceans of the world, and the first home anchorage on the return voyage. Here the Falmouth Packets would bid farewell to calm waters as they left the harbour to face the mighty Atlantic seas.

In those distant days, long before ship could talk to ship and ship to shore by radio, visible signals and the shout of the human voice were the means of communication, and often heard on the sea routes of the world were the words: "Where are you bound?" "Falmouth for Orders"....

Sails still ride in the harbour, sails of yachts and dinghies, and the waters are still busy with passenger ferries, coasters, merchantmen and great long tankers en route to and from the docks, for Falmouth is today one of the most important tanker repair ports in the world.

DUDLEY EVANS, in *In Britain*

33. Cornish Clay

China-clay or kaolin, to give it its proper name, is hydrated silicate of aluminium. It was first discovered in China, the home of fine pottery, in the early part of the 18th century by a party of missionaries who brought samples of it to Europe. The word "kaolin" is actually from the Chinese "Kau-ling", meaning "high ridge", the name of the hill in China from which these samples were obtained.

To-day, the world's richest supply of this clay comes from the district round St Austell in Cornwall. Formed by the weathering down of the granite cliffs throughout millions of years, the china-clay in Cornwall is estimated to be sufficient to last for a thousand years to come. . . .

Cornish china-clay was first mined commercially about 1755. It was the discovery of a Quaker apothecary, William Cookworthy, of Kingsbridge, Devon. . . . Fired by his discovery, Cookworthy resolved to use this clay himself in the making of chinaware. In due course he set up a factory at Plymouth, and within a few months his handmade china was selling as fast as he could turn it out. . . .

At the present time china-clay is our most valuable raw-material export. . . . The majority of the clay allocated for home consumption goes to the paper and pottery industries. The former absorbs about half the amount, using it chiefly for giving the gloss to art-paper. Pottery takes another quarter, and the balance is distributed among many other industries— rubber, plastics, textiles, linoleum, chemicals, cosmetics, and medical supplies.

P. G. H. BAKER, in *Chambers's Journal*, Edinburgh

34. The Call of Devon

Many will hear the call from ships in Plymouth Sound, will see Plymouth Hoe again and remember Drake with the might of Elizabeth's Armada. Others ... Hartland Point ... Clovelly ... Salcombe ... River Dart. . . .

For myself, Exmoor is the soul of the West Country and, when it calls, two memories strive for mastery in my heart—one from the days when three young Hows picnicked on Dunkery, looking across to their own two beacons, miraculously called by their very own name—the beacons of Robin and Joaney How.

The other memory links me with the romance of Exmoor and Lorna Doone. Coming back to Oare one evening, I saw a picture which I know I shall never forget—the wide flowing sweeps of the moor with deep shadows hiding the valleys, the velvet fields sloping away, and the jewelled lights of heather blazing in the slanting rays of a setting sun.

There was not a tree to be seen, nor a farm. Then came a murmur which deepened to a rhythmic beat, while a different sound grew with it, louder, nearer, and the rattling and grinding of wheels mingled with a quick, hard thudding. The haze-dimmed edge of the moor thinned, parted, and out of the mist rode postilions, with an old coach lumbering behind them. After them raced a wild, menacing cavalcade.

I had seen the Doones again. I had no doubt of it; but after hurrying excitedly back to the farm at Oare, I learnt that the picture-makers who were filming "Lorna Doone" had shot their scenes on the moor that day. But still I remember seeing the Doones pass on the road to Oare, on Exmoor, high up, above the world—for me it is the call of the West Country.

R. W. HOW, in *Homes and Gardens*

35. The Sussex Downs

The Sussex Downs rise at Beachy Head, crossing the country from east to west, peaceful, protecting, friendly, with a beauty which remains serene and quiet though time and seasons pass.

To the south, they look out to the sea, distant or near, over fertile valleys where woods in changeful colour shadow the slopes, and silver streams winding through water meadows skirt picturesque villages. To the north sweep the rich fields and dark forests of the Weald, the wide parklands of mid-Sussex with stately mansions and clustered farms, the old Sussex towns with their beautiful churches.

But the steadfast Downs themselves, keeping watch over Sussex land and Sussex sea, hold the secrets of their hills as they did in ancient days. Prehistoric man, Breton, Roman, one after another, left his mark on the Downs, but only those who walk along the short soft turf of the ancient trackways on the summits, quietly, with seeing eyes, will find any trace. To any such, the long barrows and tumuli of flint and stone age will tell their story.

Saxons and Normans built downland churches, but often they

cunningly hid them in the combes or folds of the hills. Down-land villages, too, must be sought out; and sometimes only the ploughman turning the stubbles on the gentle slope of the hills, or a row of cornstacks high on the skyline, with thatches roped and weighted to anchor them against the wind, tells of downland farms.

R. W. HOW, in *Homes and Gardens*

36. The Kent-Sussex Marshes

Three marshes spread across the triangle made by the Royal Military Canal and the coasts of Sussex and Kent. The military Canal runs from Hythe to Rye, beside the Military Road; between it and the flat, white beaches of the Channel lie Romney Marsh, Dunge Marsh, and Walland Marsh, from east to west. Walland Marsh is sectored by the Kent Ditch, which draws huge, struggling diagrams here, to preserve ancient rights of parishes and the monks of Canterbury. Dunge Marsh runs up into the apex of the triangle at Dunge Ness, and adds to itself twenty feet of shingle every year. Romney Marsh is the sixth continent and the eighth wonder of the world.

The three marshes are much alike; indeed to the foreigner they are all a single spread of green, slatted with watercourses. No river crosses them, for the Rother curves close under Rye Hill, though these marshes were made by its ancient mouth, when it was the River Limine and ran into the Channel at Old Romney. There are a few big watercourses, there are a few white roads, and a great many marsh villages, each little more than a church with a farmhouse or two. Here and there little deserted chapels lie out on the marsh, officeless since the days of the monks of Canterbury; and everywhere there are farms, with hundreds of sheep grazing on the thick pastures.

Little Ansdore Farm was on Walland Marsh, three miles from Rye. It was a sea farm. There were no hop-gardens, as on the farms inland, no white-cowled oasts, and scarcely more than twelve acres under the plough.

Joanna Godden, by SHEILA KAYE-SMITH

Note. There is now a nuclear-power station on Dunge Ness (or Dungeness).

37. Father Thames

The Thames meanders through many counties from its source in Gloucestershire, and until Oxford it hardly seems touched by progress. The young, quietly flowing stream, girding up its strength, is a home for wildfowl, with a grey stone farmhouse or hamlet breaking the simplicity of the meadows. As you approach Oxford and then Reading, small industries appear on its banks, the most enchanting of all perhaps being a flour mill at Sonning which still uses water for its power. Schools and colleges, palaces and pubs, holiday-makers and lock-keepers share the river with the industries as you make your way downstream. In this age of rush and hurry, of dual-carriage and motorway, you can still make the leisurely journey from Oxford to London if you go by river—and have the time!

PATIENCE BUNTING, in *Radio Times*

38. London Docks

The "London Docks" are about half a mile in length, and, like the neighbouring docks, are used by vessels engaged in the coastal and the continental trade.... In the warehouses, however, are stored produce from all parts of the world. The warehouses are of vast extent; so are the vaults which are used for storing wine and brandy. With a small oil lamp carried at the end of a long stick, you wander along gangways between almost endless rows of barrels of port, sherry and Madeira, and your attention is called to the mass of fungi which grow on the roofs. There are $28\frac{1}{4}$ miles of these gangways....

One of the most interesting features is the ivory show floor, and as you look at it you wonder at the large number of elephants that were needed to supply that vast quantity. Here may be seen tusks eight or nine feet long, and there are always some specimens of "fossil" ivory from Siberia—the tusks of long extinct mammoths. Near to the ivory floor is the spice warehouse; the atmosphere of this is saturated with a delicious odour. There are heaps of cloves, the best of which come from the Moluccas, though the largest quantities are imported from Zanzibar, also piles of nutmegs, ... mace and pepper. Cinnamon is stored on the floor above, and above that again is kept cinchona bark.

From the spice warehouse you pass to the wool department, where there are enormous numbers of bales, and if you remember that each bale contains the shearings of about sixty sheep, you can obtain some idea of the huge number of sheep required to supply our wants. One warehouse is given up to the storage of gums and oils, and the air you breathe practically tastes of eucalyptus and other oils. A large warehouse space is now given up to the storage of rubber, gutta-percha and balata. In addition to the articles mentioned, there are to be seen in the warehouses of the London Docks mercury, iodine, dried fruits, coffee, cacao, isinglass and metals.

J. W. PAGE, in *The Geographical Teacher*

(Vol. 7, 1914, pp. 259–60)

Note. London Docks, situated just below London Bridge, were closed on May 31st 1969. The same commodities are now handled elsewhere in the Port of London.

39. London as a Financial Centre

At the heart of London lies the City, and at the heart of the City the symbols of independence and financial power: the Mansion House, home of the Lord Mayor who allows precedence to none but the Queen; the Bank of England; and the Royal Exchange. Within a stone's throw stand the great banking houses, the wealthy insurance companies and the trading headquarters that spell London to the international man of business.

If you are sensitive to the pulse of a great capital, you will notice a quickening once you step into the lively alley-ways of the City. It is a place where work comes first and the inessential appearances second. The least distinguished façade may conceal a most respected finance house that may be finding the funds for a new hydro-electric scheme in central Africa or a new harbour in Arabia. And behind the great court of the Royal Exchange—within the area bounded by Throgmorton Street, Threadneedle Street and Old Broad Street—lies a building that has very little external character of note. Its façades merge with those of other buildings that crowd the narrow streets; its entrances are undistinguished; and it offers no tribute, outside or within, to its place as one of the greatest markets the world has known. The London Stock Exchange might pride itself on its unobtrusiveness in the City scene; but its real and very proper pride lies in its simple but honoured motto: "Dictum Meum Pactum"—My Word is my Bond.

PETER BRITTAIN, in *In Britain*

40. The East Anglian Scene

Carved in the base of the tower of Lavenham Church is a strange hieroglyphic. On the beam of a cottage in Blakeney are others. They look like the cabalistic symbols on a magician's cloak and so they are peculiar things to see in such typically English situations as Lavenham, where the lovely black-and-white houses of the olden-day merchants stand amidst rolling cornfields and pastures, and Blakeney, once a seaport but now almost an inland village to which the tidal waters only come rustling up a creek amongst green marshes over which the sea-birds cry plaintively.

Yet these are really just the places in which to find the strange signs, for they are the merchants' marks of long ago. These marks were used to identify the merchants' raw materials, manufactured goods, tools, implements and so on, and they were also placed on mills, storehouses and other premises. Sometimes they were branded on sheep and even cut into the horns of cattle. . . .

So although few people notice them and even fewer people know what they are when they do see them, these marks have an important place in the story of East Anglia and of England itself. For it was the rise of the merchants that caused the growth of many towns and filled them with fine houses and other buildings, and even provided tiny villages with magnificent churches. And finally it was the great merchants, particularly many of East Anglia, who placed England in a leading position amongst the nations of the world.

F. E. EVANS, in the *East Anglian Magazine*, Ipswich

41. The Norfolk Broads

The "Norfolk Broads" is the term given to the 200 miles of

navigable waterways which occupy a large proportion of the low-lying countryside between the cathedral city of Norwich and the North Sea. The waterways consist of rivers (chiefly the Yare, the Waveney and the Bure), dykes, and the "broads" themselves, which are expanses of shallow lagoon. There are about forty broads in all, ranging in size from large (such as Hickling) to tiny (such as Upton), and the sailing in such safe and smooth waters is a delight to experienced helmsmen and novices alike. The countryside is charming, and the old villages, abbeys, castles and manor-houses which are revealed as you wend your lazy way from one broad to another are a constant source of interest. The three big towns which fringe the area— Norwich and the coastal resorts and fishing ports of Great Yarmouth and Lowestoft (the latter just over the Suffolk border)—are all well worth a visit. Anglers can look forward to plenty of good sport with bream, roach and pike; and bird-watchers will be in their element.

GEORGINA GRAY, in *In Britain*

42. Iron-Ore Mine Under a Town

Irthlingborough, about fifteen miles from Northampton, is one of the most remarkable little towns in Great Britain. The cross in its main street has stood there for some 700 years, and though its bridge is only thirty years old it makes up for its tender youth by its size: it is half a mile long. Irthlingborough has also a quite bewildering number of industries, ranging from the manufacture of boots and shoes to the making of false teeth; and they are all carried on in the full light of day with one mysterious exception—Irthlingborough's iron-ore mine.

Now that mine seems mysterious to me because, although there has always been quite a lot of open-cast working in Britain, our iron-ore mines can be counted on the fingers of one hand, and few of us know very much about them. In fact, how many of the thousands of people who pass Irthlingborough every day realize that only 100 feet below them there are 45 miles of tunnel? Or that all day long little electric trains are going backwards and forwards, backwards and forwards, carrying those jagged lumps of ironstone which eventually become our pots and pans and tools, and even the turrets of our army tanks? . . .

Each train carries about ninety tons of ore at a time in its
25 wagons. The team I watched had just broken their own
record. In one week, they told me, they had sent 953 tons of
iron-ore out of the mine.... A rival team once mined just over
1,100 tons in five and a half days—the equivalent, that is, of
about 300 tons of good finished iron.... The total produced
is about 6,500 tons a week.... All this, mechanically drilled,
mechanically loaded and crushed and mechanically put on the
railway trucks, gets to the blast furnaces in South Wales
without once being touched by the human hand.

DAVID KEIR, in *The Listener*

Note. Smelting also takes place at Wellingborough, Corby, etc.

43. The Cotswolds — and Westward

(*a*) If you are driving from London to Worcester, your travel
by way of Oxford and Woodstock; and beyond Chipping Norton
an inviting road leads through the golden stone villages of the
Cotswolds to Broadway—the first village in Worcestershire
and a most attractive one, though its Cotswold stone is more
characteristic of Gloucestershire than of Worcestershire....

You have hardly left Broadway before you notice that the
landscape has taken on a completely new aspect. Gone are the
stone villages of Oxfordshire and Gloucestershire, the steep
hills and the dark soil. Now we are in definitely lowland
country with views of hills in the distance; the houses are built
of warm, rosy brick, with tile-covered roofs of the same colour,
and it is here in the Vale of Evesham that we encounter the plum
and cherry orchards that are to accompany our route for miles
to come.

MARY FFOLKES, in *In Britain*

(*b*) All day lorries are taking into Evesham, Pershore, Badsey
and other centres heavy loads of plums; every night special
trains and road convoys are moving them to all corners of the
British Isles, the Channel Isles and Eire.

The stream started with a trickle of Prolifics and Czars. Now
the main surge is on, and thousands of tons of Pershore Eggs—
the chief crop of the Vale—are making their way to jam-makers

and other processors. Later will come the dessert fruit, and then, from Gloucestershire, the Blaisdon Reds and the fruit from the high Cotswold orchards. But the Pershore Egg is the backbone of the industry. . . .

There are about one-and-a-quarter million plum trees in Worcestershire commercial plantations—648,000 more than in the other eight West Country fruit-growing counties combined. The majority are around Evesham and Pershore and on the slopes overlooking the Vale.

"J. W.", in the *Birmingham Post*

(*c*) Many qualities go to make a mountain. I never thought, when I came to the Midlands, that I should find them assembled in a bump boasting no more than 1,395 feet of vertical height. Yet I can never get out of my head that the Worcestershire Beacon, rearing itself 900 feet above Malvern town, is a mountain range. . . . But however much a mountain it may look from Worcester, you cannot help discovering soon enough that a very easy half hour from Malvern Priory will take you to this highest summit. . . . On a fine summer's afternoon you'll meet upon its slopes a cross-section of the Midland world: hikers booted and spurred . . . immaculate college prefects . . . bank managers and motor magnates—all gazing over the woods and fields and silvery Severn towards the distant Cotswolds. . . .

But you can wander a few yards off, on to North Hill, the Beacon's brother and more sequestered outpost; there you will be alone with the martins and kestrels. Or you can tramp the whole grassy crest of the ridge as far as Chase End Hill about eight miles south, and meet not a soul except at British Camp.

WILFRID NOYCE, in *The Listener*

44. "Brum"

It is evening. The sun has retired resentfully into a sullen mist of smoke. Imperceptibly the lovely green fields of Warwickshire have merged into black acres; grim streets lie to the skyline; factories with yellow windows flash past; and the eye takes in a dreary ant-hill of endeavour in which men and women are just ending the day's work.[3]

The commercial traveller puts down an empty glass on the green baize table and says: "Birmingham is unlike any other town. They make every blessed thing but ships—from pins to railway carriages. That is why Birmingham can never feel unemployment like a city with one big staple industry: there is always so much happening. . . ."

Soon after dawn there is a whine in the air. . . . It is as if a monster has been fed. From workshop and factory there comes a whirr of bands, a scream of machinery. The great jig-saw puzzle of the Midlands is at work: they are making jews'-harps and corsets, rivets and buttons, steel pens and cartridges, saddles and wedding-rings, motor-cars and cutlasses, rifles and cradles. . . .

For me the great thrill in "Brum" is the Town Hall. It stands there as if attempting to make up its massive mind to walk down Hill Street and catch the last bus back to Rome. Its solemn, classic grandeur kills every building in the locality stone dead. The shadows play between its tall columns, and the darkness is kind to its rather solid proportions. If you fed the Madeleine in Paris on underdone rump steak for a month it might look like Birmingham Town Hall. . . . Down the steep hill of the Bull Ring is a church. . . . In the chancel four stone men sleep, three in full armour, one in full canonicals, the de Berminghams, the old lords of the manor. They lie, deserted, forgotten, the men who pegged out the claim, who had no idea that they had founded anything larger than a green village.

The Call of England, by H. V. MORTON

45. The Peak District

The so-called "Peak" of Derbyshire is really a tableland, attaining a height of about 2,000 feet. . . . The edges form wild craggy cliffs, with deep river gorges winding far back into the heart of the plateau. The upper surface is covered by a considerable thickness of peat, through which, however, bosses of grit project, and have been worn into wild and fantastic

[3]Much cleaning-up and tidying-up has now taken place here, as elsewhere in Britain.

forms.... Many of these rocks are undercut by the sand driven by the high winds. The scenery is very wild and impressive, especially about the Downfall, when the stream after heavy rains falls over a high precipice of grit, round which fallen masses of rock are strewn in wild profusion.

The Scenery of England, by LORD AVEBURY

46. Manchester — Hub of the North

Ranking among the great cities of the world, Manchester has a good claim to be regarded as the capital city of the north of England. It is the commercial hub of a dense and highly productive industrial area and provides a vast range of industries with their banking and insurance facilities, together with transport, shipping, packing and all other vital amenities. Manchester has a wholesale trade worth some £688 millions per annum and the second largest bankers' clearing house figures in Britain (£585 millions a year), the city's trade being second only to that of London. Only in London, I might mention, does land in the principal streets command a higher price.... Manchester is the nerve centre of one of the world's greatest industrial concentrations. In "Greater Manchester" may be included half-a-dozen large towns and more than a dozen smaller ones, and four-and-a-half million people live within a twenty-mile radius. Nearly half-a-million converge upon the city each working day to earn their livelihood or for shopping and entertainment....

Among many evidences of the transformation of Manchester from its past image as "Cottonpolis" to its present status . . . is the tremendous upsurge of major new industries in South East Lancashire—engineering, electronics, chemicals, plastics and other new-age industries. Cotton, once the life-blood of the city, is now just "one of Manchester's industries...." Manchester is, in addition, an important seaport, for it is linked to the sea by the Manchester Ship Canal, capable of carrying ocean-going ships up to 15,000 tons.

DUDLEY EVANS, in *In Britain*

47. Liverpool's Links with the East

It is hard to believe today that Britain's second biggest port had

D

to fight for the right to send its ships to do trade with the East. Today more than a dozen shipping companies operate regular services from Liverpool, but once, and not so long ago, there was none. The turning point was in 1814. This was the year when the first Liverpool ship to trade direct with India sailed from the Mersey. And it was more than a turning point, in fact. The 516-ton "Kingsmill" set out well armed and well manned, a signal victory after a battle spanning no less than three centuries; for through all these years the struggle had gone on to allow the wooden ships of Liverpool to trade freely with all parts of the world.

Up to that vitally important year of 1814, trade between Britain and the East had been dominated by the merchants of London, through a charter granted to the powerful East India Company. If a Liverpool merchant wanted to trade with the East, he had to leave Liverpool and work with the East India Company; and some did. But most stayed at home in Liverpool, to campaign, to petition, to carry on a running agitation against those unwholesome and impolitic if not unjust restrictions. . . .

And then, at last, in 1813, came partial success. The East India Company's long-time monopoly was broken, but still Liverpool ships were barred from the China trade. However the city was quick to see the new-found opportunities in the East Indies. The trade between Liverpool and India grew steadily, but it was to be another twenty years—1833—before the East India Company's monopoly was broken completely.

TOM HEANEY, in *The Listener*

48. Halifax

My native town, Halifax, lies in the heart of the Pennine hills. There is scarcely a yard of level ground in the town except for one road, the New Road, whose name reveals the man-made origin of its contours. Halifax is an old woollen textile town. The reason for this lies in its geography.

Standing on the infertile Millstone Grit hills, Halifax could not grow rich crops or pasture many cattle, but it could feed sheep on its rough grass, the "bents" from which my own name is derived, while the water tumbling from the millstone hills was devoid of lime and therefore kind to woollen fibre. So it had sheep and streams, the wool and water needed for the cloth trade. When the Industrial Revolution came and brought the power of steam, we had iron nearby to make the boilers, and the coal at hand to put steam in them. Presently the cloth trade attracted other complementary industries, which developed on their own lines, and so today Halifax is a place of many manufactures, a teeming, bustling, industrial town of about a hundred thousand inhabitants[4]. . . .

My house stands only a mile from the Halifax G.P.O. But I can see hills from my windows, and seven minutes' walk takes me to an open promenade with a superb view of innumerable Pennines. The urban landscape, too, the houses and mills and chimneys, because of the varying contours of the land, is dramatic, exciting. . . . At night, with all the chains of road lights rolling high over the black velvet hills, the West Riding landscape has a startling and dynamic, if slightly satanic, beauty.

PHYLLIS BENTLEY, in *Homes and Gardens*

49. York: City and County

York does not belong to any of the three Ridings; it is not just a city but a county as well. It is a treasure house of the past yet thoroughly modern. Although Yorkshire's great showplace, it is also one of Britain's main tourist attractions and perhaps the best example of a fortified city in Europe. . . . What is this strange magic which captivates us at York? To me it consists largely of colour and freshness and beauty of form. Age generally has its associations of decay and ruin, but rarely so with York. The ancient walls and the glory of the Minster are clean and sparkling in the sunlight. The walls are so silvery-white they seem to have been built but yesterday. The smooth, green slopes, the gleam of daffodils in springtime, the trees and the gardens infuse an air of perpetual youth. The stately Ouse does not grow old either. . . .

Yet, on close inspection, this air of youth is mellowed with the dignity of age. . . . But the past is so cleverly intermingled with the present that even the most satiated tripper cannot fail to take notice of it. In short, York is not just for the dis-

[4]In 1967 the population was estimated at 94,770, and in 1968 at 94,280.

criminating connoisseur but for everyone—and the history of
this noble city is very largely the history of England....

York is not without its industry, but what a pleasant industry
it is! Chocolates! The famous houses of Rowntree and Terry
have given pleasure to millions for generations.... York is also
noted for railway carriage building and the manufacture of
optical equipment.

G. DOUGLAS BOLTON, in *Yorkshire Illustrated*
(now *Yorkshire Life*), Leeds

50. The Winding Tees

One of the most interesting rivers in the north of England is
the Tees, and it is doubtful if a more appropriate name than
Tees could have been found for it, the name being derived
from an old Anglo-Saxon word "Taoi", which means "winding".
This typically describes its course from source to sea....

Away on the lonely slope of Cross Fell (the summit of which is
2,892 feet above sea level) the Tees first meets the eyes of
man.... Its song and chatter are full of mirth as it seeks its
way through the smooth odd-shaped boulders in the early stages
of its existence. Then swiftly it dashes down a succession of
cascades at Cauldron Snout, foaming and seething in a mad
whirl of excitement into a pool 200 feet below, calming down
again until it reaches High Force, where it tumbles over the
75 feet precipice with a roar which deadens the voice of Thor
in the clouds....

Leaving the parent dale with its picturesque white-washed
farmsteads behind, the Tees soon reaches Barnard Castle, where,
after passing Towler Hill, it flows over the rocks and under the
bridge at the foot of the tower built by Bernard Baliol....
Following along its course, again the scene changes. Now we
see it passing on to Egliston Abbey and Rokeby, through glades
immortalized by Sir Walter Scott, then into industrial areas,
mixing with the tide as it laves and frets against the busy docks
at Middlesbrough, and finally we leave Old Father Tees in
harness, nearing his journey's end, travel-stained and slow, but
bearing on his heaving breast the vessels that link Tees-side with
the commercial world.

WILLIAM LANGSTAFF, in the (Yorkshire) *Dalesman*,
Clapham, Yorkshire

51. Northumberland — History in the Present

In Northumberland, away from the busy towns, we still have the feeling of being in an outpost. This is the countryside of the Border ballads, which commemorate the age-long feuds between the Douglases on the Scottish side and the Percys on the English side, and the battles fought at Otterburn and Chevy Chase. On all sides, too, there is evidence that this was a countryside continually on its guard. Hidden in the folds of the hills, standing in strategic positions along the banks of the Tyne and Coquet, are a formidable array of tall, gaunt, strongly fortified castles, pele towers and farmhouses, all battlemented with immensely thick walls and narrow slits of windows, built to withstand siege or raid. Some of these are now in a ruined state, but a surprising number not only still stand intact but are owned and lived-in by descendants of their original builders.

The most magnificent is Alnwick Castle, for centuries the principal home of the Percy family.... Bamburgh Castle is vastly impressive whether seen from the coast or from the little village that clusters at its foot.... It looks out to the Holy Island of Lindisfarne.... Under St Aidan and his successors, this island became a beacon of Christianity from which missionary work spread to the mainland.... Northwards along the coast is the ancient walled town of Berwick-upon-Tweed....

But, for the antiquarian, the crowning glory of Northumberland is the Roman Wall, originally built by the Emperor Hadrian between A.D. 122 and 126 from Newcastle to Carlisle, a distance of 73 miles, as the northern limit of the Roman Empire.

S. P. B. MAIS in *In Britain*

52. Edinburgh

Living in Edinburgh there abides, above all things, a sense of its beauty. Hill, crag, castle, rock, blue stretch of sea, the picturesque ridge of the Old Town, the squares and terraces of the New—these things seen once are not to be forgotten. The quick life of today sounding around the relics of antiquity and overshadowed by the august traditions of a Kingdom, makes residence in Edinburgh more impressive than residence in

any other British city. I have just come in—surely it never
looked so fair before! What a poem is that Princes Street! The
puppets of the busy, many-coloured hour move about on its
pavements, while across the ravine Time has piled up the Old
Town, ridge on ridge, grey as a rocky coast washed and worn
by the foam of centuries; peaked and jagged by gable and
roof; windowed from basement to cope; the whole surmounted
by St Giles's airy crown. The New is there looking at the Old.
Two Times are brought face to face, and are yet separated by a
thousand years. Wonderful on winter nights, when the gully
is filled with darkness, and out of it rises, against the sombre
blue and the frosty stars, that mass and bulwark of gloom,
pierced and quivering with innumerable lights. There is
nothing in Europe to match that, I think.

A Summer in Skye,
by ALEXANDER SMITH

53. A Pentland Shepherd

John Todd, when I knew him, was already the oldest herd on
the Pentlands, and had been all his life faithful to that curlew-
scattering, sheep-collecting life. He remembered the droving
days, when the drove-roads, that now lie green and solitary
through the heather, were thronged thoroughfares. He had
himself often marched flocks into England, sleeping on the
hillsides with his caravan. . . .

I think I owe my taste for that hillside business to the art
and interest of John Todd. He it was that made it live for me,
as the artist can make all things live. It was through him the
simple strategy of massing sheep upon a snowy evening, with
its attendant scampering of easy, shaggy aides-de-camp, was an
affair that I never wearied of recalling to mind : the shadow of
the night darkening on the hills, inscrutable black dots of snow-
shower moving here and there like night already come, huddles
of yellow sheep and dartings of black dogs upon the snow, a
bitter air that took you by the throat, unearthly harpings of
the wind along the moors.

Memories and Portraits,
by R. L. STEVENSON

54. In and Out of the Clyde

At Glasgow the Clyde is just a river, but farther downstream it begins to broaden out into its estuary—the far-famed Firth of Clyde which follows a winding, and ever-widening, course to the sea amid some of the finest scenery of its kind in Europe.

The best way to explore this region of mountainous coasts, long narrow sea lochs, picturesque islands and lively holiday resorts is, of course, by boat. It may be your own boat, for conditions are ideal for the amateur sailorman; the Clyde is one of the leading yachting centres in Britain. But, for enjoying the scenery, there is no better vantage-point than a leisurely seat on the deck of a pleasure-steamer. . . .

Best of all the Caledonian Company's cruises, in my opinion, is the one which starts from Glasgow itself, taking you first of all past the docks and shipyards for which Clydeside is world-renowned. The Cunard liners "Queen Elizabeth" and "Queen Mary", the two largest passenger ships in the world,[5] were both launched on the Clyde. From Gourock, the ship crosses the Firth to Dunoon and Rothesay and then continues through the "narrows" of the Kyles of Bute to Tighnabruaich. Here an hour can be spent ashore before the return to Glasgow. I go on this trip at least once a year and find it a constant source of fascination.

Some of the passengers take the opportunity of disembarking at Dunoon or Rothesay. . . . Both of these beautifully-situated places, which offer an abundance of holiday attractions, are worthy of a prolonged stay. Dunoon is the principal centre for the grand region of hills and lochs which is known as Cowal . . . Rothesay, backed by its wooded hills, is the capital of the verdant Isle of Bute, one of Scotland's loveliest holiday kingdoms.

GILBERT T. BELL, in *In Britain*

55. From a Hebrid Isle

This is an island of the Inner Hebrides, eight miles long by three miles wide, lying bare to the Atlantic, to wit, the Isle of Colonsay. A gem of an island, once you get to it, rock-bound

[5]At the time of their respective launchings.

but luxuriant with even tropical growths; home of the heather,
yet hospitable of fuchsia, rhododendron, and even palm tree;
seared with rain, yet set in azure seas; bastion of the North-
West, yet warmer in winter than London. Here, frost never
penetrates, and snow never lingers.

But if winter is kindly, it is summer's tooth that is keen. . . .
The breezes are not "spicy", but rainy, and over-boisterous to
be kindly. Occasional days of sheer beauty have slipped through
the vigilant cordon of "depressions" that ring us about. . . .
So the fine weather for a week is compressed in this island to
a single day, but such a day makes one forget the six wet
ones for sheer delight.

Today the grey curtain of nimbus cloud has lifted, and we
are receiving our weekly ration of blue. Sodden hay, that should
have been stacked six weeks ago, is being tossed hopefully yet
once again. The panorama in every direction is superb. . . .
Westwards the Paps of Jura tower above ten miles of as blue a
course as ever "white horses" galloped over. Islay, flat and
sleek, lies to the southward. Opposite, and to the north, are the
huge mountain masses of Mull, while Iona gleams mystically to
the north-west. On the distant mainland rise peak after peak
fading into the farthest haze beyond Glencoe. The western
ocean is already aglow with "the light of setting suns", and clear
on the horizon the lonely lighthouse of Dhu Heartach stands
solitary between us and the New World.

EDWARD VERNON, in the *British Weekly*

56.   A Ride in the Western Highlands

I had seen a little of the Highlands in bygone years, but it was
my companion's first visit. His supply of enthusiastic adjectives
—such as "wizard", "incredible" and "gorgeous"—was soon
in danger of running out, and my larger store also reached the
point of exhaustion. Often we simply looked at the scene spread
before us and said nothing, which, perhaps, was wiser.

The day's run was from Helensburgh to Fort William, and
our route took us through Arrochar, Inveraray, along the shore
of Loch Fyne to Lochgilphead, and then northwards to Oban,
where we spent a few hours before pushing on through
Ballachulish to Fort William. Skirting Loch Linnhe most of the

way we were favoured with an endless panorama of mountain and water. It was then that we began to realize what the Highlands really are. . . .

From Mallaig we crossed by ferry to Skye—a forty minutes' trip—and spent the day driving round the island. Skye, whose Gaelic name means "the isle of mist", is noted for its misty and wet climate, but we struck it on a day of brilliant sunshine. To visit Skye for a day sounds absurd, but it was sufficient for us to realize something of its charm. Its lovely lochs, its sweeping moorlands, and, above all, the Coolins, a range of hills of solemn and rugged grandeur, would be hard to beat. . . .

Returning to the mainland by the shorter ferry to Lochalsh, we spent the night in that beautiful village; and then made our way to Fort Augustus and so back again to Fort William. We had traversed the Pass of Glencoe on the outward journey, but were glad to take the same road on our return.

REV. J. A. PATTEN, in the *British Weekly*

57. On the Trail of the Kipper

"The herring are running," Skipper MacLeod mutters, through a battered pipe. "Let go, there!" In Indian file the drifter fleet noses from Stornaway towards the fishing grounds, perhaps only five miles off shore, perhaps 30 miles out in the Sound, once again to write the first paragraph in the story of the only dish pre-war Continentals envied us—kippers. . . . The drifterman's job is neither spectacular nor particularly dangerous. He seldom sails far from shore, and his seamanship is such that he can handle any situation likely to arise. . . .

Basking-sharks are the bane of the drifter fleets. Feeding on the same minute organisms as the herrings, and swimming through the shoals with their mouths open to trap their prey, they frequently cause havoc with the nets. . . .

Stornaway can kipper some 300 crans per day. To the kilns flow the prime herrings netted in the famous Castle Bay fishing grounds south of lonely Barra in the Hebrides, and at Mallaig, on the Highland mainland, sawdust smoke drifts over further kilns. Three "kipper boats" serve Stornaway during the season. They're the link between Hebridean kippering kilns and Mallaig railway station, where the "kipper special" waits. The

"Naviedale" is one of them; her 383 tons were about to edge from the pier as I dropped on to her decks. Nine hours separated us from the mainland. . . .

Midnight saw the "kipper special" draw out for Fort William and Glasgow. Eight hours later I was unloaded in Glasgow with 100,000 kippers. Tired out, and smelling of kippers, I arrived at the hotel to be greeted with the words: "Bacon for breakfast, sir, or kippers?"

FRANK ILLINGWORTH,
in the *Weekly Scotsman*, Edinburgh

58.   "White Coal" in the Highlands

In the Highlands summer visitors are noticing new roads climbing to lochs where great dams are being built. They see lorries grinding up the mountain sides carrying cement, steel-work and plant. They notice droves of engineers and workmen in lonely places.

These are among the numerous signs of the activities of the North of Scotland Hydro-Electric Board, whose schemes, on which £100 million are being spent, will transform many aspects of Scottish life.

From Loch Lomondside in the south to the Orkneys in the north, more than 100 stations are being built to generate electricity. A network of 1,000 miles of transmission lines on the Highland grid will convey power and light. Instead of burning coal needed for export, the new power stations will derive their energy from the rain and the wind. . . . As the years pass, most if not all of the scars made by the engineers will become healed and little scenic beauty will be lost. . . .

The road to the Isles "by Tummel and Loch Rannoch and Lochaber" will soon be under the waters of a larger Loch Tummel, which eventually will feed a power station. A new road up to 100 feet higher will replace the submerged highway. . . . At Loch Sloy, Dunbartonshire, a two-mile tunnel through Ben Vorlich is nearing completion. It will take the water from the dam to the power station 900 feet below, on the shore of Loch Lomond. . . . On the Tummel-Garry scheme, in Perthshire, another 2,000 men are driving hard like those at

Loch Sloy to complete the first section of the plant at Clunie. . . .
With a section at Fannick, Ross and Cromarty, it is hoped to
bring in additional capacity totalling 63,000 kilowatts.

HENRY BATE, in the Daily Telegraph

59. The Spell of the Shetlands

See the Shetlands once, and they will haunt you for ever. They
are mad little islands, like a mountain range sunk below its
timber line, forming a teeth of rocks between the Atlantic and
the North Sea. There is not a spot in the whole hundred of them
that is more than half a mile from salt water.

Their coast line is crazy. It is a sort of geologic debauch
where the rocks have gone mad indeed. They shoot out of the
sea in sheer cliffs—Foula's Atlantic side is one sheer cliff 1,300
feet high. . . . The islands along the Atlantic coast are often just
spear-points of red rock. There are rock arches through which
one could sail a full-rigged sailing ship. The Atlantic rushes up
to them, flings itself high up their sides and falls back in a
lacery of white, broken seas. . . . For six hours each day the
Atlantic sets through the Shetlands, sweeping in great swirling
eddies to bring the flood tide. Then it ebbs, and the North
Sea races after it, leaping and thrumming through the rips of
Yell and Blue Mull Sound, so that even the connecting
motor-boat has to fight to win the other side.

But inland all is monotony. Black peat, bogs and lonely moors.
A sheep is visible on the sky-line for miles. There are no real
streams, only gurgling burns, which run almost unseen through
the black channels they have dug among the peat, to empty
into shallow wind-swept lochs, where the water lies black as
coffee; and the lonely cry of the curlew is the only sound as you
moodily cast your flies for the speckled Shetland trout. . . . They
are lonely and dreary little islands; they are windswept and
battered; and yet, if you have stood on their wine-red moors
at sunset and seen the great swells of the Atlantic pounding in,
you will never forget them.

Way of a Transgressor, by NEGLEY FARSON

Continental Europe

60. Norway's Fjords

(*a*) Bergen is a town of fairy-tale beauty, with the blue arms of the fjord reaching to its centre, and multi-coloured houses creeping up the forested slopes of the surrounding mountains. Buildings are a fascinating mixture of the traditional-timber and the ultra-modern concrete of our own country, but design and workmanship are generally so admirable that it is difficult to find the eyesores which offend here—the ugly, the shoddy and the neglected. And the standard of cleanliness everywhere is astonishing.

CHERRY VOOGHT, in *Home and Country*

(*b*) It was a lovely summer's day when I looked from my verandah over the fjord and drank my morning coffee in my pyjamas. Cultivated fields occasionally led down to the water's edge where several islands jettied into the lake, but the slopes were mostly wooded or cloaked with clumps of fir. Both shores met in the mid-distance where the tortuous waters seemed to be blocked by brown foothills which were topped by forests, hazy blue in the distance, which led up to grey mountains, their summits shining in the everlasting snow.

In such peaceful scenes I spent a lazy Sunday paddling about in a row-boat or loafing in the flower-scented garden. . . . Travelling north by steamer to Trondheim one is soon introduced to what is the more typical scenery of Norway; a recurrent view of one of the deeper fjords may be described as a vista of grim precipitous cliff rising straight from depths, often half a mile down. But the lights and reflections in unruffled waters add romance to the sadness of harsh rock and dark forest.

Sting Fish and Sea-Farer, by H. MUIR EVANS

61. Telemark

Two hours or so by rail south-west from Oslo brings one to the threshold of the province of Telemark. It is a region of mountains and thick forests, of innumerable lakes caught in clear pools at high altitudes or in sinuous twists along valley floors.... An idyllic boat excursion starts from Skien, capital of the province, taking one through the locks and waterways to Dalen, sixty miles away. And there is a three-and-a-half hour bus trip via Bö (another rail point) to Morgedal. This tiny resort ... can claim to be the father and mother of all winter sports resorts; for it was here that ski-ing as a modern sport was born. Over a hundred years ago the young men of the village hurtled down the steep slopes and ski-jumped over cottage roofs, the slalom developing from their hair-raising zigzag descents through the pine trees....

The road beyond Morgedal is, for the most part, above the tree line ... before plunging down to Rjukan. Rjukan is one of Telemark's biggest surprises. Once it was the name of a water-fall thundering down from the mountains to the valley floor. Today, it is the name of a unique industrial community which has come into being as a result of the taming of these waters and the fantastic network of dams, power stations and pipe lines which stretches back to Skinnarbu. Buried deep in its valley, modern, industrial, vigorous Rjukan does not see the sun for five to six months of the year.

SYLVIE NICKELS, in *The Lady*

62. Oslo and District

Oslo, the Norwegian capital, is thirty-six hours distant from Newcastle by the steamers of the Fred Olsen Line. Twenty-two hours after leaving the Tyne, the Norwegian coast at Cape Lindesnes, the most southerly point of Norway, is sighted. After that the ship steams along the rocky southern shores calling at Kristiansand, and through the lovely scenery and calm waters of the Oslo Fjord.... This wide fjord provides the finest yachting region of Norway. Both shores are in-dented with innumerable snug little bays. Anchorages are safe, and the islands and the forest-covered hills of the mainland give a wonderful setting for the white sails of the yachts....

The 1,100-years-old Viking Ships at the Bygdöy peninsula, and the 900-years-old Gol Stave Church at the Folk Museum are among the chief features of Oslo and its immediate vicinity. High up on the hills—reached in half-an-hour by electric train —are Holmenkollen and the Frognerseteren Restaurant, and close by the Ski Museum containing, among other interesting exhibits, Nansen's and Amundsen's original Polar outfits. The view from the Frognerseteren over the town and fjord is alone worth the visit. . . .

The loveliest valleys of Norway lie in the eastern part of the country. From Oslo the railway systems lead out to meet them from the south. The town of Lillehammer, four hours by train from Oslo, forms the gateway to the Gudbrandsdal, one of the most historic valleys of the country. In all the valleys of Norway the peasant tradition lingers on strongly, and nowhere more so than in the Gudbrandsdal. Many of the timbered farms, built of heavy forest logs, are centuries old, and their sites go back to the earliest days of Norwegian history.

Norway: Nature's Wonderland (a booklet issued by
Norwegian State Railways)

63.   Across Southern Sweden

All along the western coast of Sweden are quaint and curious rock carvings, picturing sailing craft and sailors and weapons of 3,000 years ago. Of the actual civilization they represent, little or nothing is known. And almost in the midst of these pictorial reminders of an age long since past stands Gothenburg (Göteborg),[1] a busy thriving modern seaport and the most important commercial centre of the country. . . .

If you are in a hurry, you can reach Stockholm from Gothenburg in about six hours by electrified express train. . . . Otherwise, by choosing the far-famed Göta Canal route, a veritable stairway of water that takes your steamer upgrade by a long series of locks and then descends again 300 feet to the level of the Baltic Sea, you will have a leisurely three-day enjoyment of quiet countrysides. You view the majestic grandeur of Trollhätten Falls, where modern engineering converts the tumbling cataracts into electrical power for Central and Southern Sweden and for Denmark as well. . . .

Whatever your approach to Stockholm, the commanding
[1]Gothenburg is Sweden's largest city.

beauty of castles and islands meets your eye. . . . Stockholm is often referred to by travellers as the most beautiful capital in the world. As you wander through the narrow lanes of the old "City between the Bridges" their medieval quaintness serves as a reminder of the early beginnings of the capital in the middle of the 13th century. No less striking is the modern Stockholm with its new architecture in churches, libraries, offices, and waterfronts of imposing apartment houses. . . . And sooner or later you reach the water's edge, for the gleaming natural waterways are the main thoroughfares of the city. Your ear catches the faint chugging of motor launch or steamer.

Sweden (a booklet issued by the Swedish Traffic Association)

64. Journeys from Stockholm

From Stockholm we drove four-hundred-odd miles due north, and our first stop was the old university town of Uppsala, where Queen Gunilla's silver bell rings out across the gabled roofs and turrets night and morning as it has done every day since the fourteenth century. Our second stop was at a Vandrarhem. These are shilling-a-night hostels for hikers. We couldn't have been more comfortable. The third stop was at Lulea, and eight miles away we found the eeriest of all ghosttowns—Old Lulea, a vast medieval church and 500 houses with not a single inhabitant. For centuries, till the coming of railways and motor-cars, people would assemble from all over the great parish of Norrbotten for the church festivals. They would stay a week or more, feasting, drinking, dancing, going to church; and, as a Swedish friend of mine said, "There was much wooing". Now these great festivals take place no more, and the town, instead of being empty between them, stands empty all the year round. . . .

[On returning to Stockholm] we motored across prosperous south Sweden to Hälsingborg, from where on a clear day one may see the fantastic twisted spires of Hamlet's Elsinore. . . . The drive itself was lovely, with green and gold country on the verge of winter, old churches with their bells not hung in their steeples but in belfries some distance away. Each night the evening sky was fantastically beautiful. . . . At the cost of a few shillings we drove the Bugatti straight on to the ferry at

Hälsingborg, and in twenty minutes we were passing through
the narrow old-world streets of Elsinore.

DAVID SCOTT-MONCRIEFF, in *Chambers's Journal*, Edinburgh

65.   Kiruna and the Iron-Ore Mountains

Directly you put your nose out of the aeroplane after landing
at Kiruna you know you have come a long way from the parts
of Sweden most people are familiar with. The air, even in the
summer, has a bite in it; it has a cool freshness like mountain
air, which is not surprising since Kiruna, as well as standing
fairly high up, is 100 miles inside the Arctic Circle. Its remoteness will surprise anyone who has forgotten what an elongated
country Sweden is. Kiruna lies almost as far away from Malmö,
on the southernmost tip of Sweden, as Rome would be if you
travelled south instead of north—not far short of 1,000 miles.

As you drive from Kiruna airport into the town, as I had
occasion to do recently, you are aware also, coming from
southern Sweden, of the very different quality of the landscape. The town stands above the growth of trees, except for a
few small ones in sheltered valleys, on a bare, brown plateau
spangled with lakes and swelling into rocky hills. Some of these
hills have a strange broken outline as though bits had been
grabbed out of them by giant hands—which is in fact just what
has happened, for Kiruna lives off iron-ore. It contains the
largest underground iron-ore mine in the world, and, to begin
with, open-cast mining was the rule. The town sits between
two iron mountains that have been gnawed away by mining
into deep clefts, and their sides shaped into giant terraces. . . .

The modern growth of Kiruna began in 1903, when the
railway was built that carries the iron-ore across the mountains
to the Norwegian port of Narvik. . . . Now it is a thriving,
expanding town, with a population already of about 20,000,[2]
set down miles from anywhere in an utter wilderness, and full
of fascinating contrasts. In most ways it is highly sophisticated
and yet . . . it still has something of the air of a pioneer settlement. . . . One feels one might be in a gold-rush town of the
American far west.

J. M. RICHARDS, in *The Listener*

[2]26,804 in 1961.

66. The Lapps and Their Reindeer

Later in the day, while ski-ing on the slopes above the village, I heard the distant tinkling of bells, and soon, over the brow of the hill, I saw the arrival of a long caravan of laden sledges. They were in single file, each drawn by a reindeer, which was fastened by a leather thong to the back of the sledge in front. The caravan was divided into many "strings", the latter consisting of ten to twelve sledges and reindeer linked together as described, and each string being in charge of a Lapp driver whose business it was to keep the traces disentangled.... He is helped by his dogs, which find the track....

The reindeer is the Laplander's most valued possession and his main support, providing him with food, milk and clothing, and being the sole means of transport through the winter snows both for himself and his goods.... A rich Lapp will often own a thousand deer or more....

Reindeer are wonderful swimmers and, when the great spring migration takes place, thousands may be seen swimming the fjords, which they must cross before they can reach one of the islands near Hammerfest, where many of them spend the summer months. The Lapps are forced to follow where the reindeer lead. It is impossible for them to keep back the herd when it decides to move; their movements are thus ruled by their deer. The animals do not all migrate to the coast. Many of those in Swedish Lapland merely cross the border into Norway, spending the summer up in the high fells of Finmark, while others move towards Tromsö. The calving time is in May, when the herd is generally moving to its summer quarters.

Across Lapland, by OLIVE MURRAY CHAPMAN

Note. Since the invention of the snow-scooter and the snow-tractor, the way of life of the Lapps has become much less nomadic.

67. Finland: Her Lakes and Forests

Other visitors to Finland may have had different first impressions, but for those who don't know this unusual country I would like to share mine.

Still, deep, seemingly endless, Finnish forests are mysteriously beautiful. Roads slice cleanly through a tree-filled landscape of

E

solid impenetrability. . . . I can't imagine a more relaxing holiday than one spent on the necklace of lakes that winds through
these dense forest regions.

A little two-deck steamer glides over silent waterscapes, only
its wake breaking the silver surface: one just sits and watches
the water and the trees pass by. For intermittent excitement
there is the slow negotiation of the narrow channels that link
one lake to the next, or the passing of the long "trains" of logs
chained to a quietly chuffing tug.

Travelling in Finland is not just an escape to the forests;
there are busy towns, and in them and in the countryside, too,
buildings of great architectural interest. Old houses have
weatherboarded walls painted white or strong earth colours,
reds and ochres or sun-faded blues, and ancient churches are
roofed in a fish-scale pattern of tarred wooden tiles.

For me, however, it is the soaring imagination that charac-
terizes so many modern buildings, particularly the new
churches, that is most important. Here the creativeness of the
Finns seems to blend with their almost spiritual regard for
the forests. Identification with nature is something about which
they feel very strongly—there is a saying that you can judge the
depth of a man's soul by the distance he travels into the forests
for his holidays.

PSYCHE PIRIE, in *Homes and Gardens*

68.   Finnish Education and Culture

Finnish education is democratic and realistic too. . . . Over
ninety per cent of the population are educated at primary
schools. These are free and attendance is compulsory from the
age of seven to sixteen. Afterwards there are ample facilities
for vocational training at technical and agricultural schools, also
at the people's high schools where men are instructed in agriculture and handicrafts and the women in domestic subjects.
Since the economy of Finland is based on the timber, pulp and
paper industries this form of education is obviously appropriate
for the majority. . . .

In Finland initiative is encouraged and demonstrated even
in small matters. . . . The most outstanding example that I saw
is the group of buildings belonging to Helsinki University

which have been erected outside the city by the students of Architecture and Engineering. An extension was needed and its building has provided these students with a practical exercise in their future professions, including the economics, since they had to raise the money to pay for the materials.... The church is constructed from wooden blocks and has an altar, organ and seats, but no decoration whatsoever. An enormous window, which almost fills the eastern end of the building, and gives a wonderful view of the surrounding forest, relieves this stark simplicity as well as admitting light. Sited behind the altar the window forms a kind of natural reredos which changes with the seasons.

The foregoing is just one illustration of the way the Finns, like other Scandinavians, know how to make use of natural beauty in their building schemes. Another example is the cathedral at Tampere which has mountain ash trees planted all around it, and the roof tiles exactly match the berries.

MAY LANCASTER, in *The Rostrum*, Liverpool

69. The Danish Scene

New countries fascinate most when they heave in sight for the first time. This land is Denmark. It must be different, we think. Somehow or other it will have "Denmark" stamped all over it. But it hasn't. To our first disappointed gaze it looks just like the East Anglia we have left behind.... As we swept through the countryside we noticed the East Anglian counterpart—hummock hills crowned with beech and pine, broads and breckland and flooded valleys by the sea. We noticed the village-deserted churches in their rings of trees, whitewashed with high gabled towers and the eternal domestic pantile. The Danes build *up* their houses, while the East Anglian builds *along*, the Dane looking out, the English hiding.

Then there was the grass. There are grass countries and non-grass countries. England and Denmark are grass countries —indeed the best of the grass countries. The Danes think of a garden in terms of lawn, the garden landscaping the house....

The tidiness of mind that produced Aarhus University and our host's house and garden tends towards realism in sculpture. The Danes are accurate rather than interpretative and love to take the familiar and perpetuate it in stone. Thus the sow and her litter in the forecourt of Aarhus Town Hall—a fond tribute to Denmark's first export—and the fishwife in Copenhagen which is at first indistinguishable from the real fishwives who stand by it working.

GEORGE BARKER,
in *Home and Country*

70. Farming in Denmark

As one travels through the lush, rich folds of the countryside, dotted with whitewashed farmsteads, prominent against that patchwork landscape which denotes intensive agriculture, one becomes immediately conscious of the farming "atmosphere" of Denmark. Where crops do not grow, cattle and horses graze; where pasture-land gives way to bog, peat is cut and stacked. There is very little waste land. In the immediate vicinity of the farm, pigs and poultry complete the agricultural scene. . . .

The farm cluster usually consists of four thatched buildings standing in a square enclosing a courtyard, with the dwelling-house facing south. The village concentration of farms, so well known in England with land stretching away over the hills and dales, is unusual in Denmark. . . . Today, much of the land is State-owned and the farmer rents his property from the State comforted by the knowledge that his son will be able to do likewise. . . .

Grain has been largely responsible for Denmark's dairy-farming reputation, for it has been found more economical to put a large proportion of crop production into the barns of the dairy farmer for feeding the ever growing number of cattle, pigs and horses than to compete in the export market. In the course of a few years, Denmark ceased to be a grain exporter and concentrated her own resources and imported grain and other cattle foods upon the development of dairy-farming. . . . Owing to the co-operative system, there is less individual marketing in Denmark than in England, although horse-dealing is an exception.

KENNETH HARE SCOTT, in *Sport & Country*

71. Copenhagen

(*a*) Whether approached from south or west, the island step-ping-stones to Danish Zealand, on which Copenhagen is situated, are visible from the continent, and Zealand itself from the intermediate islands. Once reached, the advantages of Zealand for the original headquarters of a maritime State under the conditions of boat navigation must have quickly become apparent. They could, indeed, hardly have been surpassed. Not only is the island remarkably fertile, but its area was suitable for the purpose.... The position of Copenhagen is inter-mediate between Stockholm and Oslo by the sea route, and before the development of metalled roads and railways the sea route was the best.... Copenhagen is the only insular capital from which considerable possessions are still held on the continent of Europe.

The Great Capitals, by VAUGHAN CORNISH

(*b*) Copenhagen is so much a city to be walked in that it was the first to bar traffic from one of its main shopping centres and turn it into a pedestrian precinct. The result is wholly delightful.... The sea, of course, is very much a part of Copenhagen, adding greatly to its attraction and rugged character.... It is a solid city, a working city. This is not to suggest that the normal diversions are not to be had. They are indeed. The Tivoli is one of the biggest playgrounds in Europe; but for my money, the streets which end so abruptly because a ship is anchored across them, the old houses, and the popu-lace pedalling about for dear life, are much more engaging. Copenhagen is, in fact, a very natural place.

FRANCES HOWELL, in *Homes and Gardens*

72. The Dutch Scene

Of the landscape in the provinces of South and North Holland, long vistas of unrelieved flatness are unrolled before the eye. The outstanding feature of these provinces—as in those border-ing the Ijsselmeer or Zuider Zee to the north—is the com-plete absence of trees. Considerably wooded however, are the southern provinces of Limburg and Brabant near the Belgian border. Villages in these provinces south of the rivers do, indeed, begin to resemble villages in Belgium, with their long cobble-streets framed on either side with carefully trimmed trees. All the movement and activity in Holland is to be found in the intricate network of canals which connects the main rivers, the Lower Rhine, the Maas and the Waal, not only with one another, but also with the ports of Rotterdam and Amsterdam and with lesser harbours.

Without a study or a knowledge of the Dutch canal system the real Holland cannot be fully understood. Indeed all the romance lies there. All life seems somehow to find an outlet in these mathematically straight stretches of calm water. To glide majestically between canal banks, slowly passing men, houses, steeples and cows, fills the mind with placid contentment. . . .

In the summer months the inhabitants busy themselves with water craft of every description. Skiffs, small yachts and rowing boats are all handled with skill and loving care by young and old alike. Whole families spend long periods in houseboats anchored near the banks. It is not difficult, therefore, to understand the reason for the Dutch being known as a maritime folk.

Free Europe

73. Holland for Holidays

With some force, a Dutch holiday might be described as a holiday abroad without leaving home. Even first-time visitors get an indefinable feeling of having been there before, for many people speak perfect English, the way of life is very similar to our own and the food and drink are not very different either. Yet many contrasts with Britain are soon apparent. The canals criss-crossing the country are well maintained and in constant use, the ancient city of Amsterdam retains much of its traditional Rembrandtesque charm, and in spite of its status as the country's commercial capital manages to remain curiously tranquil. . . .

But Amsterdam is not the whole of Holland. The bulb fields are one of the sights of the world in spring. . . . The seaside resorts are excellent holiday centres . . . Scheveningen is the most popular resort of all, with a fine sandy beach, and has the advantage of nearness to The Hague, one of the most attractive cities in Northern Europe.

Years ago towns on what used to be called the Zuider Zee depended entirely on fishing, but as that industry declined tourism began to flourish. Volendam is a quiet place, very popular among the Dutch at weekends, and ideal for boating. The local inhabitants continue to wear traditional costume. . . .

The Dutch flower industry does not cease suddenly when the bulbs are finished for the season. All through summer, flowers are auctioned at Aalsmeer and visitors can look round the huge covered market there. The cheese markets at Edam and Alkmaar are points of interest, too.

HAROLD CHAMPION, in the *Yorkshire Post,* Leeds

74. The Netherlands Delta Plan

The Dutch are engaged on a new campaign against the sea, beside which "the enclosing of the Zuider Zee was child's play". The essence of the Delta Plan is the conversion into fresh-water lakes of the deep tidal channels in Zeeland by which the River Maas and the Waal and Lek distributaries of the Rhine reach the North Sea. The first major stage in the Plan was completed on 24th April, 1961, when the Veeregat channel between the islands of Walcheren and North Beveland was closed. . . . There is no plan to close the Western Scheldt because this is the main approach to the port of Antwerp. . . .

The Delta Plan works will simplify the outline of the coast between Walcheren and a point west of Rotterdam, and reduce the length of the sea-dykes from 454 to 19 miles. . . . The objectives of the scheme, however, extend far beyond the prevention of floods. . . . The Plan will serve the port of Rotterdam by making it possible to direct an increased proportion of the waters of the Rhine and Maas through the New Waterway. . . . Fresh water will serve the expanding petro-chemical and other industries of Rotterdam. . . . The prospect of ample water supplies will also contribute to the expected success of Europoort, at the seaward end of the New Waterway opposite Hook of Holland. . . .

The new dams across the Delta are to carry roads which will end the age-long isolation of the south-western islands of

Zeeland.... A direct road from The Hague and Rotterdam to
Middelburg in Walcheren and the "Benelux Road" linking
Rotterdam to Antwerp by way of Bergen-op-Zoom are pro-
jected.

G. B. G. BULL, in *Geography* (Vol. 47, 1962, pp. 87–89)

Note. Rotterdam, already the largest port in the world, is planning to
extend its dock facilities still further on land reclaimed from the sea.

75. Brussels

Through its position in Europe, Brussels has found itself the
centre of a system of great continental traffic arteries, and the
city and its people know well how to meet the needs of its
visitors, for the Bruxellois are both discriminating and know-
ledgeable. Refreshed, perhaps by a leisurely and substantial
meal or the speciality of some café with a teasing name, the
visitor may join the vigorous life of Les Marolles (a city within
a city, with its own traditions, even its own language) and
expose himself to irresistible bargains. He may share the native
love of entertainment, for in addition to the theatre, ballet
or concert, Brussels offers carnivals and processions, marion-
ette theatres, and archery of a high order where the spectator
can see the longbow and even the crossbow practised with
mastery by members of the ancient "Serments".

Tradition flourishes also in the city's trade skills, and the
superb results of modern craftsmanship can be enjoyed in
many shops. Miss Willcox[3] describes the pleasures of trips by
tram to the outlying countryside—to Laeken, a Royal country
home, to Waterloo, to the thirteenth century chateau of Beersel.

from a Phoenix House book list

76. Belgium's Barges

What would our splendid port of Antwerp be without our
"batellerie", or inland shipping? Remember that one of the
great advantages of Antwerp as a port is that a cargo ship
arriving there in normal times can always find a return freight.
Thanks to the "batellerie" the transport of goods to and from

[3] In her book *Brussels*, published by Phoenix House.

the interior can be made very cheaply. . . . The barge will take goods from Antwerp to Paris and come back, say, with a load of gypsum ready for loading on to some ship sailing for the Far East. . . .

Many of our barges are now motor-driven, but this is only mainly on the regular services—the transport of merchandise of all kinds on the Antwerp-Brussels, Antwerp-Ghent and Antwerp-Liége itineraries. The little 75-ton "baquet" of Charleroi was just the right size for the locks between Brussels and Charleroi—before this canal was widened. . . . At present, a type which is very common is the "Campinois", of 500 to 600 tons, something over 150 feet long, twenty feet wide and eight feet draught. They are known as Campinois, because they are well suited to the locks of the Campine Canal. Then there are the majestic Rhine barges, some of which will carry a cargo of 2,000 tons and go right up to the Ruhr. Those of 1,500 tons go as far as Strasbourg or even Basle when the depth of water permits. . . .

There is at Antwerp, in the old canal dock, a shelter dock or "Schuildok", where some 300 barges were always to be found: that is to say, a floating population of more than a thousand inhabitants. When a marriage takes place among them you can see the Belgian flag hoisted on every mast and the riverside village takes on a festive air.

JEAN BANEUX, in the Belgian magazine *Marine*, published in London

Note. In the 1960's, the port of Antwerp doubled in size to become the third largest port in the world.

77. The Ardennes

A glance at the map of Belgium will show that the region of woods and hills watered by many rivers and streams, known by the name of the Ardennes, extends from the prosperous towns of Namur, Liége and Spa in the north as far as Luxemburg and Germany in the south-east, and to the valley of the Semois and the French frontier on the west. It is one of the most beautiful regions in all Europe, and also one of the most romantic. Legend and history, poetry and fiction, provoke an interesting reminiscence at almost every turn. . . . Ruined castles ever and again recall the days of feudal chivalry, and there will be no need to remind the traveller that he is treading upon ground consecrated by the genius of Sir Walter Scott. . . .

At one time the whole of the Ardennes was an immense forest . . . Caesar mentions the forest as stretching from east to west, from the Rhine nearly to the Rhone. Now there is comparatively little left of it.

The Romans caused swords, shields and other weapons to be made in the Ardennes. At the present time Liége is noted for its manufactures of fire-arms and cutlery, and the latter industry flourishes in Namur. Till the middle of the fifteenth century, Dinant and Bouvignes were celebrated for articles in brass and copper, called "Dinanderies". In Dinant, such articles are still produced. . . .

Three lines of railway pierce the Ardennes from north to south. One line runs from Namur to Dinant and into France at Givet, following the course of the Meuse. A second runs from Namur to Marloie, Arlon and Luxemburg. The third, having its course through several valleys, runs from Liége to Spa, Diekirch and Luxemburg.

Belgium (a Ward, Lock Tourist Handbook)

78. Paris

(*a*) The importance of Paris as a crossing place on the great south-west to north-east avenue of the European plain is due to its position below the confluence of the Marne with the Yonne and Seine, and above the place where the Seine begins to make wide meanders. The distance between these two obstructions is only about six miles, and here lie islands, on one of which the original city was built and which had been provided with bridges by the Romans. . . . The "Ile de la Cité" had not only the advantage of facilitating the crossing of the river but also of providing a natural Stronghold for the defence of the crossing and for securing a monopoly of the local navigation.

The Great Capitals, by VAUGHAN CORNISH

(*b*) Paris is a city of seven hills, or even more—Montmartre, Montsouris, Montparnasse, Mont Valérien, the Buttes Chaumont, the Montagne Sainte Geneviève ... and there are many others. Upon these hills and between these hills are the towns or villages which make up *the* town. For example, the Palais Royal, where I live, is a little town walled in by ancient and decayed buildings, and to reach the big city, centring round the Opéra, one has to make one's way up steps, through gateways and along a series of cloisters and arcades.... Paris, for the zealous explorer, because of its ramshackle beauty, because of its mixture of propped-up old age and modernity underlining the squalors, because of its medieval tangle of tumbledown dwellings, is like an enchanted loft in a child's story book.

JEAN COCTEAU, in The Observer

(*c*) No one can fail to depart from Paris with the feeling that he has been visiting the world's greatest cultural centre, with an incredibly stimulating atmosphere of history and beauty. He will carry away with him undying impressions of the architectural monuments of the seventeenth and eighteenth century greatness of France; the unsurpassed treasures of art collected in the metropolis and exhibited under the best possible conditions; the functional simplicity of its new buildings; the beauty of its parks and flower gardens; the exquisite taste that pervades its arts and crafts and the wonderful display of luxury articles in its shop windows; the importance of street markets in the city's life; the charm and elegant dresses of the Parisiennes; the density and well-regulated speed of the motor traffic; the efficiency of the Métro and bus systems; the excellent quality of the meals served in the numberless restaurants; and the politeness and helpfulness of all engaged in catering for the needs of visitors.

Paris for Everyman, by H. A. PIEHLER

79. French Fields and Roads

As you travel through the French countryside certain sights become familiar, until they seem to be essential, eternal parts of the landscape: a decrepit bike or two lying by the wayside and a few bent figures working in the fields, a pair of ploughhorses silhouetted against the sky, a thin church spire poking upwards from a distant cluster of buildings. In spite of the great variety of the country, the different scenery, these sights persist and impress themselves on the mind.

They change a little with the region; in the north, the figures are weeding their fields, in the south they are bent pruning their vines; the horses are replaced by oxen, the spire changes to a tower. The bent figures and the horses become fewer on the large wheat-growing plains where tractors are more in evidence, but you may travel the length and breadth of the country without touching such areas. In any case there is always evidence of a passionate attachment to the fertile earth. Noticeable, too, is the scarcity of large towns and the preponderance of agricultural life.

The main roads are broad and noble, gently descending and effortlessly rising again with almost mathematical precision; they point ahead purposefully, possibly bending a little once every two or three miles, concentrating on their task of getting to Paris as quickly and as directly as possible. These, the Routes Nationales, with their clear, well-placed signposts and red-topped kilometre stones, are the responsibility of the State; each is much like another, and is kept in good repair.

The Gallic Land, by LEN ORTZEN

80.　Alsace — A Lovely Garden

Louis XIV, looking down on Alsace from the summit of Ste Odile, cried: "What a lovely garden!" The natural wealth enriched by the labour of the inhabitants has, indeed, made Alsace one of the most prosperous of the French provinces. ... Alsace is a country of mountain and plain, and the soil is extremely fertile. The climate is very mild and the predominating westerly wind brings in its train a great deal of moisture. ... The land is divided up into relatively small holdings. It is this feature that has long given the Alsatian peasant the self-esteem, love of freedom, sense of responsibility and passion for work which have made Alsace a province unsurpassed in agricultural prosperity....

The chief factor contributing to the prosperity of Alsace is the balance between the agricultural and the industrial wealth of the country. The textile industry is one of the oldest in the world, and it was inside the mills of Mulhouse that the first steps towards the social progress of France and of the world generally were initiated. . . .

Alsace has also a very rich subsoil. Her potash mines are estimated to be capable of producing 1,500 million tons of crude salt, whilst the annual production has been about 400,000 tons. At Pechelbraun, about 80,000 tons of petroleum a year are obtained. There are also railway-building works at Grafenstaden, breweries and large mills at Strasbourg, sugar refineries at Erstein, and so on. The centre of all this activity is the inland port of Strasbourg, which handles the export of coal, grain, petroleum and wood, as well as iron from Lorraine, along the Rhine.

CAPTAIN WIETZEL, in *Entente,* London

81. The "P.L.M."

On a recent journey from Paris to the South we passed the time trying to decide exactly at what point you see what. Just when and where do you realize that you are leaving the Foggy North irrevocably for the Sunny South?

Well, soon after Dijon you have the vines, which are the first pleasant signs of a warmer climate. Then, somewhere near Macon, the deep-brown roofs of Burgundy give way to Mediterranean curved tiles. At this stage the tiles are a mottled, washed-out cream and pink, and only later do they assume the richer, crab-coloured hue which every traveller on the train is waiting to see.

Lyons comes and goes, and the Rhone Valley opens up with its narrow, cultivated strips, sheltered from the Mistral by bamboo screens. The poplar trees, which stand like sentinels in the flat valley, get darker and darker, but they do not actually become cypresses until after Valence. (It was *before* Valence that you passed that famous landmark of the journey south, the wonderful vine-clad Hermitage Hill.) The landscape now shows every shade of green. On your right the Massif Central looks menacingly near, just across the river; while on your left, the Alps are impressive at a distance.

It is after Avignon that you get the first olive trees, and from there the country changes every five minutes. At one moment you might be in England; the next you're in Africa. Here it's cultivated; there it's hardly more than "garrigue" (bushes sprouting from the bare rock). You must wait till after Arles to see the "pins maritimes" and those long lines of cypresses bordering the Etang de Berre. Just where the train meets this great inland lake, you can observe the finest (if not the first) "village perché" or hill village.

So this is the record of a journey south, as we see it:

> Vines after Dijon.
> Tiles after Macon.
> Cypresses after Valence.
> Olives after Avignon.
> Pines after Arles.

"Jean Qui Rit", in *Men Only*

82. Marseilles: Port of Seven Seas

Tourists see many museums and historical monuments, and some of the finest can be found in Marseilles, the famous "port of seven seas"; but the tourist who keeps his ears as well as his eyes open will find an even richer field for exploration in the sights and sounds of the crowded streets....

The city was founded in 600 B.C. by Greek navigators pushed out of their Phocea colony by the Persian invaders.... In its early days Marseilles was called Massalia, which was the name given to that area by its original inhabitants, the Ligurians, a pastoral people who were not interested in maritime commerce, which was the Greeks' speciality....

Settlers from many other parts of Europe and the world established their home in this truly cosmopolitan city during the twenty-five centuries of that history.... The Romans called the Transalpine region where Marseilles is located "Provincia", a name which turns up in the modern geographical vocabulary as "la Provence". It was also during the Roman domination that the name "Massalia" was corrupted into "Massilia", and the new version has lived down to us on the official emblem of the city: "Massilia civitas".

FRANÇOIS PASQUALINI, in *The Linguist*

83. The Camargue

The flat country of lake and marsh at the Rhone delta is well known as the home of those French cowboys, the "Gardiens", who look after the herds of wild black cattle rather as a traditional duty and sport than as a matter of economic necessity. The main use of the cattle is to attract tourists—and to provide bulls for the mild French form of bull-fighting—milder to the bull but exciting enough for participants and spectators.

The Camargue earns much of its income from tourists and from fishing, but round its edge attempts have been made at rice-growing since the seventeenth century, and since the last war modern methods have enabled the area to satisfy practically the whole of France's rice requirements.

But the heart of the Camargue, the Etang de Vaccares, is a Nature Reserve, and often over the emerald green rice-fields fly skeins of pink flamingoes. Here, 600 miles from London, is the most exotic and un-European corner of all Europe. To add still further to this exotic character, gipsies from all over Europe make a pilgrimage there each spring, to the tomb of their patron saint, Sarah, in the crypt of the ancient church of Saintes Maries de la Mer.

For the ordinary visitor it is exotic enough to look out from the roof of the church to the great lakes of the Camargue on the one side, and the blue Mediterranean on the other.

"W.C.", in the *Yorkshire Post*, Leeds

84. The Bretons at Home

(*a*) To the average tourist the name of Brittany conjures up memories of cider and pancakes, misty foreshores and picturesque little farms—and perhaps also the half-heard music that always seems to be in the air. For Brittany is the country of Magic, where water-sprites and witchcraft are as much a part of the landscape as the tall standing stones that are the legacy of a previous occupation.

The Bretons came to Brittany from the other Celtic lands about sixteen centuries ago. . . . Ignored by France, the Bretons developed their own culture. In the inland region, known by the Bretons as Ar Coat, the Mountain, the traditions embraced work and religion: songs for dancing, for calling in the sheep, and for spinning flax, reflected the day's toil. On the coast, Ar Mor, the songs were of the sea, the dancing for enjoyment, accompanied by the biniou and the bombard.

JEREMY NICKLIN, in *Radio Times*

(b) The ancient duchy of Brittany ... consists of undulating plains, divided into two unequal parts by the Arrée mountains, extending from east to west, of which the culminating point is 1,282 feet above the sea. The western coast is singularly wild and picturesque, bordered with great masses of rock and precipitous granite cliffs. It is on this coast and the coast of the adjacent islands that the best sardines are caught, the curing of which forms the most important industry of the small ports, extending from St Nazaire northward to Brest.... On the elevated tablelands of the interior are reared cattle and sheep; while the more favoured plains and valleys produce large crops of cereals and excellent fruit, among which tons of strawberries and green peas are sent to England.... The best butter in France is said to come from the farms between Rennes and Prévalaye, two miles south.

Brittany and Touraine, by c. B. BLACK

Note. Brittany grows 70 per cent as much farm produce as Belgium and 40 per cent as much as Holland.

85. "The Loire is France"

On the banks of the Loire, rather than upon those of the Seine, was elaborated the essential French tradition of attitude, of manners, of comportment and of expression. No real understanding of the French people is possible without an attentive pilgrimage to the lands watered by this broad, shallow, pale, shifting river, whose ever-changing lights reflect a graceful and subtle sky.

For the full 600 miles of its course from the shiny, micaceous rocks of the Marenc and down to the sea beyond Nantes, nearly every league of the way holds something to evoke a phase of the French story.

When the Loire, swollen to a majestic width, enters Tou-

raine, then every village and castle, every manor and town upon
the banks beckons us to linger, to listen and to admire.

But though the lower valley of the Loire is often described
as the "Garden of France", it is not a garden all flowers
and greenery. As a French geographer once defined this region,
it is a robe of sackcloth fringed with gold. The sackcloth robe
is the arid uplands separating the golden fringes of the vales.

"Touraine", Vol. 2 of *The People's France,* ed. A. H. BRODRICK

86. Changes in the Dordogne

Like the small shopkeeper in Britain, the small farmer in France
finds it hard to keep going, and the mountain farmer of the
Dordogne and Central France, who often farms fields that his
grandparents carved out of woody hillside, is leaving in growing numbers for an easier and safer job in the towns.... This
despite all the Government has done for the area, with ambitious dams across the once-turbulent waters. Electricity gener-
ated here supplies the whole of France, and is abundantly
available around the Dordogne itself....

In the pretty mountain town of Le Mont-Dore, where the
streams of the Dore and the Dogne meet, there is no suggestion
that the bubbling waters, fed from the melting snows and
summer rain, will soon become a chain of artificial lakes. But
only a few miles away the first dam straddles the river at
Bort les Orgues, so named because of the organ-pipe erosion
of the hillsides....

Electricity is not the only benefit brought to the region by
these concrete barrages; fish, fat and plentiful, thrive in the
new deeps.... A further benefit is the end of the flood
menace. Even in the wettest season the number of successive
barrages on the river is so great that the flow of water can
always be kept in hand....

Another boon to the Dordogne economy is the growth of
winter sports. The waters of the Dordogne originate in the
hills of the Puy de Dôme, where, just outside the village of
Besse, a new streamlined ski-ing resort has been opened....
Perhaps the most celebrated attractions in the Dordogne in
recent years have been the Lascaux caves and their prehis-

F

toric paintings. Unhappily they are now closed ... mosses and
mildew have started to grow on the rock surfaces.

JOHN SMALLDON, in the *Daily Telegraph*

87.   About Forests — and those of Gascony in particular

Cutting trees is an agony unless one assures one's Heart that
cutting a crop is comparable to any other harvest. Mature trees
must be cut, save specimens left for scenery. And the tree-
cutter's conscience can be salved by steady, undeviating planting. There is planting for ornament, planting for game, planting
for commerce, and, most important of all, planting the wastes
and swamps to steady the fall of water and check flood and
erosion. ....

It is not good land that need be taken up by forestry. The
benefactor of his people makes two blades of grass grow for
one, but a true economist is the forester who makes trees grow
in swamp, or on the stony ground which baffled the Sower in
the Parable. The great example of this rescue of Nature herself
is the Gascon Plain, which French engineers and foresters
planted when nearly two million acres lay derelict and ague-
ridden. An immense district was brought out of poverty to
wealth by the Maritime Pine. Sand can be stayed by Corsican
Pine, so it is not useless to plough the sands if you plant trees.

SIR SHANE LESLIE, in *Homes and Gardens*

88.   Andorra

Right in the heart of the Pyrenees is Andorra, the smallest
country in the world.[4] It contains about 430 square kilometres
of mountain, and less than twenty of them are tillable land and
that mostly in the form of hand-made terraced fields. Although
under the guardianship of the President of France, who is still
ceremonially referred to as His Imperial Majesty, and the
Bishop of Urgel in Spain, this country, with its elected parlia-

[4]In actual fact, Liechtenstein is smaller, not to mention San Marino,
Vatican City, etc.

ment of twenty-four members, called the General Council of the Vall[ey]s, is still completely independent.

It has remained practically the same, with the same primitive virtues (and no doubt a few primitive faults as well) for the last 700 years. Probably it changed very little in the 700 years before that, and for who knows how many centuries back. . . .

Andorra La Vella is the capital, the smallest city you could ever imagine, though development has merged it into neighbouring Les Escaldes, once noted for its mineral springs. There is a Parliament House, The House of the Valls, proportionate to the size of the capital. It is tucked away in a square approached by narrow cobbled streets, which are what all the streets must have been like once upon a time. . . . The mountains tower above the town in superb majesty, tree-clad nearly to the summits, brilliant in the early morning sunshine, glowing richly at evening. . . .

If you want to see Andorra, go out of season if you can. But unless you approach from Spain it cannot be done before May, for the passes on the French side are snow-blocked until then.

JOHN HEREFORD, in *Homes and Gardens*

89. The Biscayan Provinces of Spain

Galicia is, even today, more nearly allied to Portugal than to Spain. . . . A "Gallego"—really a native of Galicia—means, in common parlance, a porter, a water-carrier, almost a beast of burden, and the Galicians are as well known for this purpose in Portugal as in Spain; great numbers find ready employment in the former country. . . .

Although they lie so close together, the Asturias differs widely from its sister province both in the character of its people and its scenery. The Romans took 200 years to subdue it, and the Moors never obtained a footing there. The Asturians are a hardy, independent race. Like their neighbours, the Basques, they are handsome and robust in appearance; they are always to be recognized in Madrid by their fresh appearance and excellent physique. For the most part they are to be found engaged in the fish trade. . . .

The Basque Provinces are, perhaps, the best known to English travellers, since the latter generally enter Spain by that route, and those staying in the south of France are fond of running across to have at least a look at Spain, and be able to say they have been there. The people pride themselves on being "the oldest race in Europe", and are, no doubt, the direct descendants of the original and unconquered inhabitants of the Iberian Peninsula. . . .

The northern ports of Spain, in the Atlantic, are the most important; that of Bilbao, a most unpromising one by nature, has grown out of all recognition since the close of the Carlist War. The railway to the iron mines was already in course of construction when it broke out. . . . With peace and quietness came one of the most extraordinary revivals of modern times.

Spanish Life in Town and Country, by L. HIGGIN

90. The Catalan-Speaking Countries

The Catalan-speaking countries extend from the Pyrenees to Alicante, and include Catalonia, Valencia and the Balearic Islands, apart from the French département of "Pyrénées Orientales". The Catalan countries in the Peninsula have a population of about six million, larger than that of Norway, Eire, Denmark, Finland, Switzerland or Scotland, and about the same as that of Bulgaria, Sweden or Greece.[5] These countries include the largest city in the Spanish state, Barcelona,[6] and Valencia, the third largest. The density of population is high, in most parts from sixty to 250 per square kilometre, although in some districts round Valencia with highly developed intensive cultivation it rises to 450, and in industrial districts near Barcelona to 820. . . .

Agriculture is highly developed in the Catalan-speaking countries, particularly the cultivation of Mediterranean products like olives, grapes, oranges and other fruit. The land is usually divided into small plots, each farm belonging, some-

[5] In 1967 the population of Bulgaria was 8,334,000; in 1961 Sweden had 7,495,000 people; in 1965 the population of Greece was estimated at 8,550,000.

[6] Madrid is now the largest, with an estimated 3 millions in 1967 (Barcelona 1,656,000).

times for generations, to one family. But industry and trade have reached a high degree of development, and the fact that Catalonia—like the Basque Country—has experienced the Industrial Revolution along with other European countries helps to mark it off from Spain. Economic conditions different from those of Spain have produced not only an industrial working class but also a large and wealthy middle class, whose influence is preponderant in the life of the country. This explains the strong support still given to the traditional democratic ideas in Catalonia. This large and comfortable middle class is naturally opposed to any form of extremism, and gives balance to the political life of the country.

J. M. BATISTA Y ROCA, in *Free Europe*

91. In Old Castile

"You will soon learn that there is no such thing as Spain," says the Spaniard with a smile.... "Spain is really a collection of small kingdoms which were once independent—all different. You in England take your idea of Spain from novels and films. These all deal with the South—with Andalusia, where life is slow and lazy, and where men do sing songs and kill each other for love. But look at Castile. Look at this dead plain like a sea. Look at those mountains with snow on them. Castile is over 2,000 feet above the sea. We say, 'Nine months of winter and three of hell!' Yet this is the very heart of Spain"....

The train ploughs its lonely way through a bleak, dead, mountainous land. The early sun is already warm, but there is snow on the mountains. Far to the west the hills rise and fall towards the mountains of Cantabria; to the south, ridge against ridge, lies the Sierra Guadarrama.

So this khaki land of mountains, harsh and bleak as a moonscape, is Spain! How different from the flat, languid, fruitful Spain of popular imagination! ... I look down into deep, waterless river-beds littered with boulders.... This is Old Castile—a hard, extreme land that knows the bitterness of cold and the violence of heat, a land inhabited by frugal farmers whose little homes seem literally to grow out of the stony earth.... A flat plain, the colour of cocoa, stretches to the sky. It is as monotonous as the sea. Windmills, standing on slight ridges, ride the flatness like ships.... This is the immortal La Mancha, the country of Don Quixote.

H. V. MORTON, in the *Daily Herald*

92. Water in South-East Spain

"Rainclouds over the sierra!" On how many summer evenings of drought since the dark Iberian in the dawn of time first occupied the south-east Spanish coastline must the exultant cry have been raised, to be followed by disillusion? Towering some five miles behind the long white house between Valencia and Alicante in which these words are written, the sierra in question is everything a Spanish sierra should be: far-reaching, high, trackless, peaked and chasmed in the best romantic Doré manner; beautiful and mysterious in changing light and shadow, and above all in its grape-bloom phase near sundown.

Powdered with light winter snow it is faëry; crowned with black heavy masses of cloud it can be apocalyptic. But the sierra has an arbitrary way of shrugging off trifles. By sunrise one finds time after time the clouds all fled and the old pitiless blaze due again to mock and deride.

For us, as for the Iberian, the Celt, the Phoenician, the Visigoth, the Moor, the Spaniard of the Golden Age, the subjects of Hapsburg and Bourbon, and their present heirs and assigns hereabouts, yet another rainless night is over.... But let us not exaggerate. In this particular corner of the rich fruit garden of Spain there is plenty of water about, if it can be got at ... [it comes] chiefly from a source away up in a magic tangle of mountains....

For a few hours every four or five weeks our three acres of trees on terraced land get a thorough soaking by arrangement, via an irrigation system—a very good one—believed to be a bequest of the Moor. This is enough for the olives, the almonds, the figs, the oranges and the lemons, which seem to be satisfied.

D. B. WYNDHAM LEWIS, in *Homes and Gardens*

93. Seville: Oranges and Olives

I was fortunate to go to Seville earlier this year and to visit an orange grove at the time of the harvest of marmalade oranges. The trees are bigger and better than the ones I remember in California as a child: about twenty feet high and shaped rather like a horse chestnut and planted a little below ground level to conserve moisture, so that their graceful branches seem almost to reach to one's feet.

Donkeys carry the crop to the farmhouse, and trucks to the packing stations, where the oranges are graded and packed into half chests for shipping. . . . Those oranges which are rejected by hand sorters at the packing stations are squeezed for their juice, while essential oils are extracted from the skin for perfume manufacture.

The peaceful town of Seville beside the navigable Guadalquivir has a faint air of Cambridge about it. Yet there is enough Moorish influence for it to have been chosen for several location scenes in the film "Lawrence of Arabia". A favourite landmark is the Giralda tower, the lovely campanile beside the cathedral. Spaniards say that the best bitter oranges and the best dessert olives are grown within sight of the Giralda.

JANE KING, in *Homes and Gardens*

94. Aspects of the Andalusian Scene

(*a*) I know of few things in this life more delicious than a ride in the spring or summer season in the neighbourhood of Seville. . . . It is here that the balmy air of beautiful Andalusia is to be inhaled in full perfection. Aromatic herbs and flowers are growing in abundance, diffusing their perfume around. Here dark and gloomy cares are dispelled as if by magic, as the eyes wander over the prospect, lighted by unequalled sunshine, in which gaily painted butterflies wanton, and green and golden salamanquesas lie extended, enjoying the luxurious warmth, and occasionally startling the traveller by springing up and making off with portentous speed to the nearest coverts, whence they stare upon him with their sharp and lustrous eyes.

The Bible in Spain, by GEORGE BORROW

(*b*) Three centuries ago the Andalusian hills were covered with forests, which attracted an annual rainfall of about twice the present-day measurement. Timber being wealth only when cut down, the landowners began to denude the land of trees, and, despite warnings, continued the process—until today, apart from the cork woods around Algeciras, there are few trees left within a radius of 200 miles. Thus they reduced the normal rainfall of the province to a point at which its summers are one long drought. Modern steel bridges spanning river-beds devoid of even a trickle of water in June, testify to the tragedy of those vanished forests of Andalusia.

European Excursions, by H. HESSELL TILTMAN

95. "The Rock"

One of the best things about a visit to Gibraltar—if you go by air—is the approach and landing, especially if you come in from the Atlantic. Africa looms mistily behind the rugged spurs of Espartel, and the Straits close in upon you relentlessly, like the serrated jaws of giant pincers. There is no escape, except to turn back; and then, suddenly, the way opens again, the dark sheen of woods, close-textured, rises behind Tarifa, and the great Rock comes out of the sea, like the herald of a new continent. As you near Europa Point, the massive hump of pale limestone reaches for the clarity of a Mediterranean summer sky—splendid in lone grandeur, dominating with sure strength Algeciras Bay. The town clings in a white huddle beneath the north-west buttress, its edge hard on the water —throwing failing tendrils up the steep face until defeated by the gradients and craggy outcrops. . . .

The economy of space in Gibraltar reminds one irresistibly of Malta. There is literally no space to waste, and so the houses are tall and narrow, leaning toward one another over the con-stricted streets. Main Street is a deep tunnel, walled with these balconied houses above small shops and bars, always thickly populated with the citizenry, military police and soldiers, and, of course, the Navy. . . . Heaped mounds of oranges and bananas and melons colour and scent the warm air at the shop-fronts. Down across the slope of tall houses, a forest of masts and funnels marks the dockyard, and warships ride at slack cables on the calm waters of Algeciras Bay. Algeciras itself, a white, sunlit splash at the foot of the wooded mountains of Seville, tumbles to the water.

J. B. FOERS, in *Chambers's Journal*, Edinburgh

96. Portuguese Portrait

Portugal, a narrow strip of land nowhere as much as 150 miles wide, runs down the Atlantic Coast of the Iberian Peninsula for over 300 miles, between the ocean and the high central plateau of Spain; and combines the usual Atlantic coastal flora, common to the shores of Britain and northern France, with the exotic Iberian flowers, lovers of heat and drought. In the north, where bracken grows among the heather and pines, and damp mists hang between the hills, one might fancy oneself in Scotland, but for the blue jewel-like brilliance of Lithospermum, carpeting the roadside banks; down in the southernmost province, the Algarve, one could well be in Morocco, what with the cactus hedges, the flat-roofed houses lime-washed to a blinding whiteness, the green brooding mounds of the fig trees, and the queer, queer flowers. . . .

The true splendour of these rolling southern uplands, especially after a year of drought—which frequently occurs in Portugal—are field flowers, the weeds of the arable land. In April, before the heat of the summer sun has withered them, they carpet the vast unfenced spaces between the great cork-oaks—standing far apart, dark-green and shapely—with a tissue of white and purple and gold, splashed with patches of crimson; as far as the eye can reach, to the distant hills of Spain, the whole earth is brilliant with these glorious colours.

ANN BRIDGE, in *Homes and Gardens*

97. A Journey to the Algarve

I capture a taxi in the streets of Lisbon, and bowl along to the rendezvous from which I shall begin my journey south with friends, to Albufeira in the Algarve.

The southern coastline of Portugal reaches a hundred miles from historical Cape St Vincent in the west to the River Guadiana, boundary of Spain, in the east. The entire Algarve province, fringed by the Atlantic, is one of Europe's most beautiful, least familiar stretches.

Across the Tagus first by ferry, gliding away from the great statue of Jesus, his arms outstretched blessing all voyagers. The road leads to Setubal, and we pass a factory washed in delicate turquoise. At Setubal a British company has begun to manufacture motor-cars, and this is our last view of urban life for quite a time.

Cork forests offer upraised branches like huge dead spiders, the bark slashed and stacked in woodpiles in the fields. It is almost summer and the wild flowers are bowing their exit for another season. . . .

A short distance from Alcacer girls are walking towards us. . . . They walk as elegantly as Parisian mannequins, carrying harvested rice. And now I see that interspersed between the forests are paddy fields, the rice plants sleepily feeling their way through the water. . . . This is the great cereal-growing district, and undulating into the distance are barley, wheat, oats and other grain crops. . . . Cork trees give way to oak trees. Not majestic oaks, these have flat heads and large acorns, fodder for snouty wild pigs who scrabble in the undergrowth.

JANE BRANDON, in *Homes and Gardens*

98. Impressions of Malta

Blue, a glorious deep, rich and clear blue, with streaks of sapphire, turquoise and ultramarine—this will always be the credible sea and sky colouring which filled my eyes on a recent first visit to Malta (or Malita, the honey-coloured island). Malta covers ninety-five square miles and lies right in the middle of the Mediterranean Sea, about sixty miles south of Sicily. Its people enjoy a Mediterranean climate at its very best. For days on end I delighted in unbroken sunshine, and I am told that you can forecast the weather accurately for months ahead.

The Maltese are a fascinating people, said to be descended from the Phoenicians who colonized the island a thousand years before Christ. Many of them look like Sicilians, and they talk a language which is sufficiently like Arabic to be mistaken for one of its dialects. . . .

With a long unbroken Christian history it is not surprising
that in all the towns and villages there are such beautiful
churches, many ancient, but many new. ... I was fortunate in
being a guest at the lovely Villa Bologna, with its beautiful
garden fragrant with roses, stocks, lilies and other English
flowers, as well as lemon and orange groves and greenhouses
full of delicious tomatoes. ...

I visited children along the narrow streets of Valetta, with
their washing-festooned balconies, and out in the countryside,
much of which is treeless and very barren. The lack of rainfall
is one of the problems in Malta and the average annual fall
is only twenty-one inches.

ISOBEL HURGON, in *The World's Children*

99. Sicilian Portrait

Since the beginning of time white, yellow and dark-skinned
races have struggled for Sicily. ... The many conquering races
have left their memorials. Indeed, as so often in a southern
land blessed with plenty of sun and a fine climate, many of the
arts are here seen at their best. ...

Nature does not lag behind man. ... Vineyards hung with
purple and yellow grapes abound; the rich, sweet wines of
Marsala are famous and may be bought out there for twopence
or threepence a glass. Behind Palermo is the "Conca d'Oro",
or "Shell of Gold", one of the richest valleys in the world,
covered by an uninterrupted grove of fruit-trees and carpeted
with flowers whose beauty beggars description. ... Olive trees
flourish up to a height of 3,000 feet—the oil is carried in barrels
in little carts gaily painted with religious or historic scenes. ...

The people are often very poor despite this bounty of nature.
Until recent years they had suffered from centuries of Bourbon
misrule, its infamous robber-gangs of the Mafia and the
exactions of large, often absentee, landlords. Many of them
live mainly on bread, olives and the prickly pear which grows
wild even in the most barren parts of the island. Yet magnificent palms also grow wild, or stand like proud giants in the
city squares; over the island and out to sea wafts the scent of
hundreds and thousands of orange and lemon groves—enough
even to drown the garlic and drain-stench which on land

confront the traveller with the knowledge that his age can still perhaps gild this lily.

MARTIN MACLAUGHLIN, in the *Yorkshire Post*, Leeds

100.   Sicily and "The Bridge"

People were laughing at Giuseppe Garibaldi when, about a century ago, he dreamed of a bridge across the narrow Straits of Messina to link Sicily with Italy. Today only two things stand in the way of his dream's fulfilment. One is expense. The other is the uncertain attitude of the Sicilians....

Garibaldi's bridge appeals strongly to many Italians. Road-making and bridge-building are part of their Roman heritage. Already their famous Highway of the Sun runs from Milan to Salerno, south of Naples. They want to extend it across the Straits of Messina and not to bring it to an end before it reaches the Sicilian capital of Palermo.... Sicilians do not have this urge. Road-making and bridge-building are not in their blood. For one thing, they are not Latins. Sicily was Greek and African long before it fell to the Romans in the Punic War.... Gradually their language became Italian, but it was never Latin. The bridge may create dissension rather than greater unity between Sicilians and Italians. It may accentuate the difference of their cultural backgrounds.

There is a strong case for developing Sicily commercially through building the bridge and opening new roads. Sicilians, however, are not so sure that this is putting first things first. The scourges of their island country are the elemental ones of ignorance, poverty and hunger. Sicily needs more and better school teachers in the villages. She needs dams and an ampler water supply....

On one thing the Sicilians and Italians who face each other across the Straits of Messina are fully agreed. They are certain that they live in the world's chief beauty spot. A heartfelt question was put by a Sicilian journalist at a Press conference in Rome a few evenings ago. He asked: "Can the bridge be artistic?"

J. GLORNEY BOLTON, in the *Yorkshire Post*, Leeds

101. The People of Southern Italy

In Italy ... we were again in one of the cradles of the world's
culture, a land famous for centuries for the riches of its music,
art and literature; and yet in Southern Italy we were conscious
all the time of a deeply disturbing apathy, if that is the right
word for a state of mind which produces not only helplessness,
but sometimes a violent unwillingness to understand and accept the new world of Italian democracy. We were taken, for
instance, to see the shell of a school which had been built by
the government in a small town in Calabria two years before.
The whole building had been gutted in senseless violence ...
not by delinquent children, but by adults with a so-called
grievance against the authorities, prepared to clan up with
those who had destroyed their own democratic property. So
their own children continued to huddle in a hopeless, makeshift, overcrowded school and put up with an education which
has far to go before it can break through, in the younger
generation of Southern Italy, the apathetic acceptance of the
old dead ways and habits.

We did not find a starving people. But we found a world of
people who did not know how to grow up out of an already
dead past, and were apathetically willing to accept illiteracy,
under-nourishment and squalor.

CATHERINE KING, in *The World's Children*

Note. The poverty of Southern Italy has led to large-scale emigration,
to the U.S.A., France, and Britain in particular.

102. Naples and Thereabouts

As the visitor at Naples looks across the deep blue waters of
the bay he will see three islands breaking up the wide horizon.
To the west Procida and Ischia first take the eye, for the last-
named is an island of some size; then directly to the south
lies Capri. ... The whole of this island is composed of Apen-
nine limestone, which proves it to have been at one time connected with the mainland, and to have formed part of the
peninsula of Sorrento. These rocks form the chief interest of
Capri, and their unique beauty is worthy of record among
Europe's natural wonders. Perhaps of all the grottos which the

sea has carved out at the island's base the Blue Grotto is the most famous. . . .

To the east of Naples is the mountain of Vesuvius. Europe's famed volcano stands out sharply from the horizon, the most prominent landmark to the dweller in the city, over which it appears to preside, like some vengeful fate, waiting patiently for the appointed time when it shall overwhelm the numberless white villas crowded on the rocky slopes from the shore of the bay to Mount St Elmo. It is the bulk of the mountain which makes it appear in such close proximity, for in reality it is about six and a half miles away from the town. Nevertheless, the distance is not so great as to do away with the possibility of danger from an eruption, for the whole area is known to be extremely volcanic. . . .

Pompeii, under the shadow of Vesuvius, is a city of the dead; but it is, nevertheless, a city alive with interest, for here the destroyer has become the preserver, and the ashes which fell in fiery showers upon the doomed citizens have dealt tenderly with their habitations, their lares and penates, sheltering these from the destroying force of time until the labours of the excavator should rescue them from oblivion.

Wonders of the World, published by Odhams Press

103.   "The Eternal City"

(a)   Rome is situated in the centre of the Campagna, which extends for about forty miles parallel to the coast and for about thirty miles inland. This plain is bounded on the north-west and south-east by volcanic mountains of late formation whose extinct craters enclose high-lying lakes. . . . Eighteen miles east-north-east of Rome between Monte Ripoli and Monte Sterparo the Anio descends in a waterfall from the Apennines, at the site of Tivoli. The valley of this river (which joins the left bank of the Tiber about three miles above Rome) is a natural line of communication eastward from the Campagna into the very heart of the upland valleys of the central Apennines. . . .

Rome itself stands on a group of volcanic hills nearly two hundred feet in height which abut on the left bank of the Tiber. A smaller group of similar hills rises opposite to them about a quarter of a mile from the right bank. The present width of the river here is rather more than three hundred feet. . . . The control of the waterway was facilitated by an island of firm ground in mid-channel, an exceptional feature in the Tiber.

The Great Capitals, by VAUGHAN CORNISH

(b) In 1939 I was in Florence touring with the Old Vic Theatre Company when Pope Pius XI died. When we drove to the railway station to catch a train for Rome and the opening of "Hamlet", I noticed that the newspapers carrying the news about the Pope were all heavily outlined in black. The train to Rome was not one of those that had been speeded up by Mussolini and there was plenty of time to see the countryside. It was a lovely spring day and the sun glinted on the churches crowning the hilltops, all of them adorned with black awnings, their bells tolling at long intervals.

I was very much reminded of the classical Renaissance paintings and of artists like Michelangelo who had used the same countryside as a background for his paintings. Many of the classical biblical paintings, such as the "Flight into Egypt", had been set against these very hills and valleys, making the traveller feel as if he were part of history. This feeling was reinforced when we visited St Peter's, in Rome, to see the Pope lying in state in a side chapel.

ANDREW CRUICKSHANK, in *Homes and Gardens*

(c) Rome's largest private park, the Villa Pamphili, is for sale. This peaceful oasis of parkland, on the fringe of Rome, is bounded on one side by the ancient Aurelian Way, along which an old aqueduct runs, still in use after centuries. With its sweeping pastures, its pine forests, its fountains and formal gardens, the Villa Pamphili stretches across some 500 acres, and has been the private possession of the noble family of Prince Doria Pamphili for centuries. . . . Recently I was driven round this vast estate by the owner. We drove first through a wide gateway, past the Arch of the Four Winds, which marks the scene of battle between Garibaldi's troops and French forces well over 100 years ago. The pines, the palm trees, and the ilexes stood out bravely and clearly against the spring sky of pale blue, for all the world like a Piranesi engraving.

Sheep were grazing as we made our way slowly past the
Valley of the Deer.... Only the superb vista of the great dome
of St Peter's, framed by the trees, gave the lie to the illusion
that we were lost in the depths of the countryside.

PATRICK SMITH, in *The Listener*

104. In the North-West of Italy

(*a*) It is in the North that the real changes in Italy are taking
place, particularly in Piedmont, a province of some four million
people in the North-West of Italy, which is rapidly becoming
one of Europe's major industrial centres.... Its capital,
Turin, with its great Trade Fairs, its Motor Show, its rubber,
chemicals, engineering and motor plants, is often pointed to
as a fine example of the new Europe.... Rural progress is
also marked. Piped water is replacing the village pump; electricity is spreading. Tractors are no longer oddities, and
machines have taken most of the women out of the ricefields.
As milk and meat production rise, pizzas and spaghetti are
becoming less inevitable.... The Milanese are considered loud,
tasteless and flashy. In the textile centre of Biella there are two
distinct groups of women—those who shop in Turin, and the
smaller, self-consciously smart group who risk accusations of
depravity by going to Milan.

BRYAN MOYNAHAN, in the *Yorkshire Post*, Leeds

(*b*) Milan is a good city to fly to.... By road, especially
coming from Switzerland, it is a different thing. Switzerland
itself goes flabby and blowsy, in the Ticino, and the overrated
lakes are no recompense; Como is a real Italian town, in the
best sense, but beyond it the countryside pullulates with huge
villages separated by tiny strips of countryside. Eventually the
strips disappear altogether, and among a cloud of Fiats, scooters,
and voracious heavy lorries, you are at the edge of Milan. Half
an hour later, you may be somewhere near the centre. By the
time the car is parked, you are numb.... The gloomy straight
streets of Milan, rammed full of traffic, are the brutal inter-
action of business efficiency and the Italian temperament. If

the result is bearable, it is because of the unquenchable spirit and friendliness of the ordinary Milanese.

IAN NAIRN, in *The Listener*

105. Venice "Afloat"

It is like being four days at sea. The salt air, the briny smell, the perpetual slap-slap of water against the sides of the canals, produce an illusion of buoyancy in the land, so that it would be natural to walk along the floor of the hotel with feet wide apart, balancing against the roll. The blurred windows, outside which the water tumbles roughly among the boats, are portholes, the people in wet mackintoshes who shoulder in at the door, laughing, wiping the wet off their eyebrows, have scurried along a deck, soused by spray....

Everywhere are arches: in the tall flat fronts of palaces— rose, ochre and slate-grey—that border the Grand Canal; arches of bridges springing in every back street between the shabby, charming houses, where every time you look upwards, a balcony that might have been Jessica's, or a lion's face carved in stone, catches the eye.

Everywhere there is a sense of movement springing from the water—the upward movement of people climbing the many flights of steps, the sharp, upward curve of the prows of gondolas, the aspiring domes and towers, culminating in the great Campanile, the first of Europe that rises over the rim of water to greet those coming back by sea from the East.

LETTICE COOPER, in *Homes and Gardens*

Note. Parts of Venice are crumbling, others are sinking into the mud, especially The Rialto, the main island (with St Mark's Cathedral and the Doge's Palace) which has shorter piles than the rest.

106. Travelling in Yugoslavia

"It's like visiting ten different countries rolled into one", declared the young Frasers, who were astonished at the fantastic variety of Yugoslavia. They had joined their father who was opening a new office for his tourist company there. In doing so they encountered a land with seven frontiers, six republics,

G

five nations, four languages, three religions and two alphabets.

They began their tour in the Slovenian mountains and on the way to what were to become their headquarters in Dubrovnik they had their first taste of Yugoslavia's ever-changing variety from the business centre of Zagreb to a countryside where corn-grinding was powered by water-mills and wool spun into yarn by villagers. They thought Dubrovnik, with its monasteries, churches and palaces, all in white stone, one of the most beautiful places in the world.

Here they coincided with the city's famous six-week Festival, followed by excursions down the Montenegrin coast, with its vast sandy beaches. In contrast to the popular tourist centres of the south coast they visited the wild regions of Bosnia in the mountains of which, they learned, lived bears, wild boar, wolves and jackals, and saw also the famous medieval monasteries of Macedonia.

from a Book List of J. M. Dent & Phoenix House

Note. The book concerned is *The Young Traveller in Yugoslavia* by Sylvie Nickels.

107. Yugoslav Dreamland

Breakfast in Leeds, dinner in Ljubljana—"Beloved Place"; a beautiful city with the cosmopolitan, cultured, civilized air of Paris.... Next morning by road through mountain scenery and Baroque villages to the port of Rijeka, and by ship for nearly six hours through the islands of the Northern Adriatic to reach Zadar at midnight....

The Zadar area on the Dalmatian coast has everything, except crowds and noise. It is much less oppressively hot than the well-known resorts to the south such as Dubrovnik, and I think better suited to Britons. Dubrovnik is famous for its ancient buildings. The town of Zadar is also Hans-Andersen beautiful, with all the dignity, antiquity and quaintness of York —but much more so, and unspoiled by "development". Standing on a promontory, it is encircled by a motor road. Within the ring of that road, all wheeled traffic is prohibited. Not even a bicycle is permitted along the narrow streets.

You may stand admiring a medieval tower, and turn round

to find yourself standing beside a Roman column, or beside the steps of a fifteenth century palace—and all round oleanders in full, brilliant bloom. The centre of it all is the Cathedral and the adjoining ninth century Church of St Donat, one of the most beautiful buildings I have ever seen.... Right alongside is a Roman forum.

Wandering bemused through these venerable streets, now and again you get a view out to sea where the Kornati and other islands—more than 200 of them—ride down the Adriatic like a fleet of argosies of old Ragusa.... Here the villagers live the life of centuries past, fishing, growing olives and vines, making wines, tending sheep and home-weaving their own cloth.

DIBDIN RAGLAND, in the *Yorkshire Post*, Leeds

108. Albania

(*a*) Near the coast the land is often marshy, and one of Albania's most pressing needs is a harbour at which a ship can come up to the quay. Durazzo (Durres) is being developed as a serviceable port with some rapidity, but elsewhere conditions are hopelessly backward. At the dreary little malarial port of San Giovanni di Medua (Singjin), from where there is a road to Scutari (Shkodra); at Valona (Vlona), and at Santi Quaranta, a straggling, disconsolate village, it is necessary for a merchant vessel to trans-ship her cargo into barges at some distance from the land. Down to this desolate coast there wander a few rivers, but they are of very little navigable use. If, however, the scheme to drain the Boyana (Bojana) is carried through, it would convert Lake Scutari into a magnificent harbour.... Though Albania lies upon the Adriatic, very few of its people devote themselves to fishing. And the soil in many parts affords the peasant an exiguous livelihood.

Countries of the World, ed. SIR JOHN HAMMERTON

(*b*) Half a mile outside the towns you are back in the primitive Albania of 2,000 years ago. The herds of cattle, sheep and goats are being tended by the women folk; the two-wheeled carts, with the oxen " 'neath the yoke", date from Celtic times, and the men slouch round in the same dress;

only modern rifles have replaced the spear and the club. The Albanian men are abnormally lazy; it is the women who work, and the warriors sit round waiting for trouble.

E. ASHMEAD BARTLETT, in the *Daily Telegraph*

Note. Some progress has latterly been made in bringing the villages under "the law of the land".

109. Greece — Parthenon and Poverty

Half-a-million tourists, from Britain and America, Germany and France, and all the affluent corners of the western world, escape every year for a week or two into the romantic legend of the Greek *past*; and some 490,000 of them, I suspect, go home again without noticing much about the Greek *present*— about the problems that modern Greeks have to live with. *Their* world has not been shaped by the heritage of classical serenity but by the last 2,000 years of Greek stagnation, occupation, revolution and war.... Greece today is still a nation of as much poverty as beauty and of more bitterness than glory.

In nearly every table of European economic and social development, Greece is at or near the bottom. There are peasants scraping a living from the mountains of Epirus and the barren peninsulas of the southern Peloponnese who are not much better off than the "fellahin" of Egypt. A quarter-of-a-million Greeks are permanently unemployed, many more are chronically under-employed, and 100,000 of them emigrate every year in search of a new life abroad....

Beside the white perfection of the Parthenon such twentieth-century matters may seem banal; but ... they pose a race with history whose outcome may determine the life or death of modern Greece.

DAVID HOLDEN, in *Radio Times*

110. Greece: Light and Shade

The Greeks are a proud and dignified people who would never parade their poverty, and my tourist friends do not leave the main roads and turn aside into the villages. Even the more adventurous who do, can only half understand what they see ... the reality of distress is often difficult to recognize when the vision is blurred by the warmth and light of a summer's day....

First we travelled South West from Athens across the Corinth Canal, past the ruins of Old Corinth, stopping for a moment near that stronghold of legend, Mycenae, where a great prehistoric Hellenic civilization had its heart; through Sparta, which lies beside Mistra, a haunted city of the dead below the mighty flank of Mount Taygetos; and thence to Githion, the gateway of the Mani, which forms the central prong of the Southern Peloponnese, jutting into the Cretan Sea.

When you enter the Mani, all softness is left behind. It is a precipitous, desolate and intractable region, with little or no land available for cultivation. The much-prized water is stored in underground cisterns. Roads are little more than rough tracks and villages a collection of houses, each built in the form of a small fort, from which, until recently, local vendettas were carried out. And everywhere there are stones and boulders. The Maniots say that when God had finished making the world he had a sack of stones left over, and he emptied it all in the Mani.

J. V. HAWKINS, in *The World's Children*

111. Sponges in the Aegean Sea

The sponges are black and slimy during life and are securely anchored to shells, rocks or other solid objects. The divers of the Aegean are world famous for their skill and endurance. The diver has a life-line attached to his right arm, and thus equipped leaps overside with a 30 lb. block of marble, which bears him to the sea-bed twelve to forty fathoms below. Here he stays for about two minutes, filling a basket at lightning speed, when he is hauled to the surface, his marble "sinker" attached to another line being recovered separately. The sponges are stamped upon and beaten and then hung overside for twenty-four hours to remove the last of the slimy substance. There follows more beating, more washings, and finally a period of drying in the hot sun, the sponges being hung on lines.

A Natural History of the Seas, by E. G. BOULENGER

112. Bulgaria's Agriculture

Bulgaria, the second smallest of the Balkan states, is essentially an agricultural country, about the size of England; 82 per cent of the population work on the land, and another 10 per cent are directly concerned in the marketing or use of its products. The few industries are mainly based on agricultural requirements and have been carried on in the same places for hundreds of years: leather work at Shumba, cutlery at Gabrovo, and so on. The Bulgar has a well-deserved reputation as one of the best workers in the world, but he does not take kindly to factory life. . . .

The isolated villages are amazingly self-supporting; life is simple but healthy. . . . In recent years modern agricultural machinery has been invading the Balkans, but there are still thousands of peasants who use the methods of generations ago. And with these they try to compete with the vast modernity of Canada and the Argentine! Small wonder that their standard of living is so low. Today there is a tendency to abandon the impossible competition, and to lower the acreage devoted to grain in favour of fruit, tobacco and market-garden produce. . . . The principal crops are wheat and maize, but tobacco is increasingly important—it was often marketed as "Turkish". In the south, cotton and even rice are cultivated. Most romantic of all crops is the rose. There is a famous valley in Southern Bulgaria, the Valley of Roses. Here conditions of soil and sun combine to give a remarkable quality of scent to the flowers, and from this valley comes 75 per cent of the world's supply of attar of roses, the basis of most perfumes.

Balkan Background, by BERNARD NEWMAN

113. Across Northern Bulgaria

The capital of Bulgaria occupies the same site as the squalid poverty-stricken town once governed by the Porte. No mushroom city in Western America ever sprang so quickly into a prosperous being from the ashes of filth and a corrupt administration. At the beginning of the century the mean-looking buildings and foul, dark streets of Sofia rendered the place a nest of filth and disease, and its rapid conversion into a modern city of fine buildings, broad well-paved streets, and pleasant parks and gardens, is one of which Bulgarians may well feel proud. . . .

Not so very long ago the journey from Sofia to Plevna (Pleven) entailed some discomfort, for it had to be made in a conveyance locally known as a "Phaeton", a little box on wheels, as unlike the English vehicle of the same name as can well be. . . . Now, however, we were able to travel as far as Plevna, a sleepy little town, by the recently constructed railway, a dreary line laid through gloomy gorges and across monotonous plains. . . .

From Plevna we travelled on to Tirnova (Trnovo), with a tedious delay at Gornea-Orehovitza, where we had to leave the train proceeding to Rustchuk (Ruse) on the Danube, and take a branch line which runs south. From here we caught our first glimpse of the Balkan Range, and the scenery gradually increased in grandeur until we reached the ancient capital of the Bulgarian Tsars,[7] assuredly one of the most picturesque and interesting places in Europe. . . . On a bright April morning we left for the Shipka Pass—a drive of about thirty-five miles along pleasant country roads as smooth as asphalt. . . . The Shipka Pass is nearly 5,000 feet above sea-level. . . . From here you may discern to the north the Danube river—a tiny thread of silver over a hundred miles away—and, southward, the pretty red-roofed village of Shipka, nestling in gardens and orchards, in the centre of a vast forest of rose-trees.

Through Savage Europe, by HARRY DE WINDT

114. Rumania is Content

Rumania (properly called ROMANIA) opposes revision of the treaties, near-treaties and arrangements reached after the Second World War, even where these affected Rumania adversely. Bucharest's attitude is that it has no quarrel with Russia over the loss of Bessarabia and Northern Bukovina, or with Bulgaria over the loss of the Southern Dobruja. Perhaps this attitude is partly due to the position of Transylvania, a big slab of Northern Rumania. It has a large Hungarian minority, but is the historical heartland of the Rumanian people.

[7] Tirnova or Tirnovo, now Trnovo.

The Vienna Award imposed by Hitler handed Transylvania over to Hungary. At the end of the war it returned to Rumania. Bucharest does not want *that* revised.... Rumania has only recently entered the tourism field, but bids fair to become a powerful rival to Yugoslavia. That country has the superb Adriatic coast-line and islands, but Rumania also has splendid scenery (almost every village and town will keep the camera busy) and is making a much better effort than Yugoslavia in her cuisine....

Bucharest is a fine city, with many wide boulevards, huge squares, parks, lakes and most imaginative fountains. There are also many charming old houses in the Balkan style, with highly decorated doors, courtyards and splendid wrought-iron railings. Some of the new buildings are fine examples of architecture, but utility buildings such as blocks of flats are depressing. The colossal House of Scinteia (the party newspaper) was erected by the Soviet Union in the very worst Soviet grandiose style.

DIBDIN RAGLAND, in the *Yorkshire Post*, Leeds

115. Some Places of Interest in Rumania

The most impressive portion of the Danube is without question the Iron Gates, between the towns of Orsova and Turnu Severin. One passes in the quaint little steamer through a narrow gorge, at one point only 116 yards wide, with great perpendicular walls of rock rising majestically on either side, and the water tearing through at tremendous speed....

Braila, an important river-port on the Danube, has a large trade in petroleum and grain. Immense warehouses and elevators have been erected for the storage of the latter commodity....

Tulcea, another thriving river-port, is situated near the western fringe of the Danubian delta in Northern Dobruja, 30 miles almost due east from Braila. It is a commercial centre for the varied produce of the rich district lying south of the delta. Eastwards of the quaint flat town, whose scattered buildings house a polyglot population, the Danube divides to form the Sulina and the St George branches, their tortuous courses winding for miles through watery wastes of an indescribable desolation.... But this region is a sportsman's paradise; all kinds of water-fowl are to be found, and fish—sturgeon, carp and salmon—are plentiful. . . .

Constanta lies on the Black Sea, 140 miles east of Bucharest by rail. Despite its modern appearance, the town has many early historical associations, and fragments of the Great Wall of Trajan, at the seaward end of which Constanta lies, still stand to bear witness to its strategic importance. The clean and attractive streets are flanked by many fine buildings, while among modern structures is the Casino. . . .

Sinaia, a lovely hill resort seventy miles north of Bucharest, has two royal residences—the Château of Peleshor, built in 1903, and the Château Pelesh, completed about 1880. . . . The Turnu Rosu, or Red Tower, rises at the southern end of the Sibiu Pass in the Transylvanian Alps, which is traversed by an old Roman road still known as the Trajan road. The tower, built in 1533, guarded the entrance from what was formerly Hungarian territory into Wallachia.

Countries of the World, ed. SIR JOHN HAMMERTON

116. Life in Hungary

Mrs Varga, who is a native of Hungary, gave a very vivid account of life there. She attributed a certain slowness of industrial and social development in a freedom-loving people to their troubled history of repeated foreign invasion. The majority of Hungarians are still landless farm labourers without the help of unions against the exploitation of big land owners.[8] Although after 1918 reforms were promised, not much was done, and wages and the standard of living in the country were extremely low.

The town worker, said Mrs Varga, was slightly better off and had some trade union protection, but standards were far below those of England. Work started at 8 A.M. for everyone except the Civil Service, but there was plenty of social life and gaiety until late at night. People sat at tables outside the innumerable cafés and gossiped as they do in Paris.

Architecture, Mrs Varga continued, was disappointing compared with that of the historic cities of Europe, but the romantic situations of the towns, particularly Budapest on the

[8]Hungarian agriculture has now been collectivized.

two banks of its wonderful river, were marvellous, and many
tourists enjoy Budapest with its health-giving baths and its
facilities for boating and ski-ing, and its excellent music and
opera. The theatre performed great plays of many nations.

Mrs Varga went on to describe details of home life, the
cheapness of domestic labour, the richness of the food and the
cheapness of fruit—a pound of lovely peaches, for instance,
costing only threepence and a pound of tomatoes one farthing.

Ilkley Gazette

117. The Spirit of the Hungarian People

It is difficult to explain in definite words the sensation of mystery
and romance that the wayside traveller finds in Hungary. The
scenery seen by the light of day is uninteresting, for the whole
country is just a huge plain. But at night in the moonlight
the fields of corn, the clumps of trees, the little knolls here and
there become meeting-places of fairies. It is the mixture of races
that has given to this countryside its poetical charm. To the
Magyar mind all that country is inhabited by invisible beings
that spring to life when the sun goes down, and I have met
peasants who were afraid to wander in the light of the moon
for, as they said, the fevers descend on earth when the moon
rides in the sky.

The primitive Magyar is pantheistic in his attitude towards
nature, and translates this sentiment into the little folk-poems
he improvises to the sound of his rustic flute or the Gypsy's
fiddle. The Hungarian projects his personality on to his external
surroundings.... In the northern countries of Europe the
scenery is more majestic than the Hungarian plain, but the
peasants do not look on their country through the veil of their
own folk-lore or folk-music, nor do they associate each legend
and melody with definite events in their country's history to the
same extent as the Magyar does. Every step that the lonely
traveller makes through the plain is accompanied by songs,
dirges and dances until his mind echoes and re-echoes to a
mighty symphony composed of countless fragmentary tunes....
The shepherd tending his flocks by the Tisza river looks up at

the starry sky and thinks of his mother far away in Transylvania or his sister sweeping her room with rosemary boughs.

Raggle Taggle, by WALTER STARKIE

118. Tokay Wine

Millionaires' wine is Tokay essence, a product of Hungary and the nearest approach to the golden Elixir of Life. It is said that there is no tonic in the world so effective. Administered by the teaspoonful, it has taken the place of strychnine for medicinal purposes, and is reported to have achieved the recovery of a patient for whose life all hope had been abandoned. It is exceedingly rare and the most expensive wine of all, for it is really an extract of the quintessence of wine. It is only made in a really good year, and, however fine the vintage, the quantity produced is necessarily very small.

In the Tokay vineyards the grapes are left on the vines until the sun has dried them up into raisins. The finest of these are picked and piled up in a cask. They are left for twenty-four hours, and a certain amount of juice is squeezed out by the weight of the fruit itself. No pressure is applied. Pounds and pounds of grapes produce only a teaspoonful of the liquid which eventually becomes Tokay essence.

D. MACCLURE, in *Chambers's Journal*, Edinburgh

119. A Hungarian Playground

Hungary's Lake Balaton is fifty miles long and so wide in parts that you can't see across it. It is also exceptionally shallow on the south side, which is a drawback for good swimmers but a delight for children and their carefree mothers. An average water temperature of 69 to 75 degrees Fahrenheit should please everyone.

There is something about Lake Balaton that sets it apart, and not only in the hearts of Hungarians. Hardened British travellers enthuse about it in a misty sort of way, and one and a half million foreigners visit it each year. It can't only be because it is in a splendid setting of trees and vineyards; that the white sandy beaches are thick with children sporting with the toys, gymnastic equipment, pedalos and ponies put there for them; it can't even be that the water is said to be velvety to touch and warm from May to October. Other lakes are like that.

It might be because the Hungarians have a way of shaking up equal measures of melancholy and gaiety, and producing gipsy music; or it could be their enthusiasm and their ability to put the traveller in a holiday mood.

Round the 118 miles of shore there are resorts of various sizes. Sailing boats are available for hire, pleasure boats circulate, one can fish, eat huge Hungarian meals at old inns, or ride from the stables at Tihany. Horses, of course, play an important part in Hungarian life, and expert equestrian displays are a tourist attraction.

FRANCES HOWELL, in *Homes and Gardens*

120. Vienna

(*a*) The physical features which influenced the establishment and rise of Vienna, and helped to determine the extent and frontiers of the Dual Monarchy which the Hapsburgs ruled from that capital in 1914, are of a remarkable character, and not repeated on as large a scale in Europe.... For a distance of about forty miles below Grein the Danube flows through deep and narrow gorges.... Whilst covering this defile, Vienna also provides access to the open lands of the Middle Danube basin, closely flanks the important lowland route between the Adriatic and the headwaters of the Oder and Vistula, and also turns the natural defences of Bohemia, a region which is difficult of access from the Upper Danube basin on account of the ridge of the Böhmerwald which has its steep face to the southwest.... From Vienna can be controlled the route from the west between the Alps and Böhmerwald, that from the north by the Elbe valley between the Erz-Gebirge and Riesen-Gebirge, and that from north-east between the Sudetes and Carpathians. Vienna, therefore, is the common starting point from all German-speaking lands for the "Bosphorus crossing" to Asia.

The Great Capitals, by VAUGHAN CORNISH

(*b*) Vienna is not just a provincial German town like Breslau or Düsseldorf. Vienna has a character, a flavour, a tradition of its own. Vienna is European—the product and meeting place of various cultural and racial elements: Slavic, Latin, Magyar, Germanic. The oversized head of a dwarfish, rickety body, this once imperial city has been a headache to Europe and to itself, ever since the Habsburg Empire went to pieces. Now there may be a chance to find a new function and "raison d'être" for this problem child among the capitals.

Free World, New York

(c) City of romance, of gaiety, of tragedy: which is the true picture? Most of the popular notions of Vienna have been conjured by visitors. Christa Esterhazy's book[9] seeks to show the city through the eyes of the Viennese themselves, a people proud of their artistic and architectural heritage but enjoying present-day life and with high hopes for the future.

Music still fills the air of Vienna as it has done for centuries past as a city which has been the background to some of the world's greatest composers and performers. It is to be heard not only in churches and concert halls and Opera House, but bubbling from a myriad traditional inns and coffee houses and from private houses where the family, like Schubert's own, make their own music. Here too is the Vienna of the ornate and magnificent baroque, buildings and interiors without parallel in Central Europe, many recalling vividly a legendary personality or historic event. . . .

There is evidence that the city is alive and vibrant now as it has not been for decades. The old, drab buildings are now gay with colour, and youth and laughter are everywhere in the streets and parks. Vienna, the author says, is once more at home to all the world.

from a Phoenix House book list

121. Carinthia — An Austrian "Lake District"

It is strange but true that it is no farther to travel to Carinthia in Southern Austria than to the French Riviera, yet this Alpine region, which is just as warm and far more varied, has never swarmed with tourists. It is not that one single attraction of the Mediterranean is lacking, unless it is a small quantity of salt

[9] *Vienna* in the new "Cities of the World" series.

in the water. . . . Apart from constant good weather—a storm may come and as quickly go—the main difference between this and other mountainous regions is that on the whole, it is not majestic. It is a soft, lush countryside of verdant pastures and rushing streams, cowbells and pretty churches. . . .

It would be almost impossible to pick out the prettiest lake, although it is hard to think of anything lovelier than Weissen See. At an altitude of 3,000 feet this long narrow lake, set in national trust land, boasts an average water temperature of 72 degrees Fahrenheit, so that, although it is really outstanding for walking and for its rural, truly Austrian atmosphere, all the fun of the lake—boating, water ski-ing and swimming—are very much a part of a holiday there.

It is easier to say which is gayest and warmest—it is the largest, Wörther See. Velden, circling its western shore, is the main tourist town of Carinthia. . . . Wörther See is warmed by thermal springs, as are many of the lakes, and is quite near Villach, perhaps the chief of the medicinal spas in the area.

MARGARET HOLLAND, in *Homes and Gardens*

122. The Salzkammergut

The name Salzkammergut ... means nothing more than "Crown lands of the salt mines", and it was the mines of this region which brought wealth to the Imperial Treasury. Today they are still being worked, and are the property of the state.

Bad Ischl, reached by bus or small-gauge railway from Salzburg ... is the centre of one of Europe's loveliest lake districts, for ringing it within a radius of less than twenty miles are some thirty lakes set among thickly wooded hills and mountains.

A Fortnight in Austria, by GORDON COOPER

Note. The Salzkammergut is the region where the three provinces of Upper Austria, Salzburg, and Styria meet. In addition to Bad Ischl, the small towns of great interest and beauty include Bad Aussee, Hallstadt, and St Wolfgang (with the original "White Horse Inn"). The salt has helped to preserve many objects from the early Iron Age, so that Hallstadt has given its name to a period of Europe's development, roughly from 1000 to 500 B.C.

123. A House in the Tyrol

I do not think in all Tyrol I saw a house more lovable than that one.... Its upper storey was of grey weatherboard, the lower brilliantly whitewashed. From the side, on account of the barn, it was a much bigger house than seen from the front. On the white front wall there were the fresco of a saint and a verse praying God and the saint to watch over the house and keep from it all evil and all enemies, both of man and beast.... The dark wooden balcony, fretted at the edge in an openwork design and running the full length of the front, was gay with the crimson and gold of begonias in pots, and above it right under the eaves a second tiny carved wooden balcony opened off an attic, in the dusk of which you could make out the harness of the farm-horses hanging from the rafters.

Before a Tyrolese peasant-house one's mind slips back to the old folk-tales of beasts that talked with men.... In winter, even the fowls have their place indoors. Low down in the wall you will notice the hole cut for their entry into the kitchen. Behind the kitchen is the stable, divided into compartments where the horses, the cows, the pigs, stay snug while the countryside is white with snow. Above them is the hayloft.... When winter howls at the door there must be a really dramatic sense of satisfaction in knowing all one's possessions to be under the roof with oneself. Only the firewood is left actually out of doors. Yet it hugs the wall so close in golden-brown stacks under the shelter of the balconies, it too seems to have been admitted to the friendly alliance of man and beast.

Tyrolean June, by NINA MURDOCH

124. Liechtenstein — The Lilliput State

The Arlberg-Orient express, with its ten imposing through-carriages, from Calais and Paris to Vienna, Budapest and Bucharest, makes a stop in Swiss Buchs. There it crosses the Rhine and veers into Austria. But first, for a quarter of an hour or so, the travellers pass a smiling countryside, and by pretty, spotless villages, through the smallest independent state in the world—Liechtenstein[10]. .... Liechtenstein is entirely

[10]The writer has evidently not taken states like Monaco, Vatican City, etc. into consideration.

independent, with its own sovereign and parliament, its own
laws and judiciary. It has no army, and a regular police force
of only nine. . . .

In its way Liechtenstein is a spacious land. You forget that
it is only sixty-two square miles in territory when you stand
under the pergola of a crossroads chapel set in silver birches on
a hillside and see the smiling valley of the middle Rhine
stretched out before you. The river is the natural frontier; well
behind rise the Swiss Alps. . . . There is not a town proper in
the land, yet the village main-streets are of the most advanced
twentieth century type, in a setting which has stayed traditional.

In a state of which one-quarter is mountains and another
quarter forests, agriculture cannot provide for the entire population. Slightly over half the wage-earners are employed in
industries—factories which look like summer colonies, and
which go in for products that give much work and need little
raw material, such, for example, as artificial teeth, of which
Liechtenstein exports sixty millions annually. As to agriculture,
the sun and the warm foehn wind go to produce their staple
diet, maize, and that lovely little wine that looks and tastes like
the "vin rosé" of Anjou.

KEES VAN HOEK, in *Chambers's Journal*, Edinburgh

125. The Varied Industries of Switzerland

Although Switzerland possesses no significant natural resources
and lacks direct access to the sea, it has established its place
among the major industrial countries. Not only banking,
finance and insurance have earned Switzerland an international
reputation. Its chemical and engineering industries, its watches
and precision instruments, its food products and textiles are
also known to people in almost every part of the world.

Although the role of agriculture in the Swiss economy has
continued to decline in recent years, industries have advanced
and expanded until today they employ more than half of the
country's labour force. The Swiss firms chiefly obtain raw
materials from abroad, process and finish them, and then export
most of the products all over the world.

With a domestic market of under six million people,
industrialists and business men have sought additional selling

opportunities in other countries. . . . For example, only about three per cent. of the Swiss watch-making industry's output remains in the country. The rest is exported. . . .

Since hydro-electric power represents a key source of energy in Switzerland, the electrical engineering industry has assumed a major role in the economy. Its products have found application in power stations, factories, locomotives and other installations all over the world. The textile sector, the oldest and one of the biggest industries in the country, makes fabrics, lace, knit-wear and other clothing products.

MANFRED PAGEL, in the *Yorkshire Post*, Leeds

126. Swiss Milk by Pipe-Line

The Swiss are rapidly extending their milk pipe-line system to transport fresh milk from the Alpine pastures to the dairies in the valleys. The reason is simply that no one wants to carry the milk down the mountains. Pipe-lines are the only way to beat the labour shortage in the Alps. . . . The pipe is made of plastic, half an inch in diameter, cheap to buy and easy to install. It can be laid on the surface, or buried a foot deep where necessary; it can be carried over ravines and rivers by attaching it to a cable. The newest pipe-line in the canton of Valais is more than eight miles long and runs down from a height of 8,000 feet. The milk can be in the dairy within half an hour of leaving the cow, and this is of particular importance for making the finest cheese. . . .

How do cows come to be up in the mountains? The answer is that the inhabitants of those Alpine backwaters are nomadic. In winter the cows, housed in the valleys, cannot get fresh fodder, and their productivity declines. In the early summer they are driven up to the lower pastures; then, as the air becomes warmer, they are put right up in the high meadows above the treeline. By the end of July they are starting their descent back into the valleys, filling the air with the tinkling of cowbells. In some districts, such as the Val d'Anniviers, whole villages pack up and move, leaving behind only a few fire watchers. The priests go too, also the schoolmasters, so that the children's education will not suffer—the education that qualifies them to break away from the mountains and live in the towns!

ALAN MCGREGOR, in *The Listener*

127. Zürich

The site of Zürich is lovely, a crescent facing into the sun around the northern end of the Zürichsee, split by the river Limmat and full of short steep hills. Behind, bigger wooded hills, and behind them the Alps, usually lost in the haze. The water seems more present than in most seaside towns, almost as though it ran under the streets like electricity. However odd it may seem to those who have their Switzerland typed as bourgeois and dull, Zürich sparkles. And at the same time it is a truly international city, prepared to welcome every culture while remaining itself. For a simple example, you can get the day's newspapers from all over Europe at nine in the morning— and in few cities, even the biggest, can you do that.

The old city grew on two tiny hills on either side of the Limmat, peaceful and very solid. Zürich has made sure that it has remained there, only a few yards from the main streets and the Quai, not by giving new buildings a fancy dress but by making sure that the scale and rhythm are maintained, which is all that is needed. The part on the north of the Limmat is not as demure as it looks, like many other things in Zürich: the part to the south around St Peter's Church contains a lovely sequence of irregular lanes leading up to the Lindenhof, a leafy, somnolent belvedere overlooking the river, and a wonderful thing to have a few yards away from the commercial centre of the city. The rest is modern, and the best of it has been built since about 1950.

IAN NAIRN, in *The Listener*

128. Through the St Gothard[11]

The St Gothard series of tunnels encountered on the way from Lucerne to Milan must be seen to be believed; and even then the traveller rubs his eyes.

As it climbs the mountains the train executes a figure eight, now crossing a deep ravine, now entering a tunnel, now emerging and crossing the ravine again at a higher point. At one moment you see a village church on one side of you; at another you see the same church at the opposite side. In the American idiom, the St Gothard line is the father and the

[11]Or Gotthard.

mother of all scenic railways; and the mountain country through which the train passes is magnificent.

The tunnel is 9¼ miles long. At the highest point the train reaches 3,786 feet above sea level.

My own most vivid impression of the journey is of a dramatic change which our emergence from this dizzy sequence of tunnels on one occasion brought. We had entered it on the Swiss side amid the blinding whiteness of mountain snow; as we came out into the sunshine on the other side of the Alps we quickly became conscious that we were in a country of gentler outlines whose dominant note was a deep and restful green. There was no mistaking it; this was the true Italy.

"Northerner", in the *Yorkshire Post*, Leeds

129. The Rhine — History, Beauty, and Commerce

Take the first Rhine crossing point of the Second World War and add the yellow-haired siren of the Lorelei, the most efficient river transport in the new Europe, the medieval tower where legend says Archbishop Hatto was eaten alive by a million righteous mice, the biggest exporters of wine in Germany, and the sixteenth-century house of the bedevilled Dr Faust, mix in a "wrecker" current of twelve m.p.h. and a few reefs, and you have ... the most important waterway in Europe, and in parts the most picturesque as well. Eight hundred and thirty miles long and, even as high up as Bonn, nearly half a mile wide, the Rhine is as busy as any motorway. Nearly 9,000 boats of all nations work the river, carrying 140 million tons of cargo a year. . . .

But the Rhine is no "Old Father Thames". From Rudesheim to Bonn, seventy miles farther down, is the trickiest stretch of the river: traffic is strictly controlled, particularly past the Lorelei rock where all the boats have to take on pilots.

DERRICK AMOORE, in *Radio Times*

130. Baden-Baden

Last spring I spent a few days at Baden-Baden in Germany's

Black Forest, and was, I freely admit, surprised to find it was an experience that I am ready to repeat at any time. Baden-Baden is not the heavily Teutonic town one might expect, with solid strait-laced architecture and rather looser entertainments; nor is it faded, staid and full of querulous water-tipplers. Nor, again, is it any jumped-up post-war resort. . . .

Baden-Baden is probably the most elegant town in Germany, a fact which the Germans are magnanimous in accepting because its beauty is very largely due to the inspiration of the two Frenchmen who ran the casino in the early part of the nineteenth century. They are responsible for the exotic trees which make the Lichtenthaler Allee, sweeping through the town beside the little Oos, an experience; they put up the Pump Room and the splendid colonnaded Kurhaus which has in it the casino. . . .

But besides the sedentary pleasures, one can swim, outdoors and in the heated pool on the roof of the ultra-new Bath Centre; play golf or tennis; ride or glide, shoot clay pigeons or go motoring in the splendidly uncrowded Black Forest, where the inns serve memorable meals. A spur of the autobahn comes right into the town. At night there is dancing, gambling and the theatre.

One can reach Baden-Baden in two days of easy motoring, seventeen hours of the Lorelei Express, or two hours flying to Frankfurt and on by air taxi to the little flying field at Baden-Oos.

FRANCES HOWELL, in *Homes and Gardens*

131. Changes in the Ruhr

The industrial Ruhr, scene of dying coalmines and mounting unemployment, is seeking help from United States, British and Scandinavian investors to give the area a new role. As fuel oil forces coal out of the market and steel production drops, the Ruhr is going all-out to develop chemicals, cars and electrical goods. General Motors have already opened a new giant Opel works at Bochum. Du Pont and A. B. Metals, a British firm, are installed at Hamm and Herne respectively.

The State of North Rhine Westphalia has set up an Industrial Development Corporation to re-jig Ruhr industry. . . . The

Ruhr communities, packed tightly along the narrow coal-belt from Muehlheim to Dortmund, are all heavily engaged in re-structuring as their classical industries disappear. The problem is to get new industry on the scene before pit closures, each of which means that up to 5,000 men lose their jobs.... Ten years ago, there were twenty-one pits and 54,000 miners in Essen. Now there are only seven pits and 24,000 miners.... Gelsenkirchen became a black shell of a town overnight when its two major collieries closed down.

But Bochum is a dynamic town, according to its Mayor. "We want to forget its grimy image and become a cultural centre," he says. The gleaming skyscrapers of a new £2m. university bear witness to his intentions. Once a coal town of 360,000 inhabitants and 43,000 miners, Bochum will soon have only 4,000 left working in the pits. Already 16,000 men work at the Opel works and the town is branching out into plastics and electrical goods. But 50,000 people have lost their old jobs in the transformation process.

DONALD ARMOUR, in the *Yorkshire Post,* Leeds

132. Germany's North Sea Coast

Now it must strike you at once that it's ridiculously short compared with the huge country behind it. From Borkum to the Elbe, as the crow flies, is only seventy miles. Add to that the west coast of Schleswig, about the same distance.... Now what *sort* of coast is it? Even on this small map you can see at once, by all those wavy lines, shoals and sand everywhere, blocking nine-tenths of the land altogether, and doing their best to block the other tenth where the great rivers run in. Now let's take it bit by bit. You see it divides itself into three. Beginning from the west the *first piece* is from Borkum to Wangeroog—fifty odd miles. What's that like? A string of sandy islands backed by sand; the Ems river at the western end, on the Dutch border, leading to Emden—not much of a place. Otherwise, no coast towns at all. *Second piece*: a deep sort of bay consisting of the three great estuaries—the Jade, the Weser, and the Elbe—leading to Wilhelmshaven, Bremen, and Hamburg. Total breadth of bay twenty odd miles only; sandbanks littered about all through it. *Third piece*: the

Schleswig coast, hopelessly fenced in behind a six to eight
mile fringe of sand. No big towns; one moderate river, the
Eider.... Behind the first piece is East Friesland—a low-lying
country, containing great tracts of marsh and heath, and few
towns of any size; on the north side, none. Seven islands lie
off the coast. All, except Borkum, which is round, are attenu-
ated strips, slightly crescent-shaped, rarely more than a mile
broad, and tapering at the ends; in length averaging about six
miles.

The Riddle of the Sands, by ERSKINE CHILDERS

133.   The Herring and World Power

For centuries national wealth was created by the herring's
presence off Europe's shores. Because of the herring, men
transformed obscure fishing villages into mighty cities, which
opened up the trade routes of an expanding world and facilitated the exchange of goods between East and West. Because
of the herring, men formulated political doctrines which still
exist. . . .

About seven hundred years ago the herring, driven (it is
believed) by whales, migrated to the Baltic salt marshes. In
those days meat was a luxury in Europe, and fish was relatively
much more important than now.... With the herring fisheries
as their mainstay, Lübeck, Bremen, Hamburg, Stettin[12] and
Rostock became important centres of world trade; their fleets
grew and their business men financed trading expeditions to all
parts of Europe. To safeguard their interests, these merchants
formed the Hanseatic League in 1241; at the height of their
power they had posts in 130 towns. . . .

But the herring, cause of their advancement, was also the
source of their decay. The herring shoals, influenced perhaps
by change in sea temperature, moved into the North Sea, off the
Dutch coast, and the merchants of Amsterdam were quick to
grasp the opportunity of ousting the Hansa merchants from
their commanding position. They prospered as the Germans
had done: soon their fleets were carrying the commodities of
the world and laying the foundation of the Dutch Empire. . . .

But at the height of her power, Holland's destinies were

[12]Now in Poland, and called Szczecin.

again influenced by another migration of the coveted fish. The shoals moved across the North Sea to the English coast. The distance involved was trifling, but the historical significance was enormous.

GEORGE MELL, in *The Millgate*, Manchester

134. The Position of Berlin

Berlin is situated halfway between the Bohemian Erzgebirge and the sea in the northern plain which has here a width of about two hundred and fifty miles. This is not only a broader access to the main area of Eurasia than that by way of Lower Austria but has a more open continuation, for it lies clear of the Carpathians. Moreover it connects the only coastlands inhabited by Germans with the main interior of the Continent. . . .

[In this plain] we cannot miss the significance of the connection provided by the Elbe estuary and the Havel-Spree valley. It is a defile where the highways converge in the zone of latitude in which lie the great wheat lands which are the principal home of the European Stock both in the Old and the New World. In this zone, moreover, are deposits of coal and metalliferous ores. . . .

The lines of water-parting to north and south of the rivers Havel and Spree do not rise above the six-hundred-foot contour, and consequently most orographical maps suggest to the eye that a generally uniform plain extends from the foothills of the Kingdom of Saxony across Brandenburg to the coast of Mecklenburg. In fact, however, there are long ridges of old moraines a few hundred feet in height left in lines roughly parallel to the Baltic coast during the retreat of the ice-sheet. It is thus not merely the central position, or the acquired importance of a capital, which drew railways to a junction at Berlin, for the glacial hills to north and south make the neighbourhood of the city a desirable railway route for connection with the broader parts of the European plain which lie beyond the northern Carpathians.

The Great Capitals, by VAUGHAN CORNISH

135. Munich

(*a*) Munich, or München, owes its origin to a primeval line of communication, the Isar, which in its upper reaches joins the Inn at Innsbruck, and thus lies on the Brenner Pass route. The advantages of its situation soon made themselves felt, and it became the capital of Bavaria. It is situated amongst majestic lake scenery in forest-clad mountains, and the taste of a line of cultured rulers and of an art-loving people have kept it a city beautiful. It is a thriving commercial and industrial city, yet one of the most deservedly popular rendezvous in Europe. Its lay-out and architecture are both dignified and practical.

Countries of the World, ed. SIR JOHN HAMMERTON

(b) Third largest city of the Federal Republic, Munich was largely shaped by the extravagant, art-crazy and eccentric Bavarian kings. It has become the undisputed cultural metropolis of Germany today, in a sense her capital. Egon Larsen,[13] writing out of true affection for the city, which he has known so intimately, brings its art and music, architecture, theatre and commercial enterprise radiantly alive: for him, he says, "there are only two places in the world where one can live—London and Munich".

from a book list of J. M. DENT and Phoenix House

(c) As winter ends, Munich enjoys its "Fasching", an un-inhibited pre-Lenten spree. With daunting stamina the town dedicates itself to six noisy weeks of dressing-up and celebrating into the small hours. A few million sausages and seas of Bavarian beer sustain the revellers until the frenzied climax. Costumes incredibly elaborate or revealingly simple; flirting loudly exhibitionist or deadly earnest; fun, instant.

Radio Times

136. How Big is Germany?

The salient fact is that Germany, unlike France, has no natural frontiers. She is "a nation without a country". Sea and mountains bound her on north and south; but to east and west lie only the great rivers, bridged time and again by the historical routes of invasion. The Rhine may be held (though

[13]In the book *Munich* ("Cities of the World" series).

not by the Germans) to form a western limit; but which of the eastern rivers would define, for some future Hitler, "the last territorial claims that I have to make"?

Germany has been a prolific nation, for whom emigration, in early times, has represented a sheer necessity. But this emigration, since the Germans are a mid-continental and not a maritime people, has in the past been overland, not overseas. . . .

No natural centre emerges from the configuration of parallel zones, running east and west, which constitute German territory. The unification of the Reich has been accomplished in defiance of nature by a deliberate act of will. Artificial communications—a magnificent network of roads, railways and waterways—were reinforced, on the eve of war, by the finest internal air services in Europe.

German unity, then, comes from the people, not the land, and German nationality rests, so to speak, on "jus sanguinis" rather than "jus soli". Stability, equilibrium, contentment, are repugnant to the German. A standard of perfection, a fixed mould, is to him a prison. . . . Hence his continual fear of encirclement. "Don't fence me in" is a wail of anguish typically German.

Time and Tide

137. Poland: A General Survey

The Poles are Slavs, like most Russians, the Czechs, the Serbs, and others; but they are intensely proud of their own traditions, very patriotic, preserving their own language, and often despising or even hating brother-Slavs. History tells how there have been kingdoms of Poland before, of varying extent and power; at one time Poland ruled from Baltic Sea to Black Sea. But always it has been a story of conquest by neighbours or disruption within the kingdom; a stable Poland has seemed impossible. Today, however, the Poles are most enthusiastic for their independence and very ambitious for their future. . . .

Geographically Poland is midway along the Great European Plain; politically Poland is a buffer between the Communism of Russia, the Fascism[14] of Germany, and the democracies of Scandinavia and Czechoslovakia[14]; racially the land is between Teuton and Slav—thirty per cent.[14] of the population consists of "minorities"—i.e., people who are not Poles. Most Poles are

[14]Before the Second World War.

Roman Catholics, but towards the eastern frontiers people belong to the Greek Church; beyond the boundary eastward is the official atheism of the U.S.S.R., and westward Protestant North Germany. Economically Poland is at a stage between the industrialization of the West and the peasant-life of southeastern Europe and rural Russia; the modern scientific orderliness of the Prussian mind penetrated from the west, and the humble peasant faith from the east. Such is the new Poland—not Russian, not West European, not industrial, not agricultural, Slav yet not Slav—a strange mixture with a problematic future.

A Geography of Europe, by H. ALNWICK

138.   The Polish Land Question

In 1919 a familiar, but to me an ever-surprising, scene was the appearance of the overlord on his lawn, smooth and lovely as the softest moss.... Immediately he would be surrounded by peasants who, kneeling before him, reached to kiss his hands, his coat, even his boots, in abject adoration. To them he was the arbiter of life or death.... By 1939 the situation struck me as appalling. The years between had seen some slight improvement in the land system ... but the majority of the people were still land-hungry.

It took a Second World War to remedy the agrarian anomaly. Now the Polish Government has taken over the estates of the land owners and the tiny allotments of the peasants (who still represent three-quarters of the nation) and are busy settling family by family everywhere. The aim is to provide twelve-and-a-half to twenty-five acres for every peasant family, and the scheme includes the establishment of training centres with agricultural colleges and experimental stations. Although the land is under State control, the system of individual ownership continues.[15] The establishment of collective farms as in Russia is not part of the programme. The larger farms lie in the new territories—those parts of Germany handed to Poland to balance the eastern lands which she has returned to the U.S.S.R.—e.g. for miles round Breslau (now called Wroclaw).

MRS CECIL CHESTERTON, in *Homes and Gardens*

[15] 87 per cent of the agricultural land remains in private hands.

139. The Minerals of Poland

The mineral resources of Poland have been given little systematic study, but it is probable that scientific research will bring to light many hidden stores of wealth. The Kielce plateau contains the great coal-fields, and on it and around Cracow a great manufacturing region has developed. Here are extensive beds of coal and considerable deposits of iron and zinc ore. Lignite coal is found in several districts, also cadmium, lead, silver and copper ore. Limestone is quarried for structural purposes and cement-making is steadily becoming an established industry.

Galicia is remarkably rich in minerals, of which petroleum and salt are the most valuable. The Galician oil-fields still give satisfactory results and a great promise for the future, especially those in the districts of Boryslaw and Bitków, the richest fields of the petroleum industry, but more capital is required to meet the increasing cost in equipment. At several points in the Polish oil belt the mineral wax known as ozokerite is worked. The vast rock-salt mines of Wieliczka and Bochnia near Cracow have been famous since the twelfth century; those at Wieliczka are enormous, and contain, it is estimated, over 20,000,000 tons of salt, while the immense *under-ground* salt city, splendidly decorated and equipped, is one of the most celebrated show-places of the Continent.

Countries of the World, ed. SIR JOHN HAMMERTON

140. Poland's Grounds for Optimism

(*a*) Economically the potentialities of the new Poland are enormous. The possession of the whole of the great Silesian industrial area gives her the possibility of becoming the great coal-exporting nation of Europe in the near future. Already she is acquiring markets in Sweden previously mainly dependent upon Britain for coal.[16] The lower standard of living of her miners and the shorter sea passage across the Baltic makes it likely that she will be successful in retaining such markets as she obtains in this part of the world.

The acquisition of a stretch of coast over 250 miles in

[16]Coal is now less important in industry, here as elsewhere.

length and her firm hold on the ports of Gdynia, Danzig (which we must now learn to call Gdansk), and Stettin [Szczecin] make her a major Baltic Power. Judged from the point of view of economics only, Poland makes a very good exchange in accepting Pomerania and Silesia up to the Oder and the Neisse in recompense for the forest and marshland of which much of her Eastern territories was composed. These lost Eastern territories, however, also contain some good agricultural land and the oil of Eastern Galicia.

CHRISTOPHER BUCKLEY, in the *Daily Telegraph*

(b) When I was in Poland, I often had to make the morning train journey to Warsaw from Lodz—or "woodge" as it is pronounced in Polish—the big textile city seventy miles west of Warsaw. It was an interesting route.... Once one had left Lodz behind, one was immediately in the broad Polish plain—deserted, it seemed, at most times of the year, except for an occasional horse-drawn sledge cutting a line across the monotonous snow in winter; solitary men horse-ploughing or sowing seed by hand, acres apart from each other, in the spring. But by June the whole land was purple, and by July it was yellow with rye. This was rich land, and the villages were there.

DERWENT MAY, in *The Listener*

141. Czechoslovakia and Her Peoples

Of the western Slavonic-speaking peoples the Czechs, inhabiting the hill-girt country of Bohemia, are among the most important. They were first Christianized by the Eastern Church, but became Roman Catholic, the early religious centre being at Taus (Domazlice), at the Bohemian exit of a pass from Bavaria. Later on, Prague was founded and became the capital, and it should be noticed that in it, as in many other cities of Slavonic language, the cathedral is within the castle, typifying association between religious and political leadership, both being frequently more western (German) than the rest of the population. It was natural both that the small, compact, and distinct mass of Czechs should early attain a sort of national self-consciousness, and that their country, in spite of its physical separateness, should receive German immigrants, especially up the Elbe gap. The distinctive personality of Bohemia is illustrated by the fact that the University of Prague, founded on the Paris model, was the first University established beyond the Rhine. . . .

Between Bohemia and the Carpathians, or more strictly the Tatra, is a physiographical trough such as so often occurs between fold-mountains (e.g. Tatra) and old blocks (e.g. Bohemia). It is occupied by the March (or Morava) river, is called Moravia, and is known as the Moravian Gate, for through it Vienna communicates north-eastward not only with the Oder basin via Breslau, but also with the Vistula basin via Cracow. Somewhat more German than Bohemia, the Moravian Gate is still mainly Slavonic, with dialects grading eastwards towards Polish. . . .

Not only does Czechoslovakia include Moravia, but it also stretches along the south flank of the Carpathians through a region of Slovak speech and rural life right on to the small district where Ruthenian language just emerges west of the Carpathians.

The Peoples of Europe, by H. J. FLEURE

142. The Bohemian Upland

The uplifted block, mainly formed of crystalline rocks, which includes Bohemia, part of Upper Austria, and half Moravia, has a steep and faulted edge towards the escarpment region of Bavaria. On the north its rim is formed by the Erzgebirge and the chains that continue the high ground towards Silesia; but on the south-east, through Moravia, it drops more easily under the marine strata of the Vienna basin. . . . The Elbe rises on the south flank of the Riesengebirge and then wanders through the easily excavated basin, until it escapes, still aided by the soft sandstones, through "Saxon Switzerland" into the great plain of the north. . . .

The typical Slavonic country lies southward of the Elbe, and gives to Prague (Praha) a population that is predominantly and vigorously Czech. . . . By far the greater part of the populous upland of Bohemia lies at 1,000 feet or more above the sea, and the hollow of the Elbe basin is an exceptional feature.

Prague lies on its southern edge, where the Vltava, the Moldau of the Germans, reaches the lower ground from its source in the extreme south of the country. This river, worthy of the capital, receives the drainage of the whole plateau south of the system of the Elbe. High on its left bank the castle and cathedral of the Bohemian kings look out over Prague, as if to inspire and consecrate the passionate devotion of the Czechs.

South-west of the city, shales and limestones form a basin for the Berounka River on the surface of the crystalline rocks. Pilsen (Plzen), the great brewing centre, stands on this stream, midway between the capital and the frontier crests.... Brünn (Brno) stands picturesquely where two rivers come down from the edge of Bohemia to the fertile region.

The World We Live In, in a section by G. A. J. COLE

143. A Czechoslovak Spa

Czechoslovak Communist officials still recall with pride the days when a British king came to the spa of Marienbad to take the waters. Tourists can buy as souvenirs copies of British sovereigns bearing the head of Edward VII, most famous of the many monarchs, princes and potentates who visited Marianske Lazne, better known to the rest of the world by its former name of Marienbad, in the first decade of this century.

In those years, Marienbad was one of the brightest jewels in the Austro-Hungarian empire, then in its brilliant heyday. Today, that empire has been dismembered for half a century. The glittering figures of international society who once wined, dined and flirted there are long since dead. Most of the visitors there now are Czechoslovak workers sent there by their trade unions on a cheap holiday for medical treatment or for convalescence....

But as part of a drive to attract more foreign tourists to Czechoslovakia, spa towns like Marienbad, Carlsbad (now Karlovy Vary) and Franzensbad (now Frantiskovy Lazne) are now again courting visitors from the West who, before and after the First World War, formed the bulk of their clientele. ... A favourable tourist rate of exchange has made a Czechoslovak spa holiday an attractive proposition for tourists paying in hard currency....

Marienbad's main hotels were all built towards the end of the last century in a massive, heavily ornamented Victorian style—palatial and imposing, if not always beautiful. They stand in spacious grounds, masked from the town centre by fragrant pines.

IAN MACDOWALL, in the *Yorkshire Post*, Leeds

144. Some Features of the Russian Plain

(*a*) *An Old Russian Village.* There were the humpy barns with umbrella-like roofs of straw; stumpy log huts with their arrow-shaped straw roofs overgrown in places with thick moss; brush fences crackling from dryness; towering sweeps over open wells, the butt end of the cross-poles weighted down with stones and resting on the ground like dogs on their haunches; unpaved streets, with ditches in front of their houses to drain the waters after heavy rains and spring thaws; swells and hollows in the ground, with holes in which the mud never dried out.

Red Bread, by M. HINDUS

(*b*) *Visiting Zagorsk.* Breakfast, at our little old-fashioned Moscow hotel, was at a buffet.... It would have been pleasant to linger by the window, gazing out at the silvery expanse of the Moskva River, but, although it was only June, the heat was intense. We decided to drive out to the country, to Zagorsk, which is only about forty miles away.

We took our battered van through the city streets and came to the suburbs that sprawled further outwards with every new block of flats.... The landscape became fresh and green; the group of peasants we saw sitting in the shade of the birch-woods might have come from a Chekhov play. The women wore white kerchiefs over their heads and long, shapeless dresses; the men, middle-aged to old, wore loose, belted blouses over baggy trousers tucked into topboots, their peaked caps heightening the suggestion of uniform....

Nearer Zagorsk, a manufacturing town, the birches disappeared again and the creamy dust was everywhere. Dominating the side of a building was a huge poster, a blown-up photograph of a plain, snub-nosed woman. Reading the caption,

we learnt that she was the champion hen-tender of the district
but that she intended to increase her quota of eggs next year.

LORNA WOOD, in *Homes and Gardens*

(c) *Pripet Marshes.* In the upper Pripet basin the woods are
everywhere full of countless little channels which creep through
a wilderness of sedge. Alone, the right bank of the Pripet rises
above the level, and is fairly thickly populated. Elsewhere extends a great, intricate network of streams with endless fields of
water-plants and woods.... In the drier parts the earth is
carpeted with meadow saffron and asphodel; but over the bogs
vapours hang for ever, and among the reeds in autumn there
is no fly, no mosquito, nor living soul, nor sound save the
rustle of dry stalks. No scene is more characteristic of the
inhabited places than the infinitely melancholy picture, often
witnessed from the train itself, of a grey-headed peasant cutting reeds, standing up to his waist in water.

Provincial Russia, by H. STEWART and F. de HAENEN

(d) *Dnieper Dam.* Among the eleven million sightseers who
have travelled expressly to view the huge dams which power
the Tennessee Valley Project, have been official and unofficial
visitors from most parts of the world. One group included
Soviet engineers.... Russia already had its own gigantic
Dnieper plant, which Marshal Budenny afterwards blew up
in face of the German armies in August 1941, and which has
since been rebuilt. This powers what is probably the world's
largest steel plant and aluminium factory. It also irrigates a
block of black-earthed Ukraine territory, far larger than the
whole of the British Isles; produces building materials in unbelievable quantity; electrifies agriculture, and reconditions
farming and industrial machinery.

MAURICE BENSLEY, in *Chambers's Journal*, Edinburgh

145. Leningrad and Moscow

(a) Few towns have better bones than Leningrad. Its shape
and plan are superb. The great river pours through it a swift
flood of pale water, dividing past the island on which the

Exchange so splendidly stands, and in winter its snow-covered, frozen levels stretch from one solid granite quay to another. The streets and squares are laid out on a magnificent scale. ... Except for its river, Leningrad owes little to nature. It shows itself at once for what it is, a wholly man-made creation, but made by a superman, the superbly artificial product of a grandiose imagination.

SIR WILLIAM HAYTER, in *The Observer*

(b) Leningrad seemed a magnificent city whose glories were all in the past, its residential buildings drab with peeling paint, its great cathedrals and palaces proudly and lovingly restored. ... The people are intensely proud of the beautiful things handed down to them from past generations.... But homes are not forgotten and everywhere great square blocks of flats are going up. In Moscow, some of these take the form of giant skyscrapers on the pattern of the Chrysler building in New York. We had no opportunity of seeing inside these dwellings, but our guide told us that they consisted of one to five rooms, according to the size of family.... In spite of overcrowding, the cities have an air of spaciousness about them, because everything is on a grand scale. The streets are very wide. That known as "The Ring of Gardens" in Moscow carried sixteen lanes of traffic, and we estimated that it was at least a hundred feet across. It is the fourth concentric ring-road around the Kremlin, the centre of Moscow.

DOROTHY MORCOM TAYLOR, in *The Bible in the World*

Note. A writer in 1969 described Leningrad as "the most European city in Russia" and "still the most beautiful city in northern Europe."

146. Russian Baltic Lands

(a) The cares of this world soon encompass the Lithuanian child. He or she starts work at a very tender age as custodian of a couple of cows or a score of geese. All around circles the forest of pine, fir, birch and oak, with a thick undergrowth of berries. Each village is a little community in a forest clearing, and beyond the horizon, and beyond that again, there is ever the same alternation of forest and clearing. The Niemen is the

I

father and the forest is the mother of the Lithuanian people.
... Man is still breaking the Wild, still held in check by the
forest and the marsh, still a child of the wilderness.

Beyond the Baltic, by A. MACCALLUM SCOTT

(b)   It was with some surprise that I discovered the country
of Livonia. The name conjured up to me memories of the
heyday of musical comedy, of Daly's Theatre resplendent with
mountain maidens singing and dancing in company with lovely
choruses and colourful soldiery. Pleasant thoughts indeed as I
gazed out of the window of the local train, chugging along
from Riga towards the Soviet frontier of that time.

The scenery certainly failed to fit in with my ideas of comedy,
musical or otherwise. Forest and more forest, grim and un-
smiling; forest of that dense and deadly monotonous kind
common to Eastern Europe; forest growing in accordance with
the best modern principles—every tree exactly like every other
tree, and showing no individuality whatsoever, just serried
ranks of potential pit-props.

HENRY OATTS, in *Chambers's Journal,* Edinburgh

147.   The River Volga

This mighty artery of the Russian plain, with its tributaries,
waters most of the Russian Soviet Republic west of the Urals
—a plain of nearly 1,459,000 square kilometres, or more than
Germany and France taken together. This area, with over
150 million inhabitants, was before the war of 1914-18
Europe's granary. The Volga is the source of well-being for the
people in the whole of south-west Russia; along it and its
tributaries (in summer) you can go by boat right up to the
Ural Mountains in the east, through canals to the Polar Sea
in the north and to the Baltic in the north-west, and by the
Don Canal to the Black Sea and the Mediterranean in the
south-west....

Up and down this mighty waterway in summer there is an
unceasing movement of innumerable boats, ships, rafts, lighters
and steamers, with thousands of people, and with precious
cargoes of the crops and products of the rich land. In Nov-

ember ice begins to form; but as soon as the ice is thick enough, it makes for three or four months a splendid highway for a lively sledge traffic up and down the river or across it. The railways, too, make use of it; rails are laid from bank to bank at places where there are no bridges, and so the goods-wagons are taken over without the costly use of ice-breakers.

Through the Caucasus to the Volga, by FRIDTJOF NANSEN

148. Baku

The short flight across the Caucasian Mountains from Soviet Azerbijan, which geographically and racially is similar to Iran, presents the most striking and complete contrast I have ever seen.

Baku is to-day a great modern city; and, as it is one the Germans never reached or damaged, it seems strangely pre-war compared with Moscow or Leningrad. On rich, flat sands, the tracery of oil derricks seems as perpetual as the trees and small ships that crowd the shores of the Caspian in the certainty of safety.

There is nothing of a backwater about Baku. . . . It possesses modern buildings superior, I think, to most in Moscow. Apartment houses with flowery balconies have the air of being less crowded, and university buildings, schools, palaces of culture and art galleries stand noble and streamlined on the hill.

As in all Russian towns, theatres abound; and there is an opera house which contains singers with voices as good as those to be heard in Moscow. Some operas are the usual European ones, others are Azerbijani in music and settings.

Walking through the streets, one is struck by the fact that, though the physical appearance of the people differs strikingly from those in Moscow (here faces are all Oriental ovals), they are similar in every other way. That proud, self-confident look, as if they owned the world and knew how to mould it . . . is indicative of thorough assimilation of Soviet culture.

IRIS MORLEY, in the *Yorkshire Post,* Leeds

149. Minerals in the Ural Region

The most important of the new Soviet centres of economic

life is in the Ural Mountains, which lie where Europe and Asia meet. Here there are being worked vast deposits of iron ore, and already the Urals are the most important centre of Russian iron ore production, yielding 60 per cent of the total Soviet output. Sverdlovsk (pop. 426,000)[17] and Chelyabinsk (pop. 273,000)[18] are two of the chief centres; a third is Magnitogorsk, one of the most romantic creations of recent years. Less than forty years ago its site was occupied by the obscure village of Magnitnaya (Magnet Mountain), inhabited by Cossack peasants, and herds of cattle browsed on the slope of the Atach Mountain, which has been described as one vast lump of iron ore. Today a great city of 150,000[19] people stands there, with huge power plants, batteries of coke-ovens, and tremendous blast-furnaces.

Although there is coal in the Urals, it is not of the right coking quality for the iron works and their chemical subsidiaries. Hence Kuznetsk at the foot of the Altai Mountains, on the borders of Mongolia, comes into the picture. It is 1,400 miles from the Urals, but it has excellent coking coal. So the Ural-Kuznetsk Combine has been formed. . . .

From one end of the Urals to the other stretches a chain of oil wells, sited on an extension of the oil-bearing strata running north from Baku in the Caucasus. Derricks tower above the ice at Pechori, and they break the skyline at Cherdyn and Perm, line the banks of the Kama and the Emba, are prominent at Sterlitamak, south of Ufa, and Makat, at the head of the Caspian Sea.

E. ROYSTON PIKE, in *War Illustrated*

Note. Salt, copper, gold, silver, manganese, platinum, uranium, chromium, etc., are also found in the Urals.

[17]940,000 in 1967.   [18]820,000 in 1967.   [19]352,000 in 1967.

Asia

150. The Great Siberian Plain

(a) Truly, Siberia is a country of magnificent distances. It is almost as level as the ocean. In over 1,000 miles I do not believe the grade of the railroad varied 300 feet, and in many places it was as straight as an arrow, without the slightest curve for forty or fifty miles. Indeed there was one stretch of perfectly straight road for 116 versts, or nearly eighty miles. ... In substantially parallel courses there are many mighty rivers flowing through the entire breadth of Siberia into the Northern Sea. The chief ones are the Ob, the Yenesei, and the Lena. The main stems of these rivers usually extend southward 1,000 or 1,200 miles, when by numerous radiating tributaries they spread fan-like through an immense area of country, finally finding their source in the great, high plateaux of Central Asia.

Siberia and Central Asia, by J. W. BOOKWALTER

(b) Siberia's timber becomes useful only if it can be transported on water. And all the main Siberian rivers flow northward into the ice-bound Arctic Ocean. The logs must be taken down in rafts in the summer, cut up in Arctic sawmills in the winter, and shipped off to the world in the following year. That is the cheapest way.

Forty Thousand Against The Arctic, by H. P. SMOLKA

151. The Trans-Siberian Express

I like the Trans-Siberian Railway. It is a confession of weakness, I know; but it is sincere.... You lie in your berth, justifiably inert. Past the window plains crawl and forests flicker. The sun shines weakly on an empty land. The piles of birch logs by the permanent way—silver on the outside, black where the damp butts show—give the anomalous illusion that there has been a frost. There is always a magpie in sight. . . .

At the more westerly stations—there are perhaps three stops of twenty minutes every day—you pace the platform vigorously, in a conscientious way. But gradually this practice is abandoned. As you are drawn further into Asia, old fetishes lose their power. It becomes harder and harder to persuade yourself that you feel a craving for exercise, and indeed you almost forget that you ought to feel this craving. . . .

And now the journey was almost over. To-morrow we should reach Manchuli. The train pulled out of Irkutsk, and ran along the River Angara until it debouched into Lake Baikal. At the mouth of the river men were fishing, each in a little coracle moored to a stake at which the current tugged. It was a clear and lovely evening.

Lake Baikal is said to be the deepest lake in the world. It is also said to be the size of Belgium. Its waters are cold and uncannily pellucid. The Russians call it "The White-Haired", because of the mist which always hangs about it. To-night the mist was limited to narrow decorative scarves which floated with a fantastic appearance of solidarity far out above the unruffled waters. . . . Contrary to general belief, the railway round the southern end of Lake Baikal is double-tracked, as indeed is the whole Trans-Siberian line from Chita westward to Omsk, and doubtless by now further.[1] The train crawls tortuously along the shore, at the foot of great cliffs.

One's Company, by PETER FLEMING

152. Developments in Eastern Siberia

The Sibiryaks are a tough, independent and enterprising people of Russian blood who have colonized Siberia since the seventeenth century. They are a fusion of Don and Ural Cossacks, criminals deported for life, runaway serfs and migrating peasants seeking a more prosperous existence, and political and religious exiles. . . . The Kuzbas is an example of their enter-

[1]The Trans-Siberian line now has a double track (or more than double) for the whole of its length from Leningrad to Vladivostock, a distance of about 5,430 miles. An air route follows closely that of the railway.

prise.... Its principal town, Stalinsk,[2] in 1926 a village of 4,000 souls, has grown into a great industrial city, earning its living in the arsenals, the locomotive shops, the metallurgical plants, and in the mines.

Other large industrial areas are in the Far East (heavy industries at Komsomolsk and Khabarovsk) and at Irkutsk, close to Lake Baikal. Here a big hydro-electric dam has been built ... to provide power for the industries developing so rapidly in Eastern Siberia....

The Soviet Union's largest locomotive shops are at Ulan Udé, capital of the autonomous republic of Buriat-Mongolia; here, too, are found the most extensive wolfram deposits in the world. One-sixth of the world's gold output comes from the Lena-Vitim fields in Yakutia, the world's finest timber is felled on the banks of the Yenesei, and the immeasurable forest taiga of Northern and Eastern Siberia is the home of ermine, sable, silver fox, blue fox and other precious fur-bearing animals....

Buriat-Mongolia is the Soviet Union's most important cattle-raising country, but otherwise bad climate and poor soil combine to create the problem of how to feed the growing industrial population of Siberia. A further problem is oil. Synthetic oil is made from coal found in the Kuzbas, and at Cheremkovo, but the island of Sakhalin remains the chief source of oil in Siberia.

"J.M.", in the *Yorkshire Post*, Leeds

153. The Blacksmith's Basin

In the Kuzbas (Kuznetsk Basin), called the "Blacksmith's Basin" because it was there that the Mongol Jenghiz Khan forged his weapons before attacking the Western world in the thirteenth century, history is repeating itself. After a lapse of seven centuries, during which the Kuzbas has hardly been utilized, it is now once again the great forge of a nation. Great thriving cities have sprung up on land which is so rich that you can sow and harvest your crops in less than four months.

For hours as we approached Novosibirsk, its central city, by the Trans-Siberian railway, we passed through cities and

[2]Now Novokusnetsk.

towns black with smoke. The snow on the ground looked dirty and hard. Except for the wooden houses—arranged mostly in neat, orderly rows—we might have been going through Barnsley or Sheffield on a cold winter's day. It was not a glamorous sight—unless you suddenly reflected that the town through which you were passing simply did not exist in the 1920's.

The Kuzbas ... is roughly half-way from Vladivostok to Moscow. It lies well to the east of the Ural Mountains—a thousand miles or so—and gets much of its power from the great River Ob.... There is enough coal for the world, and the rich black soil is fertile enough almost to feed the entire population of the globe....

The ground is rich in other minerals as well as coal—particularly in some of the light metals that are so highly important in modern industry. In a steel factory at Novosibirsk I was told that all the manganese they wanted came from the near-by town of Masulsk, whereas formerly it all had to be transported from Georgia and the Ukraine, a couple of thousand miles away. And there is iron ore too, close at hand.

Trans-Siberian, by NOEL BARBER

154. The Soviet Far North

The Soviet "Administration of the Northern Sea Route" handles not merely sea transport but practically every colonizing and economic development, including mines, agriculture, forests, roads, rivers and air transport, in the region north of 60 deg.N. Lat., meaning a territory nearly as large as the United States....

The Soviet Union felt they needed a second string to their transport bow—in addition to an all-year rail route, the Trans-Siberian, they wanted a summer route from the Atlantic to the Pacific for steamers, the North-East Passage, called by them the Northern Sea Route.

The success of the Northern Sea Route needs explaining. The key word to any large development is not fight but adaptation. Instead of thinking how to overcome the disadvantages of long winters, the pioneers of the Soviet North seek to capitalize on winter cold as advantageous. Instead of worrying that glaciers are bad, Soviet flyers think how lucky they are to have them in places like the rugged and rocky Franz Josef Islands for use as landing fields. Instead of deploring that the rivers are ice-covered so many months in the year, Soviet engineers consider what fine natural highways the ice makes, permitting tractor-drawn trains of sledges to wind their way during half the year between the northern seaports and the interior of their continent—natural tractor freighting routes of 2,000 miles each along the Ob, Yenesei and Lena, 1,000-mile routes on shorter rivers.

VILHJALMUR STEFANSSON, in *Think*, New York

155. Reindeer of the Tundra

There they came, a thousand reindeer, fine animals, notably larger than Lapland reindeer. Most of them were grey coloured, some very light in colouring, others snowy white, a few spotted. Then the reindeer sledges were brought forward. They are slender and elegant and wonderfully strong, and are made entirely of birch; you will look in vain for a single nail or screw. All the joints are kept together by straps of narrow, undressed reindeer hide.

Two reindeer are harnessed to each sledge, side by side. After the sledge had been got ready, two riding animals were brought forward, and the neatest little saddles of reindeer-hide laid on them. One rides at a walking or trotting pace, never at a gallop. Reindeer are not equal to the strain involved in galloping. But in other respects they make very serviceable mounts. They will cover thirty miles with a rider and not be any the worse.

Through Kamchatka by Dog-sled and Skis, by STEN BERGMAN

156. Some Towns of Southern Asiatic Russia

(*a*)   That Russia is making progress in Central Asia according to Western European standards in general is undeniable. There is a university at Samarkand and at Tashkent, and Usbeks and Tajiks are learning to become doctors, engineers, architects, mechanics. The Central Asian Republics have their laboratories, schools, printing presses, theatres, hospitals, clubs, technical institutes—in fact all the modern amenities. . . .

Modern Samarkand is as proud of its factories as of its university. It has leather factories, flour mills, distilleries, brick works, pencil factories, cotton cleaning mills, and outside the town, a new silk factory. . . .

Tashkent is like Samarkand, with its modern Russianized new town, and its old town where the century-old Asiatic civilization still flows on its leisurely tea-drinking way. . . .

Krasnovodsk revealed itself as a desolate dust-heap of a town surrounded by fierce mountains of solid reddish rock. As a seaport of the Turkmen S.S.R. it has some importance, being the link between Central Asia and European Russia. To it come the products—chiefly raw cotton and dried fruit—from Turkmenistan[3] and western Usbekistan.[4]

South to Samarkand, by ETHEL MANNIN

(b) Charjui is the centre of Turkmenistan's cotton production. A number of new factories have recently been built. Most of them are ginning mills, where series of circular saws, ranged alongside each other, separate the seed from the fibre. The latter is then compressed into bales and dispatched to Russia to be spun. The seeds are pressed on the spot to extract the oil. It is coal black as it flows from the presses, but when purified turns a golden yellow like olive oil, and is welcomed for all kinds of cooking. The refuse yields a valuable cattle food, and is also sometimes used as fuel for heating.

Alone through the Forbidden Land, by GUSTAV KRIST,
translated by O. LORIMER

157.   The People of Russian Turkestan[5]

The life of the people is a simple and monotonous one, and withal frugal. Their diet consists almost wholly of meat and cheese. They have a peculiar drink called ayran, made of boiled milk diluted with water, and then allowed to stand until it slightly ferments and turns sour. It forms an excellent and most refreshing summer drink. Their various products of the

[3]Or Turkmenskaya S.S.R.   [4]Or Uzbekiskaya S.S.R.
[5]See note on Extract 156.

dairy are kept in goat-skins. Their clothing and bedding they make themselves, and mostly from the felt and wool of the sheep and goats. The curious tents in which these people live, called yurts, are well known. They are made of a coarse felt, fully an inch thick, composed of the coarser varieties of sheep's and goat's wool. The tents are round, with a dome-shaped cover, in the apex of which is a small aperture through which the smoke escapes from the fire built on the ground in the centre of the tent.

Siberia and Central Asia, by JOHN W. BOOKWALTER

158. The Tarim Basin

(a) We were looking down into the great enclosed basin which occupies the very centre of the continent. Within the ring of encircling mountains, the basin floor is composed of a broad desert zone of gravel surrounding a zone of vegetation in which most of the villages and towns are situated, and which in turn surrounds a great central desert tract of sand and salt. The entire basin, which is three times as large as Great Britain, drains to the salt lake of Lob Nor. At least it would drain thither, if most of the streams did not wither to nothing in vast slopes of gravel and plains of sand. The principal river, the Tarim, or Yarkand, flows along the western and northern sides of the basin. In many places the sands of the Taklamakan have buried the ruins of ancient villages, which could have existed only when the climate was moister than now.

The Pulse of Asia, by ELLSWORTH HUNTINGTON

(b) Most of the irrigation depends upon an elaborate system of Karezes, or underground wells and canals, which tap the subterraneous drainage from the mountains. The climate of the basin is extremely arid and, owing to the low level of the trough, very hot during the greater part of the year. The warmth of climate, together with the assured supply of water, makes it possible in the oases of the basin to reap two annual harvests. The fertility of the soil, when irrigated under such favourable conditions, is great, and accounts for the abundance of produce in cereals as well as in fruit and cotton.

On Ancient Central Asian Tracks, by SIR AUREL STEIN

159.   Conditions in Sinkiang

Yarkand is the richest oasis in Sinkiang or Chinese Turkistan,
but we did not appreciate this fact until we had left the city
and saw the open country covered with wide stretches of rice,
maize, wheat and millet. Khotan is famous for its silks and
felts, its cotton cloth, carpets, paper and jade. The native-
woven silk is coarse in texture and dull when compared with
that produced from European looms, but when dyed with
deep vegetable colourings it has an indescribably rich appearance, and much of it is exported to India. . . .

Millet and rice are regarded as the best paying crops, the
former occupying one half of the total area cultivated. Apricots,
grapes, peaches, nectarines, quinces, cherries . . . grow in great
profusion; and pumpkins, which are the staple vegetable, are
supplemented by carrots, onions, cucumbers, garlic and fennel.
Donkeys are found in thousands and take the place of the
wheel-barrow and the cart in England, besides carrying the
bulk of the internal trade. Sheep are usually of the fat-tailed
species. All animals, as a rule, are miserably thin owing to
the almost entire absence of grazing.

Through Deserts and Oases of Central Asia, by
ELLA AND SIR PERCY SYKES

160.   On the Tibetan Plateau

We reached a pass on the Tibetan plateau, and gazed eastwards over a bare and gloomy scene. It was five o'clock on a
grey February evening; nothing was visible but wide earth
plains, chequered with tufts of coarse grass, and beyond that
the jagged rim of snow-striped mountains; an icy wind snored
over the bare gravel. Up a glen we noticed a small stone
village, almost invisible against the boulders, but said to be
inhabited all the year round; as it is well over 16,000 feet, this
is truly remarkable. There is a hot spring hard-by; and indeed
such a concession would be necessary. . . .

It seems curious even in August, to be able to lie on the
grass at an altitude of 16,000 feet and picnic comfortably, but
it must be remembered that at these great heights, in summer,
it is very hot in the sun and cold in the shade. One must get

out of the wind of course, and a storm may burst almost without warning, otherwise it is delightful. The winters are hard and long, desperately hard and very long, and the wind makes one gasp. Indeed crossing the plateau in March, one might believe it was a desert, completely devoid of plant life. But during the brief summer it is astonishing the number of plants which revive.

The Riddle of the Tsangpo Gorges, by F. KINGDON WARD

161. Two Tibetan Towns

Lhasa is prettily situated at a little distance from the bank of the River Kyi, in a large valley with a commanding horizon of high barren mountain ranges. The huge palace of the Dalai Lama[6] is erected on one of the two summits of a small isolated ridge that shoots up in the middle of the valley. Even the best photograph will fail to convey a true idea of its imposing appearance, as it stands, a red palace, capped with golden roofs, uplifted high in the blue sky, on a shining pedestal of dazzling white buildings. . . .

Jakyendo is built on a rise at the foot of a chain of mountains. Above it, looking down on the laymen's dwellings from a rocky spur, stands a monastery, the building decorated with red and white lines. Dominating the crest on which the monastery rises, a magnificent background of summits bars the distant horizon.

My Journey to Lhasa, by ALEXANDRA DAVID-NEEL

162. A Glimpse of Mongolia

No town in the world is like Ulan Bator (formerly called Urga), the capital of Mongolia. The most conservative eastern life and customs, and western innovations like the telegraph, telephone and the motor car, exist side by side in motley combination. The houses of the Russians cluster around the church with Byzantine cupolas; colossal Buddhist temples rise high over thousands of felt-covered Mongol tents. Mounted Mongols, slippered Chinese, long-bearded Russians and smiling Tibetans swarm. . . .

[6]Now in exile in India. His palace was called the Potala.

In the course of my travels in Mongolia I have come across herds of horses so large that they covered the steppe as far as eye could reach. The richest Mongol I met owned 14,000 horses. The Mongols derive most of their food from cattle; meat is their main diet. Sheep also are indispensable to the Mongol; from their wool he gets material for felt stockings and for his tent, and their meat is a delicacy.

Tents in Mongolia, by HENNING HASLUND, translated by
E. SPRIGGE and C. NAPIER

163. The Two Worlds of Japan

At an open air restaurant in Hibiya Park, Tokyo ... my attention was caught by the sight of a beautiful young Japanese woman in full traditional dress. This in itself was not remarkable; many Japanese women, though few men, still wear the kimono, at any rate occasionally. But this woman was standing by a juke-box, feeding it with coins, listening to Elvis Presley and the Beatles at full blast.

Contrasts like this are typical of present-day Japan. Tiny wooden houses, with sliding paper walls instead of windows, with mats and cushions instead of chairs, have TV sets (perhaps several) and a refrigerator (though hot water from a tap is a rare luxury)....

The countryside is still a patchwork of tiny irrigated rice fields, but the new super-express train to the South covers over 300 miles in three-and-a-half hours (not long ago the journey used to take ten hours).

The mixture of old and new, of East and West, struck me particularly during a day's excursion from Kyoto recently. Kyoto is surrounded by wooded hills. The highest, Mount Hiel, of about 2,500 feet, is bound up with the history of Kyoto and of Japan; for centuries, off and on, the city was dominated, sometimes terrorized, by the warrior-monks of the great monastery of Enryaku-ji, high on the mountain. Nowadays, Mount Hiel is a favourite place for picnics and outings, easily accessible by cable-cars and motor-roads to the very summit.... A roar of engines in low gear became heard, and a confusion of shrieks and laughter.... Yet inside the vast temple, the great hall, open on its long side, was filled with

Japanese tourists and children, kneeling and listening quietly
as a monk related the temple's history.

MICHAEL FUTRELL, in the *Yorkshire Post*, Leeds

Note. A writer in 1969 referred to the "brash, confident, but still deeply
spiritual culture of the new Japan." He mentioned "a beautiful temple
garden, a miraculous oasis in the dirt and industrial din of Osaka."

164. In and Around Tokyo

My programme allowed me to see a great deal of Tokyo itself
and the surrounding country, and to make the eight-hour
journey by the famous Tsubame train from Tokyo to Osaka.
I should point out that this wonderful train is a "limited
express" and provides the traveller with every possible comfort. He is told, for example, the time of day at regular intervals and the state of the weather immediately ahead, whilst
interesting places along the route are pointed out as he speeds
along. On this particular run an exceptionally fine view of
Mount Fuji may be seen, and the line takes you through
Kyoto, the splendid ancient capital of Japan. . . .

Tokyo itself, with a population of well over seven millions,[7]
is said to be the third[7] largest city in the world; and I have
read that it is increasing at the rate of 400,000 a year. Apart
from Hong Kong I have never seen such crowded streets,
shops and buses. Two million children enter the primary
schools in Japan each year. No wonder there is the ever-
present problem of food, buildings and living room for these
people.

REV. J. T. WATSON, in *The Bible in the World*

165. Life in the Kansai

The Kansai is the west central area of Japan. Its heartland is
one of the few plains of mountainous Japan, about sixty miles
long and twenty miles broad. Its overworked soil has known
the farmer's plough and the warrior's boot for generations too

[7]The 1965 census gave the population of the city of Tokyo as 8,893,000;
and of Greater Tokyo as 10,869,000. This makes it the largest city in the
world. (Greater Tokyo was estimated in 1969 to have 11,353,724 people.)

numerous to count, for here it was that Japan's first central government was established a few centuries after Christ, here that the first Korean and Chinese emissaries set foot with their gift of a mainland culture which raised ancient Nihon (Nippon) from barbarism to civilization, here that arts flourished and civil wars raged while the present capital, Tokyo, was but a backwoods frontier outpost.

The twentieth century has wrought great changes in this remnant of old Japan, however, changes best illustrated by the growth of three mammoth cities. Osaka, with its three million people, has become the industrial and commercial capital of Japan; a million people tramp through its central railway station every day, many of them boys and girls fresh from the villages of Shikoku and Kyushu, looking for a steady job in the bustling factories of the metropolis, but often falling in instead with the racketeers and other bad characters whom the city also breeds. Kobe finds its life dominated by a busy port, the gateway to South-East Asia, and by the ruthless fact that Japan must export or perish. The ancient capital of Kyoto, on the other hand, lives at a slower pace, with the traditional (and too often feudalistic) silk and handicraft industries absorbing the energies of its workers.

ROBERT SUKEDA, in a Japanese Church
"Labour Letter"

166. Japanese Mulberry Trees

The Japanese fields are surrounded with hedges of mulberry trees, with broad shining leaves, which add immensely to the general appearance of the country. The mulberry trees are in leaf just as the worms are hatched from the eggs which have been carefully kept during the winter, and, when once hatched, the grubs must be carefully and constantly tended and fed. Shallow bamboo crates are piled up on stands in the great upstairs apartment, and in any other quiet place that is available, and here the grubs are allowed to feed to their hearts' content on the broad mulberry leaves which are constantly being brought in, fresh and crisp from the fields. Great care must be taken during this period, for the silkworms are easily disturbed, and the country people say that if they hear bad words spoken, or words of ill omen, they will shrivel up and die. Silence therefore is observed in all rooms where there are silkworms. When the grubs have done eating, they go to sleep in the cocoons which they have spun for themselves, and a little later, when the right time comes, the cocoons are taken and the silk thread is spun from them.

Everyday Japan, by ARTHUR LLOYD

167. Round the Coasts of Japan

One peculiarity of the seas surrounding the Japanese Archipelago is the presence of two gulf streams, the one cold, the other warm. The Kuroshiwo, or Black Current, is produced near the Equator by the action of the Trade Winds, flows along the coasts of China till it strikes the shores of Japan, follows the Japanese coastline as far north as about 38 degrees N., and thence bends eastward across the Pacific Ocean, where it spends its remaining strength in washing the coasts of British Columbia. The other current is a cold one[8]: it rises near the mouth of the Amur River, and, flowing southwards between the mainland of Asia and the island of Sakhalin, washes the western coasts of Hokkaido and the main island of Honshiu. One result of these two contrary currents is to produce surprising differences of climate and temperature between places which are really only a few miles apart and which lie almost on the same parallel of latitude.[9]

Everyday Japan, by ARTHUR LLOYD

168. Chinese History and Influence

China is the oldest civilized society on earth, fifty centuries old and covering three million square miles, a quarter of all Asia. She has been speaking the same language on the banks of her rivers for 5,000 years. She was an ordered country when the people of our islands were painting themselves like savages. She has been swept by tyrants, torn by dynasties, ruled by

[8]Called the Kurile Current.
[9]Another result is to cause fogs.

K

hundreds of emperors, has suffered unthinkable calamities, but has survived. . . .

How many of us realize that China, far off and remote from us all, has woven itself into our lives and ideas? She was greatly affecting our ways of life, was preparing the visible glory of our royal pageantries, when two monks brought out of her strongly guarded frontiers a bamboo cane with the eggs of the silkworm hidden inside it, and so gave silk to Europe. Her furniture, said the late Laurence Binyon, gave ideas to Chippendale, her pottery captivated the mind of Western Art and set all Europe at China's feet. She was making beautiful things ages before the thought of beauty began to dominate our lives on this side of the world. . . .

Her simplicity of art comes from a deep love of birds and flowers, and through it she has, says Binyon, expressed a philosophy of life in the work of sixteen centuries of gifted artists. Long before our great painters found their inspiration in the beauty of the landscape the Chinese had found it; they knew Nature as part of their consciousness of the continuity of all life. To them "Man was not the centre and hero of the universe", but just one part of it, and so it is that in Chinese Art the figures on the stage have never dominated it, but have been merely a part of the whole.

Wonderful Year, by ARTHUR MEE

169.   The Great Wall of China

A rough stairway leads to the top of the Wall, which is about twenty feet wide, with a crenellated parapet on each side, and you can walk along it as far as you can see, with here and there a scramble where it has fallen in a little. Every half mile or so is a little square tower of two storeys. The Wall itself varies a good deal in height according to the nature of the ground, averaging probably about forty feet. On one side Mongolia, as you see it, is a vast undulating brown plain; on the other side China is a perfect sea of brown hills in all directions, and across these stretches the Great Wall. Over the hill-tops, through the valleys, up and down the sides it twists in an unbroken line, exactly like a huge earth-worm suddenly turned to stone. And as you reflect that it is built of bricks, in almost inaccessible places, through uninhabited countries, that each brick must have been transported on a man's shoulders enormous distances, and that it extends for 2,000 miles, or one-twelfth of the circumference of the globe, you begin to realize that you are looking upon the most colossal achievement of human hands.

The People and Politics of the Far East, by SIR HENRY NORMAN

170. The Approach to Peking

Day by day the steamers pass in long procession; and passengers, craning eagerly from the side, catch a first glimpse of fabulous and ancient China—railway station, flour mill, mud-built houses which accompany the windings of the stream and are clustered above ramshackle wooden piers.... Each house is a one-storeyed yellowish cube, the colour of unbaked pottery, of the soil; every village suggests a grouping of mud pies, newly cut by some child with a sharp spade....

We steamed up towards Tientsin and our wake, as the river grew more narrow, sucked and gurgled along the crumbling mud banks. Presently there was a great roller sweeping behind us, a hissing wave which brimmed up on to the fields, flooding the crops, clawing away and tearing down big slabs of the jealously guarded earth. This attack was repeated by successive steamers; it happened, I suppose, with every tide. Here was a field, carefully dug and planted, in which their backwash had channelled a slimy creek; here a house, cracked through and ready to fall, sagged over the yellow swirling water....

The day was over when we reached the suburbs of Tientsin, and a factory whistle blew dismally from a yard.... Next morning we caught the eleven o'clock to Peking from the shabby desolate station across the river.... The train itself was comfortable if rather grimy; attendants brought us tea and steaming face towels, and for three hours we jolted on towards Peking through a landscape nearly identical with yesterday's. The river, it is true, was not in sight, but the ground was as flat and carefully cultivated; everywhere the

same families of conical graves, the same pallid soil and leaf-
less branches.

A Superficial Journey through Tokyo and Peking, by
PETER QUENNELL

171. The Loess Highlands of North China

(*a*) In Shensi the peasants live in caves scooped out of the
porous yellow earthen cliffs. Their fields are poor. Every fall
of rain carries off land which goes to heap up the bed of the
Yellow River. To make up for the losses caused by the rain,
the men work tirelessly, like ants, bringing new earth in
baskets.

Forbidden Journey, by ELLA K. MAILLART

(*b*) Absolutely treeless, with never a suggestion of even brush
or grass, these loess regions were everywhere for day after
day the same bare yellow brown. Of cave dwellings cut far
back into the cliffs there was no end, by far the majority of the
population having only such homes. Much of the way lay high
and gave us splendid views across mountainous country
fantastically broken, as only loess can break.

Wanderings in Northern China, by HARRY A. FRANCK

(*c*) I had little desire to see the gaol. You reached it by a
winding road without any shade. The sun beat down on the
dust, and the dust made life miserable.... I was in a rebellious
mood when I went to the prison, but the mood did not last
long. The sun was pitiless, the prison caves were higher up the
mountain than I had imagined, but the prison itself, with its
high walls cut out of the loess, was curiously impressive.

Journey to Red China, by ROBERT PAYNE

172. China — North and South

In the winter it is cold everywhere in China and in summer it
is hot everywhere. This applies to the tropic south and the
temperate north. Peking has snow and ice while at Hong Kong
it never actually freezes, but it takes the same warm wardrobe

in the wintertime, north or south, to keep your teeth from chattering. And in the summer you will need a tropical wardrobe not only in the tropical south but in the "temperate" north. . . .

One of the amazements of a visit to China is to discover the radical differences between the northern and southern halves of the country—differences in the landscape and differences in the temperament of the people. I think of Nanking as a city marking the borderline. North there lies a brown and dusty world of thirsty plains. To the south spreads the green and watered country of the illimitable rice fields.

Finding the Worth While in the Orient, by LUCIAN S. KIRTLAND

173. China's Inland Waterways

The spate of official reports describing new developments in China has revealed increased government interest in the construction and renovation of inland waterways. The well-publicized extension of the railway network has been rapid, but it has involved the use of much iron and steel, vital commodities of which China is still desperately short, and also a relatively large capital expenditure. In September 1959, the Chinese Communist Party Central Committee and the State Council issued a directive . . . which stated in part, "In all localities where there are rivers, an active effort should be made to harness them in order to make them as navigable as possible.". . .

Dredging is going on to rejuvenate the 2,400-year-old Grand Canal, and construction work has begun on a 110-kilometre extension from it at Tientsin eastwards to Tangshan in order to serve the Kailan coal-mining area. Work on the Canal itself is at present concentrated on that part of the channel between Tsining in Shantung and the River Yangtse, a 510-kilometre section.

But the most significant improvements concern the 5,500-kilometre River Yangtse itself. . . . The well-known bottleneck at Tienhsing Chow, near Shasi, where silt used to pile up during the low-water season, is now navigable at all times. At Kungling, above Ichang, the bed of the river has been widened from thirty metres to sixty metres by blasting. A system of over 5,000 navigation lights, based on Soviet methods, has been working along the whole navigable length of the river since 1954, making it possible to pass through the gorges between Ichang and Chungking by night and reducing the duration of the steamship voyage between those two places from four to two days.

D. J. DWYER, in *Geography* (Vol. 46, 1961, pp. 165–166)

174. In Western China

(*a*)   Szechwan has so much rain and cloudy weather that the province bordering it on the south is named Yunnan, which means 'South of the Clouds'. . . . Chungking is the largest city in western China. It has an imposing position on the north bank of the Yangtse. In the lower part the streets are narrow and ascend in steps. The shops offer a great variety of wares, notably silks, for which the province is famous. Tatsienlu, the "Gateway of Tibet", lies at an elevation of 8,500 feet in a narrow valley with mountains rising thousands of feet on each side. That the town is progressive was shown by the recent installation of a hydro-electric lighting plant.

Men Against the Clouds, by R. L. BURDSALL and A. B. EMMONS

(*b*)   The Cheng-tu plain, with its three or four crops a year, is the richest and most populous district in the whole of China. This extraordinarily productive plain supports a population estimated at no less than four millions. Among the crops are rice, wheat, tea, tobacco, maize, the opium-poppy, and the yellow rape that turned hundreds of acres of land into seas of bright gold.

From Peking to Mandalay, by R. F. JOHNSTON

175. Life Along the Si Kiang

(*a*)   Canton is the human ant-hill of South China, with a population variously estimated upwards to four millions, and the city is substantially today what it was a thousand years ago. Its narrow tunnel-like streets are beehives of activity: every man, woman and child works and notwithstanding the daily wage of a few cents are quite good-natured about it. Everything under the sun seems to be manufactured in some shape or form by the Cantonese. The river life also presents an amusing spectacle, and after you have looked over the hundreds of sampans, you are not surprised to hear that more than a million of the city's population live on the water.

A Million Ocean Miles, by SIR EDGAR BRITTEN

(*b*) Up the Si Kiang, or West River, I have seen seemingly contented Chinamen, always ready with a quip or a grin while swaying at their sweeps, or, more laborious still, eternally walking up a tread-mill in the stern of a junk—truly the case of a man being turned into a machine. Then there are the sampans, the prerogative of pushing them along being often reserved for gnarled and ancient women, who, standing up, facing for'ard, one foot swinging back and forth, shove the craft through the water. . . .

Further up-stream lies the customs-port of Wuchow, where half the population of the close-packed city live in boats, moored fifty-deep along the shore-line. The lives of this floating concourse of people are at the mercy of the treacherous river, its turbulent waters having a habit of rising forty feet in a night, when the floods pour down from the hills.

LLEWELLYN PRIDHAM, in *Chambers's Journal,* Edinburgh

176. Chinese Outside China

The Chinese are a most industrious, energetic, resourceful people; they are born traders and not afraid of hard work. In many respects they can be compared with the Jews—a people loving to settle in towns, though they are not afraid of living in the country if need be. The majority[10] of Singapore's population of 1,200,000 is Chinese; in Indonesia, Chinese number something like a million and a half,[11] and are largely to be found in the towns. The same is true of the Chinese in India, and of course in the United States.

Moving away from China, however, has not meant for them

[10]Nearly three-quarters (1,454,500 out of 1,995,600 in 1967).
[11]Now about three and a half millions.

ceasing to be Chinese, and here the comparison made above
with the Jews is of interest. For like the Jews (though with
certain notable exceptions, as in Malaya) the Chinese seem to
resist assimilation even when, as in some cases, they have
forgotten to speak their own language. Their ties with the
homeland, their attachment to one another, and the fact that
frequently they have been persecuted in exile, all these factors
have contributed to make and keep them a people apart. . . .

From what has been written above it will be easy to see how
the new situation in China itself is having a profound effect
upon the Chinese of the Dispersion. Though large numbers
of them can have little sympathy with the régime now dominant in China, their country (i.e. China) is today a world power.
They are citizens of no mean city. There is in consequence a
new interest in Chinese culture and the Chinese national
language. Education is one of the great questions of the moment
for all Chinese outside China.

REV. J. T. WATSON, in *The Bible in the World*

177.   Hong Kong and the Chinese

In Hong Kong, on the edge of the Chinese mainland, three-
and-a-half million Chinese are crammed into a crazy capitalist
boom-town within sight of the Communist frontier.[12] But
Hong Kong is a British Colony; how different are the Chinese
here from the 700-million on the other side? There are superficial differences, of course. In Hong Kong you can work for a
profit and gamble and spit in the streets. In China you work
for the State; gambling is illegal and spitting anti-social. But it
is doubtful whether fifteen years of Communism have really
changed a race with 4,000 years of culture.

And in some ways Hong Kong's "laisser faire" allows us to
see the Chinese as they really are, because as far as they are
concerned Hong Kong is part of China. Ninety-seven per cent
of its population is Chinese. Most of them do not speak English;
to them the British Administration is simply a convenient local
boss whose presence leaves the Chinese free to get on with
the serious business of living. It is undoubtedly Chinese enterprise and hard work that has transformed Hong Kong into the

[12]The total population of Hong Kong is now nearly 4 millions.

thriving industrial centre it is today. And it is here in Hong Kong, inflated many times over by the mass exodus from China since Communism arrived there, that we can mingle with greater freedom than anywhere else among Chinese people who were born and brought up in China. . . .

What is it like to be Chinese? One person in every four on the face of this earth is Chinese, yet Western knowledge of them is strangely blurred. . . . The Chinese themselves are largely to blame for our ignorance. Traditionally they have closed their doors to the outside world and brought up their children to look upon all other races as inferior beings.

RICHARD CAWSTON, in *Radio Times*

178. Life in Hong Kong

As we neared Hong Kong we were quickly surrounded by dozens of little boats. Many were manned by children, who dived into the swirling currents after coins. Others had large nets, suspended on long poles, to catch an orange or a bread roll which someone might throw.

In the Philippines we had found the world was passing by— the country was forgotten—and little was being done to revive the economy. What a contrast Hong Kong turned out to be. Here was a hive of activity. Here among the refugees was hope. A colony previously dependent on shipping had become a manufacturing centre. In a city renowned for its cheap cottons, exquisite formal dresses and coats were now being made from beautifully hand-sewn silk.

It was encouraging also to hear the widespread praise for the far-sighted British Colonial administration that governed the colony. A crash programme to build massive apartment blocks was well advanced, and nearly half a million people had been rehoused.

Yet many still lived in hillside shacks or on the rooftops. Thousands more lived their entire lives on sampans. Most of these disease-ridden rotting craft were in two groups, both surrounded by a massive sea wall which acts as a typhoon shelter. Typhoons come to Hong Kong every autumn, and while many bring disaster they do also bring rain, and rain, however it comes, is welcome in a colony where water pressure

is on for only a few hours every few days, even in the rainy
season.

ROBERT PERRIN, in *The World's Children*

179.   Indo-China[13] — "Pearl of the East"

Indo-China's geographical position makes it the focal point of
South-East Asia.... This great, rich and beautiful country—
often called "The Pearl of the East"—covers 286,000 square
miles, so that it is one and a third times as big as France.....
It is a land of vast mountain ranges clothed with thick forest,
huge stretches of jungle, the home of rhinoceros, elephant,
tiger, bear, leopard and panther, and of mighty rivers which
literally rise above the clouds. The Mekong, almost 2,000
miles long, is one of the great rivers of Asia, and the Red River
passes through some of the most majestic areas on earth....

Its warm, moist climate results in a luxuriant growth of all
vegetation and cultivated crops. The resources are immense
and, in normal conditions, tea, maize, pepper, rubber and,
incomparably the most important of all, rice, are exported....
In Cochin-China one can motor for a whole day without losing
sight of the rice-fields.... The country is a storehouse of
mineral wealth, whose riches have hardly been scratched as
yet. Anthracite coal, iron ore, zinc, tin and wolfram are the
chief....

Saigon, on the river of that name, forty miles from the sea,
is one of the finest cities of the Far East, beautiful with large
numbers of trees and parks, and with many notable public
buildings. A first-class university was established there after
the Second World War. Only four miles off is Cholon, with a
large percentage of Chinese. It has extensive rice mills.

J. L. FORSTER, in *The Trident*

180.   People of the Great Lake

The Tonle Sap river reverses and for five months runs backwards to its source; thousands of forest acres are flooded fifty

---

[13]Now divided politically into North Vietnam, South Vietnam, Laos,
and Cambodia. Cochin-China is now part of South Vietnam.

feet deep. And this occurs each year around the Great Lake of Cambodia. The cause of this unique freak lies far away in the Himalayas of Tibet. When the snows melt in early summer the huge Mekong river, that flows through South-East Asia, rises so high that it backs up its tributary the Tonle Sap and causes the Great Lake to swell to four times its normal extent.

The Cambodian villagers must either ride the flood like Noah or perch their houses on stilts fifty feet high or higher.

I went and lived with these people, both when the Lake was low and when it was high; it was water, water everywhere and a wonderful lot of fish. But the thing I remember most was the blinding heat from that shimmering sheet of water in the middle of the great Cambodian plain.

It is fine for the fish. They come swimming up the Tonle Sap to lay their eggs in the green shade of the inundated forest. The food supply is rich. The concentration of plankton (microflora and microfauna) is the greatest in the world and so is the concentration of fish.

When the waters begin to subside in October the fish are fat and they set out on their journey back to the main river, the Mekong. This is the fine time for the villagers, who set traps on a really colossal scale.

HUGH GIBB, in *Radio Times*

181. The Ruins at Angkor

I have been spending a couple of days looking at the ruins of an ancient empire at Angkor, in the middle of the Cambodian jungle. This empire flourished at about the time of the Second Crusade, but then gradually declined as the land was invaded from neighbouring Thailand and Vietnam. The great stone temples and palaces were left empty, and the jungle closed in; now it is a famous archaeological site and is being painstakingly tidied up again by experts, and many of the buildings restored. . . .

To enter a temple compound where the jungle still reigns is like suddenly coming across the results of a bomb explosion; heavy sandstone pillars are heaped in all directions; arches lurch drunkenly; stone floors bulge and sag. Then one realizes that all this is caused by the roots of the great trees, twisting among the pediments and around the stone window-frames, slowly wrenching the heaviest buildings apart, thrusting aside supporting columns, till a whole façade crashes in a disordered heap. But here and there, the detail of a carving seems marvellously preserved.

Elsewhere the presence of the jungle is less dramatic; the big trees have been cleared and the courtyards levelled; and, before the midday tropical heat makes movement intolerable, it is as pleasant to stroll through some of the ruined temples of Angkor as through some ruined abbey in a forest of Europe.

The local people, descendants of those who built Angkor and its empire, are smiling, simple villagers. They play on pipes which harmonize with the liquid sound of their bamboo cowbells and with the almost overpowering song of the forest birds.

ANTHONY LAWRENCE, in *The Listener*

182.   Bangkok: "Eastern Venice"

The capital and chief port of Siam (Thailand) is situated on the River Menam, some miles above the Gulf of Siam. It is a picturesque city, with flimsy wooden houses, thatched or tin-roofed, which jostle each other along the river-banks—indeed many houses are actually built out over the river on stilts or on floating pontoons, and many people live in houseboats moored along the river. The city is criss-crossed by a network of canals and creeks, on which ply numerous native boats called "prahus". These are propelled by one oar at the stern, and many have a tent-like cabin made of woven matting for protection against the tropical sun and rains.

The hot and damp climate favours the growth of trees, which line the canals and often meet overhead to form a dark tunnel through which the boats glide silently. For many years the canals were the streets of Bangkok, and so it has been called "the Eastern Venice". Nowadays, however, roads have been built to allow easier movement within the city.

Bangkok is a long narrow city, extending for about ten miles up the river, but only about a mile wide. The buildings and vegetation are so dense that it takes a considerable time to get through in some places. There are some modern concrete buildings in the middle of this native eastern town—commercial houses, an up-to-date hospital, shops, and a University, for instance. In fact, modern Bangkok is a fashionable city, with a gay cosmopolitan life. It is difficult to know how many people live in Bangkok; but a recent estimate suggests a population of 700,000 at least.[14]

Bangkok possesses many old Buddhist temples, called "wats". With their steep ornamented roofs and spires, their images and tinkling bells, these are most impressive to the stranger.... The industries of Bangkok are rice-milling and boat-building, and there are many sawmills where logs of teak, which are floated down the river, are cut up into planks for export.

Vol. III of the Oxford Junior Encyclopaedia, ed. by
LAURA E. SALT and GEOFFREY BOUMPHREY

183. Marvellous Malaya

Malaya means palm-lined coves with the surf trickling, layer on layer, to the white sand; like an American film about the South Seas. Malaya means the blaze of a monster orchid in a rain-drenched forest alive with the chatter of ringtailed monkeys. Or dying sunlight on lacquered dragons at the pagoda gates; or fantastic limestone bluffs leaping out of the plain; or towering ranges of rock steps behind pools of lotus flowers at the cliff temples of strange gods. Malaya means pretty laughing faces under the laced mantillas of sixteenth century Portugal, and solemn turbaned faces turned west to Mecca when the call to the faithful rings above the splash of fountains in the courts of many mosques.

And more than all, Malaya means opportunity for people and peoples—copra and tin, a third of all the tin in the world and half its rubber. There are three and a half million acres of rubber trees in Malaya. They look like slender beeches.... The Malays live in villages, and fish and cultivate rice and tapioca and coconut palm. The Chinese and Indians live in towns, buy and sell and follow the professions, and often read the latest books and plays from London and New York. Often,

[14]The population in 1963 has been given as 1,608,000, and in 1966 as 1,577,000.

too, the Malays say, they send the money they make to India
and China. European government has cared for the Malays;
given them schools and hospitals, and opened the government
service to them and to them alone. In fact, till the Japs came,
politics in Malaya revolved around a tussle between the European commercial community, who favoured the Chinese because they made Malaya rich, and the European administrators
and planters, who favoured the Malays because they kept
Malaya peaceful and content.

The *Evening Standard*

Note. In 1963 a federation called Malaysia was established, consisting
of West Malaysia (eleven Malay States) and East Malaysia (the Borneo
states of Sabah, formerly North Borneo, and Sarawak). This federation
is independent, with a British High Commissioner. Singapore was a
member until 1965.

184. The Malay and His Country

The Malay, dwelling on the bank of a river, his only highway
from village to village, and clearing no more of the dense jungle
than was necessary to provide rice-fields and orchards for his
needs, had no thought for panoramic views over the fair land
in which he lived. If he climbed forest-clad hills, it was in
search of jungle produce; the idea of felling trees to get a vista
of his country never occurred to his utilitarian mind, and the
open highlands of the Taran and Larong Mountains were
closed to him by stories of the genies and dragons ready to
destroy trespassers near their domain.

The Malay fisherman saw more. Beyond the mangrove belt
or the tree-lined sands he could descry distant hills now in a
purple shimmering haze capped with white billowing cumuli,
now dark under a pall of thunder-clouds. But from fisherman
and rice-grower alike the glories of this small tropical country
were hidden, and even now are only partly unfolded to those
who have had the fortune to climb the highest peaks, drift
down the largest rivers and explore the islands of either coast.

Malaya, by R. O. WINSTEDT

185. Singapore

The island of Singapore, which is only about twenty miles long and some twelve miles broad, gives its name to the city and port on the southern shore to which most people refer when they speak of Singapore. It is linked to the State of Johore on the Malayan mainland by a causeway which carries road and rail traffic....

Vast areas of jungle were cleared and planted with rubber trees after the Para rubber plants, imported first from Brazil to Kew in 1873 at the instigation of Lord Salisbury, and subsequently in 1877 to the Botanic Gardens at Singapore, had been found to thrive in the Malayan soil and climate. From two cases of these plants which survived the ocean voyage was laid the foundation not only of Singapore's, but of the whole of the Malayan rubber plantations.

Not the least of the achievements on the island has been the suppression of the malaria-carrying mosquito. It has meant years of unremitting effort, but this was rewarded by an almost complete absence of malaria from Singapore's bill of health.

Wise administration kept the port and dock facilities expanding on a scale commensurate with the ever-growing volume of shipping.... The port served not only as a clearing house for most of the trade of Malaya and the surrounding islands, but also as a calling place for ships of all nations passing through the bottle-neck of the Malacca Straits.... The fine harbour is one of the largest in the world, befitting a port ranked commercially among the world's ten greatest.

The development of air travel and airways has further established Singapore as an island of paramount importance. The airways converge on the Colony just as the sea lanes do, before once more branching out to serve widely scattered areas.

"Artif", in *The Trident*

Note. Singapore is now a republic, but is still a member of the British Commonwealth.

186. Some Impressions of Indonesia

Three main and contradictory impressions stand out in the mind of the traveller on his first visit to Indonesia. First is the wide diversity of the country. Indonesia is formed by four main islands,[15] but also embraces thousands of others, many of them not insignificant in size; there are four or five ethnic and linguistic groups (150 languages!); the cultural life of the country is based on four or five different strata of civilization, as evidenced in the Hindu and Buddhist temples, the mosques and the churches, yet even these witness to only a part of the many influences which have left their mark. . . .

But underlying this variety there is among the people a solid homogeneity which strikes the visitor. Faiths and religions have come, and sometimes gone; the old tenacious animistic beliefs still lie close to the surface and the gods and spirits still receive their offerings at the corner of the rice field. Indonesia —with a population about half[16] that of the whole of Africa —has preserved its traditions. As one gazes at the rice fields, cultivated in terraces up the mountain slopes, one admires the age-old skill and tenacity of the peasants; one also wonders at the slow method of harvesting the rice, the spikes cut one by one with a small knife hidden in the palm of the hand, which the silent harvester must not drop lest the protecting spirit should be disturbed and flee away.

And, finally, there is the feeling of exhilaration. A new nation is coming into being. . . . Thousands of students from all parts of the country can be seen cycling in the streets of Jakarta, the heart of Java, which is the spiritual centre of the new Republic.

OLIVIER BÉGUIN, in *The Bible in the World*

187. Life in Sarawak

Two days on a boat from Singapore brought me to Sarawak, where I arrived on September 1st. My friends very kindly came to meet me at the first port of call down-river, and brought me the last forty miles up-stream to Sibu in a speedboat, a thrilling introduction to travel in Sarawak. There is no railway here, and few roads. Most of the country is jungle, the thick vegetation pierced only by rivers and creeks. Communication is chiefly by water or by air. . . .

[15]Borneo (in part), Java, Sumatra and Celebes. West Irian (formerly West New Guinea and a Dutch colony) came under Indonesian administration in 1963.
[16]It is now well under half.

Sibu seems to me one of the wettest spots on earth. I am writing this to the sound of torrential rain which blots out all other noises. The garden has become a swamp, and the water is creeping up and threatens a minor flood. As this is possible at any time, most of the houses are built on stilts. The country presents very great contrasts; within a short distance we can see tribal people living under the most primitive conditions, and in the towns, modern buildings with all the latest amenities. There are few towns of any size. Sibu is second largest to Kuching, the capital, and is developing fast. New roads and buildings are being built all the time. The riverfront is always busy, with hundreds of small craft coming and going, as well as ocean-going ships up to about a thousand tons, which tie up at the wharf and look as though they are just at the end of the street, as indeed they are.

DORIS WEBB, in a Methodist Missionary
"Monthly Letter"

188. Amboina, in the Spice Islands

Amboina is the easternmost point on the Indonesian Airways span of the archipelago. The little Dakota that had flown me and my interpreter from Macassar swooped down in sudden ecstasy to one of the oddest-shaped islands I had yet seen. And I had seen some very odd shapes in the Celebes.

This island had two green crescent lobes that were thick with coconut palms and tropical shrubs, and it was almost cut in two at the centre except for a thin stretch of honey-coloured sand. As we flew above the elongated horseshoe bay we could see one-winged "praus" (outrigger boats) gliding ethereally over the surface of the water.

For a moment I thought the sea was filled with blood, but as I peered closer I saw that it was coral. As for the brilliant red patches on the hills, they must have been the descendants of those rhododendrons that had attracted English botanists two centuries ago.

Amboina is one of the fabulous Spice Islands (the Moluccas) —a romantic-sounding name, evocative of adventure on the high seas. Both Drake and Raleigh came here and took back perfumed cargoes of spices that preserved our forefathers' meat

L

in the days before refrigerators. Amboina still exports cloves, although I did not recognize the clove tree when I saw it. It seemed so strange to see light green clusters of cloves actually growing on branches! I only recognized them when I saw them lying out to dry on bamboo mats in front of the houses on the road from the tiny airport to the town of Ambon. . . .

There was a wonderful perfume in the air for, in addition to the cloves, there were camphor trees and flowers of every description.

NINA EPTON, in *Home and Country*

189.   New Guinea — Primitive and Modern

In a fertile valley of New Guinea, hemmed in by the high range to the north and by the limestone belt to the south, are the Kiapou pygmies, living today under conditions that prevailed in the Stone Age. I came upon them cutting down huge tracts of mountain jungle with their stone axes, and clearing the land for their crops of taro and sugar-cane. For a while I took stock of them: square, light-brown faces, receding foreheads, tufts of hair, long arms, and not one of them more than 4 feet 10 inches in height. They are, without doubt, wonderful little men; better bowmen would be hard to find anywhere in the world today. True, they are primitive, very primitive, but they live well and make large gardens; among the crops I saw were taro, bananas, sugar-cane, native corn, sweet potatoes, spinach and celery. . . .

Beyond the valley lay the rolling timbered slopes and grasslands. On every slope were cultivated squares, while little columns of smoke rising in the still air revealed the homes of the people. They were like little farm-houses, oblong in shape and built low to the ground. They grew potatoes, spinach, etc. and bred pigs in large numbers.

Through Wildest Papua, by J. C. HIDES

Note. Port Moresby, the capital (in Papua, the S.E. quarter of the island of New Guinea) now has its University, hospitals, etc.

190.   The Haunting Beauty of Burma

It is a never-to-be-forgotten moment when the newcomer, after

a long and tedious voyage, enters the brown waters of the
Irrawaddy and suddenly sees floating in the far distance be-
neath a sky of faultless blue the great golden dome of the
Shwe Dagon Pagoda.

From that time, if he has any soul, Burma will have captured
him. . . . And as he sails down the river for the last time, he
will look over the side and will see hundreds of blue water-
hyacinths floating down with the tide to be lost in the waters of
the Bay of Bengal, and he will remember the vivid green paddy
fields, the muddy creeks, the deep teak forests and the white
pagodas perched on every hill, with their attendant saffron-
clad monks, that he is leaving for ever. . . .

I have flown from Rangoon to Moulmein—one cannot get
there direct by car—and I well remember the enchantment of the
scene as I came down over the town in the early morning. The
brown waters of the Salween made a vast, deep stain far out into
the sea, the mountains of Thailand were lost in the blue haze,
and the river was a mass of picturesque junks, paddy boats and
gigs, which made no effort to make room for us to alight. Behind
the town was a low ridge of tree-clad hills, crowned with many
white and red pagodas. . . .

It is south of Moulmein that the Tenasserim coast becomes
really mysterious. It is a coast of thick jungle, broken only
by deep, silent-running creeks, up which sturdy little motor-
boats tow the barges of the tin companies whose activities take
place in rigid seclusion in the secret hinterland that very few
white men have penetrated.

PHILIP BATEMAN, in the *Cape Times*, Cape Town

191. The Road to Mandalay

At Rangoon the traveller would get in one of the paddle steamers
and come up the Irrawaddy, that slow river with its enormous
mahseer fish, its string of white egrets on the silvery sandbanks,
its riverside washing places and temples, its green jungle lapping
the water's edge with shadow and silence.

And the rice going down to be milled, the enormous teak
logs in a stage of the journey that will end with them planed and
polished as decks in Her Majesty's ships. And around this great
river, around its tributaries and their tributaries, the elephants

hauling down these great logs from the inland forests—piling them at the river's side, in this sludgy creek, with the roof of the jungle above, and indeed silence and the green shade hanging about the unhurried elephants like a cave. Silence, until that moment dusk brought when the soft feathering bamboos would rustle like a skirt ... as the children went into the great Arakan Pagoda and knelt to the gold Buddha, leaving flowers in small vases before the god—pink and white carnations that filled the temple with their clove scent; as moneylenders and the jade sellers packed up for the day; as the cooking fires were blown into life again and the heart of the town seemed lustrous and warm and friendly with these small points of fire and the swaying bead curtain beyond them, the bamboo houses....

All over the country the white spires of the temples gleam among the trees and on the hills. Their thousands of tiny bells with their leaves are so made as to catch the smallest breeze. And each whisper of a tinkle is a prayer to Buddha....

You can smell and you can feel this road that leads to Mandalay. The weedy, damp smell of the paddles as they turn over slowly, trundling up the still river to Mandalay, to the great red fort and the hill. The newly disturbed mud where the elephants are at work. The hot bazaars with the sweet smells of candies, the "spicy garlic smells" of curry, the warm bitter smell from cheroots, be they black or white.

BERNARD GUTTERIDGE, in *The Listener*

192. The Changing Face of India

The big changes that are going on around us are imperceptible and immeasurable.... I suspect that a re-orientation towards a new Humanitarianism is going on in millions of minds ... Gandhi's stress on ethics and non-violence has permeated Indian thinking and has survived him.... The village does not change, save that in some provinces it is more militant than it was, and bent on achieving a social transformation. In the great towns the eye detects at once the ugly march of industrialization. Factory chimneys in Delhi share the skyline with the minarets of the Moghul mosques. Bombay has expanded in straggling suburbs of concrete. Since the war the bigger cities have doubled their population, and in the slums the congestion would rouse a less patient people to the wrath that makes revolutions. As before, the homeless poor spend the night sleeping on the pavement with a rag of sacking under them, but they seemed to me more numerous than they were.... Dispersal of industry is the accepted plan, to raise the level of village life.

H. N. BRAILSFORD, in the *New Statesman*

Note. In the north-east, great "steel" towns like Durgapur have arisen. In the south, Coimbatore has become the "Manchester" of South India. These are typical of the developments.

193. Indian Peasant Life

India has many types of agriculturalists. There are places in the South where undersized, black, primitive families live elemental lives on the land. In the North are tracts where auburn-haired, copper-complexioned giants fight and raid, and hastily turn to the ploughshare when "punitive measures" are heralded.

Let us look for a moment at an average farmer in the United Provinces. He is neither a weak freak nor a swashbuckling bully. He is strong, industrious, home-loving. He is poor, but better off than many others; a good average in respect to race, geographical position, economics and character.

Gonda Lal is thirty-seven. His village is near the ancient town of Ayodya. To this day, few Europeans are seen there. It is a place of medievalism and romance: elevations of gods, processions of virgins, public mortification of Hindu penitent ascetics, and so on. Gonda Lal has nothing to do with all that. It is all run by a multiplicity of religious people. They may be Moslem, Jain, or Hindu. They may be mendicants or hierarchs. Somehow they live on the likes of Gonda Lal; just how, he has never thought out.

As he goes and returns from his bit of poorish arable land he salaams to the temple of his Hindu upbringing; but he makes a little acknowledgment of other deities. Why risk a mistake and lose possible eternal joy just for the sake of a little politeness...?

All days are much the same to Gonda Lal. No Sunday, no week-ends; no cinemas, no dogs, no football.... It is a slow life, but it would be idyllic and quietly contented, but for the fact that almost all over India the tiller of the soil is in debt to the owner, and the latter takes care he never gets out.

E. W. R. STONE, in *The Wheatsheaf*, Manchester

Note. Despite the vast exodus to the towns, and with the reduced power of the land-owner, village life still predominates in India. A writer in 1968 said, "India is a land of striking contrasts, side by side — modern cars and ambling bullock-carts; giant office blocks and ancient tumble-down bazaars; ostentatious wealth and abject poverty; technical colleges and women in industry still carrying loads on their heads; agricultural institutes and barren fields".

194.   The Forests and Animals of India

The forests are the favourite haunts of the big game of India, more especially the damp forests of the Western Ghats, of the Terai, and of Assam, still the home of the wild elephant, the rhinoceros and the bison. The only lions to be found in India are a few in Gujerat. India's characteristic beast of prey is the tiger. Far more common than the tiger is the leopard or panther, which is just as dangerous. The black or sloth bear is fairly common wherever there are rocky hills or forests, but is, as a rule, harmless to man, living on ants, honey and fruit. Crocodiles haunt nearly all Indian rivers. Sometimes they bask in the sun near the water's edge; sometimes they lie with just the head above the surface of the water, motionless as a piece of wood, but at the very slightest sound they disappear.

Living India, by LADY HARTOG

195.   Cows in India

Even more alarming than the unchecked increase in the human population is the unchecked increase in the bovine population. When I close my eyes and think of India, the first thing I see is cows. Cows wandering in groups along the road, cows grazing on the garbage across from the Grand Hotel in Calcutta, cows jay-walking somnolently past Lloyd's in majestic defiance of all traffic regulations, cows as numerous and multi-shaped and multi-hued as the rats which once tumbled after the Pied Piper of Hamelin, cows with sores and protruding ribs and tiny one-quart udders. Holy cows, all.

Because the cow is holy, no attempt has ever been made at husbandry. For centuries the diseased and unproductive have interbred with the healthy, so that today the Indian cow is probably the poorest of its breed in the world. And as the land grows more crowded, the breed grows constantly poorer.

That something must be done about the cow problem even the most orthodox Hindus will agree.... I suggested to my Hindu friends that it would be to India's advantage if the Hindu religion could be modified to permit the slaughter and consumption of beef. If, under the supervision of village committees, a programme of selective slaughter and scientific husbandry could be enforced, so that the bovine population could be reduced from 225 millions to 150 millions of improved breed, India would have more than enough to provide her with dairy animals and draught animals. If, in conjunction with such a programme, some miracle could induce the Indian masses to abandon their ancient superstitions, then overnight the national diet would almost be doubled in calorie and protein content.

DAVID CARPENTER, in *Tribune*

Note. As India becomes increasingly more urbanized, industrialized, and secular, the taboo on the killing of bulls and cows is much less rigid, but scientific husbandry, taught at new agricultural institutes, is not yet widely applied. Meanwhile the human population approaches 500 millions, at the rate of one million per month.

196. Calcutta

In certain quarters of Calcutta the aspects of the streets, the costumes of the passers-by, the fronts of the buildings, give the impression of some rural metropolis in the interior of England. Great factories—low buildings spread over vast areas—lift a forest of brick chimneys to the sky, or thrust great wharves out into the river, and networks of railroad, fan-like, over the plains. All these are connected in one way or another with the preparation and weaving of jute, the staple product of Bengal. Almost all the burlap used in European and American agriculture comes from these great industrial centres that line the banks of the Hooghly below Calcutta. The corn of Argentina, the sugar of Cuba, the potatoes of Idaho, are distributed in bags that have passed through the looms of these Bengalese establishments.

A Novelist's Tour of the World, by VICENTE BLASCO IBAÑEZ

197. The Ganges – Brahmaputra Delta

It is a fertile, semi-aquatic plain, rich in crops of rice and jute, and covered with a net-work of rivers, streams and creeks. Boats take the place of carts, the waterways serve as roads. The land is subject to annual inundation and silt fertilization. The slope of the country is away from and not towards the chief rivers, and the water in the minor channels flows from and not towards the main streams. In the rains a volume of turgid water spreads itself over the country; low-lying areas are inundated to a depth of eight to fourteen feet, the water covering everything but the river banks and the artificial mounds on which the villages are built.

Bengal, Bihar and Orissa, by L. S. S. O'MALLEY

198. From Calcutta to the Hills

Calcutta was unbearably hot and stuffy. I longed for cool fresh air and to get away from the crowds, so I took the train to Darjeeling in the Himalayan foothills. The train jogged along on its leisurely way, through endless rice paddy dotted with clumps of palm, bamboo and an occasional luxuriant dark green group of mango trees. A ferry across the Ganges and then the train continued through the night towards those tempting hills.

At the foot of the hills we changed into the "toy train" to climb the last fifty miles and 3,000 feet. It looked for all the world as if it had been transported out of the children's section of some amusement park, but had a powerful little engine and an enormous fog-light on the front.

It ran on single-track two-foot gauge and without benefit of cables or ratchets, simply by one long gradual pull; was hauled round loops, backed up hair-pin zigzags, and passed right along the main streets of small towns. Men were dotted everywhere—

on the cowcatcher in front, on top of the cab; and the guard sat on top of the roof of the last coach, in what seemed to me to be a rather hazardous position. The air became cooler, invigorating, and squat cheerful hill folk smiled as we went by.

Darjeeling, clean and cool, situated on the edge and the steep western slope of a narrow ridge at about 7,000 feet, lived up to its promise. I walked through the steep narrow streets looking for a place to stay, and at the other end of the town I came to the New Elgin Hotel, a white wooden building set among lofty evergreens.

IAN THORNTON, in the *Yorkshire Post*, Leeds

199. From a Himalayan Ridge

After four hours of constant ascent, we reached a pass at a height of about 14,000 feet. Here a glorious view opened before us. To the west towered the mighty mountain tongue which, projecting from the north, separates the Nubra from the Shayok Valley. Its lower portion, for several thousand feet above the valley, presented every variety of colour, from the "café au lait" of wide bands of clay, interspersed among the rock slopes, through many shades of brown, grey and red, to rich maroon and purple. From the general level of this colour complex, perhaps 20,000 feet, shot up 3,000 to 5,000 feet higher, peaks of every imaginable size and shape. Some of these were cones, wedges and pyramids of solid dark blue and purple rock, with jagged apexes, whose sides were so steep that snow could not lodge on them; others of greater size, covered with eternal driven snow-fields running down into glaciers in the angles between the slopes, shone before us in dazzling splendour in the wonderfully clear air, undimmed by the slightest suggestion of haze.

In the Ice World of Himalaya, by F. B. and W. H. WORKMAN

200. Nepal: Land of the Gurkhas and the Sherpas

Five hundred miles in length and a hundred miles in breadth, Nepal embodies much of the great Himalayan range, including

most of Everest and Kanchenjunga. Wild, savage, and virtually
unexplored for the most part, the little state is yet one of the
best governed in the whole of Asia. The topography falls
naturally into four distinct zones, each running east and west.
Bordering on the plains of Bengal is the Terai, a region of dense
tropical forests and jungles, abounding in wild animals and
forming the worst malarial region in the whole of the Indian
sub-continent.... North of the Terai is the country of the
Doons, foothills of the Himalayas, rising to nearly 3,000 feet,
and beyond that are the Uplands reaching to 10,000 feet. North
of this is the Himalaya itself, the wildest and grandest country
in the world, reaching to the slopes of Everest.

Although comparatively extensive in a geographical sense,
Nepal restricts its political life to one very small area, the valley
of Katmandu. In this little region, bounded by mountains
10,000 feet high, live the King and all the national leaders.

Like so many races in the East, the Nepali is a mixture of
various peoples.... The Gurkhas came to the land only in the
mid-eighteenth century, and there is no mistaking their connection with the Rajputs of Central India. Unlike the latter,
however, they soon identified themselves with the other peoples
of the country, intermixing and marrying.

The Contemporary Review

Note. A writer in 1970 described Katmandu as "a fascinating mixture
of magnificent temples, priests with prayer-wheels, flute players, young
Tibetan carpet makers and outdoor markets".

201. The Markets of Delhi

In the markets of Delhi products of the whole earth are spread
out before the eye—shawls of Kashmir, cuts of English broad-
cloth, corals of the Red Sea, gems from Ceylon, gums and spices
from Arabia, rose waters from Iran, watches and clocks from
Switzerland, perfumes from Paris, candied fruits from China,
Worcestershire sauces from England. The animal marts offer
horses, elephants, camels, buffaloes, dogs, cats, monkeys,
leopards, bears, deer, stags of all species. And especially tigers—
cubs barely weaned with all the charm and grace of playful
kittens, and majestic bloodthirsty full-grown beasts which
proudly boast the label of "royal Bengal". World-famous are

the gold workers of Delhi, and the designs they execute on cloths are sought through all the Orient. The nearby state of Kashmir exports huge quantities of shawls to Delhi where artists embroider them with ornaments in silver and gold.

A Novelist's Tour of the World, by VICENTE BLASCO IBAÑEZ

202. The Gang Canal

Since the opening of the Gang Canal (from the Sutlej River to the Thar Desert) over 500 new villages have come into existence. They were all planned and built on systematic lines with proper roads, drinking-wells, and other amenities of village life. The population, as a result, jumped from a bare 28,000 in 1921 to 180,00 in 1934. The phenomenal increase in population and the development of cultivation have resulted in the establishment of suitable marketing centres, which have grown into important trading towns. The most flourishing among them, Ganganagar, called after the Maharaja, although only a few years old, compares well with the long-established canal marketing centres in the Punjab in respect to population, trade and industries. Along with this, considerable industrial development has also taken place. Four ginning-factories, three pressing-factories and two sugar-factories have already sprung up in the canal area. More than a dozen flour-mills and many oil-extractors are in operation.

H. H. The Maharaja of Bikaner, by K. M. PANNIKKAR

Note. Many similar irrigation canals have been constructed in the Punjab, notably the Jhelum, Bari Doab, Chenab, Sirhind, and Western Jumna canals. The result is what has been called "the finest system of irrigation canals in the world".

203. The Taj Mahal

The Taj Mahal is a building in the Arabic style. It is just a mosque much larger than other mosques, square, with a great dome, and with four minarets at the corners of the enormous platform which serves as its base. And yet it is entirely different from all other buildings of the Arabic school, because of the peculiar quality given it by the marble, the only material used in its construction.... There is something diaphanous, something unreal, about it. A red building with arabesques in different colours serves as a huge gateway to the gardens of the Taj Mahal. Beyond the gate opens a long rectangular garden with walks and paths paved with marble.... In the centre of the rectangle is a vast water-course that reaches as far as the stairway leading up to the monument. The whole gigantic mass, with its dome and its minarets, is reflected upside down in this silent pool. As the breeze flecks the surface of the watery mirror, the edifice trembles in the depths with a pearly luminousness that banishes all thoughts of death.

A Novelist's Tour of the World, by VICENTE BLASCO IBAÑEZ

Note. The Taj Mahal is a mausoleum rather than a mosque, and is near Agra. It was built about 1629–50 by Shah Jehan as a tomb for his wife, Mumtaz Mahal.

204. The Central Deccan

Saris, scarves and other smaller articles are made from the silk of the Tasar worm gathered in the jungles in the eastern and southern parts. Cotton carpets and rugs of a superior description are manufactured at Hyderabad.[17] Gold and silver tissue cloth are also made. The texture of some of it is almost as fine as muslin. It is used for veils, head-dresses, bridal robes and saris by the wealthier classes. Oil pressing affords employment to a very large number of persons. The chief oils are made from coconuts, mustard seed, castor-oil seeds, ground-nuts and linseed. There are oil pressers in every village who supply the requirements of the community and send the balance for sale at the nearest bazaar. The oil mill is a simple affair, consisting of a wooden screw press, to the lever of which a blindfolded bullock is yoked and driven round in a circle. The most important minerals in the region are the ores of iron which are widely diffused.

H. H. the Nizam's Dominions,
by S. H. BILGRAMI and C. WILMOTT

[17]Hyderabad and Secunderabad, Andhra's twin industrial cities, now have well over one and a half million people.

205. Ceylon

All the wealth of an exuberant tropical Nature seems to have been concentrated on the Island of Ceylon, which Brahmin poets called "the pond of the red water lilies"; the Chinese, "the land without sorrow"; the Greeks, "the land of the jasmine and the ruby"; the bards of Buddha, "a pearl eternally unstained resting on the bosom of India"; and, centuries later, the Mohammedans, "mankind's consolation for the loss of Eden". Ceylon has grown of late years to be one of the most popular winter resorts frequented by Europeans....

Towering over the hills behind Colombo (capital of Ceylon) we could see an almost vertical cone, Adam's Peak, the summit of which appeared quite inaccessible. Lying some fifty miles inland, this mountain is climbed only by those who visit it on a sort of pilgrimage during the summer months.... The last few hundred feet of the mountain are almost perpendicular and must be traversed with the help of chains, which at times have broken and dashed pilgrims to their death on the rocks below.

A Novelist's Tour of the World, by VICENTE BLASCO IBAÑEZ

206. Exotic Plants of Ceylon

Everywhere in Ceylon there are plants with strange pods, fabulous fruits, or unexpected blossoms. This tree crowned with a cluster of green melons is the pawpaw, and this bush hung with claret-coloured nuts is the cocoa plant. The nut-meg tree is tall and straight with a dark green trunk and dark green leaves. The tree that bears the clove mimics it in less sombre foliage. On the hillside is a tea plantation; in the plain is a field of ragged cinnamon bushes hemmed in by sago palms. There are many rubber trees. This great tree, with unwieldy fruit budding out of its trunk and branches, is the bread-fruit. It would need one learned in plants to name the cactus and the ferns, to recognize the pimento and the pepper tree, or to tell which among the many unruly creepers bore the vanilla bean.

The Other Side of the Lantern, by SIR FREDERICK TREVES

207. Srinagar: Venice of the East

We left Calcutta on a breathless afternoon in June, travelling to

Rawal Pindi, and then by car to Srinagar. Most people who read travel books know about Srinagar—"the Venice of the East" and so forth. It is all true. The place is beautiful and haunting. You see forget-me-not coloured mountains in the distance; the colours of the bazaar overhanging the river are exquisite, and there are times when you feel you would be happy to stay there all your life. Lotus-eating. That is all life in Srinagar amounts to. . . .

After lunch the "Bund" is deserted, while the population goes to sleep. At about 4 P.M., out come the picnic parties, floating by in the flat-bottomed, attractively cushioned punts that are called "shikaras". Placidly these drift down the Jhelum river, and out by way of tributaries to the lovely spots that exist beyond. Slipping through narrow, leafy water lanes, they force their way through the lilies growing in such profusion, out on to the lakes that are without a ripple, where the pink lotus lilies grow. . . .

Many people maintain that the country is spoilt by the Kashmiri. . . . Let us admit that he is dirty, loquacious, idle, a liar and a thief, knowing not the meaning of gratitude. But he is also a natural craftsman, adorning his creations with few of the crudities found further south. . . . And he is a wonderful waterman. He will guide a shikara through narrow congested channels, leaving a fraction of space to avoid a collision. He may infuriate you, but always you will want to look at him. He is a rascal, but to some his charm is potent.

Mountain Magic, by EVE ORME

208. Climbing in the Pamirs

The climate during our visit to the Pamirs in June and July was one of the most changeable in the world. It was always cold when we left camp between six and seven o'clock in the morning, the sky often grey and cloudy and the mountains veiled in mist. At noon it was often extremely hot. There are no trees on the Pamirs, and I have vivid memories of halts on the hillsides where there was not even a boulder large enough to give shade, and where, in spite of my pith-hat, sun umbrella and thick clothes, I felt as though I were slowly being roasted as we lay exposed to the fierce sunshine. It was always very cold

when the sun went down, and in camp I wore all the clothing
I could muster and pulled a fur coat over all.

Through Deserts and Oases of Central Asia,
by ELLA and SIR PERCY SYKES

209. The Khyber Pass

If you travel eastwards across the Khyber Pass towards
Peshawar—and you can do so by ordinary motor-bus from
Kabul in Afghanistan—you come suddenly upon one of the
most dramatic prospects in the world. You are still in a wilderness of jagged red mountains whose strange shapes only a
Gustav Doré could have imagined. The road before you
straggles down into the jumbled chaos, and disappears. But far
below, through a chance gap between distant precipices, you
catch just a glimpse of a green and level countryside, with tiny
trees and roads, houses and silvery streams. It is called, with
majestic simplicity, "The View into India"; and it is quite
unforgettable.

You can tell me, if you like, that those trees and houses are,
in strict political fact, not now in India at all, but in Pakistan.
You can say that they are part of the Vale of Peshawar, whose
meadows and rose gardens are far from typical of the Indian sub-
continent as a whole, beyond the Indus. But *here* is the Khyber,
and *there* is the beginning of the plains, and something tells
you that you are now about to cross one of the great dividing
lines or watersheds of human geography.... Behind you, for
thousands of miles, stretches the harsh and impenetrable
mystery of Central Asia—and of Russia. Immediately about you
is the lawless tribal territory where the "King's writ" has never
run, except in the hours of daylight on the narrow highway on
which you are now standing. But in front, through that distant
peepshow in the rocks, another world begins. It is, in the
official phrase, "settled territory". Its people go about their
business unarmed, it is flat and fertile and civilized, eminently
lootable—the eternal rich prize of India.

DOUGLAS BROWN, in *The Listener*

210. Afghanistan

Afghanistan is a wild and mountainous country, in the eastern part of which the peaks of the Hindu Kush rise to over 21,000 feet. Deep gullies pierce the mountains, and on the wide plateau not a speck of green is to be seen for days at a stretch. In summer the sun beats mercilessly down on the rugged mountains; in winter, they are wrapped in snow, and for nearly six months the route through Central Afghanistan is completely closed to traffic. . . . It is only of recent years that we have heard much about the lofty peaks of the Hindu Kush, bleak and wild as they are, with not a speck of green to refresh the eye. The daily extremes of temperature cause fissures in the rocks, while avalanches blot out the cliffs and fill up the valleys. The Hindu Kush lies like a mighty barrier round the (former) North-West Frontier Province of India, cutting straight across Afghanistan to the westward. Earthquakes devastate these mountains, cleaving them apart and forming deep gullies, through which torrents of melting snow rush down. . . .

Kabul, the capital, is situated in a large fertile plain surrounded by high hills. There are fine wide streets lined on either side with poplar and mulberry trees, but there are also many gloomy narrow lanes. The banks of the river, which flows through the town, are picturesque.

Through the Heart of Afghanistan, by
EMIL TRINKLER, *translated* by B. K. FEATHERSTONE

211. Travelling in Iran (Persia)

Physically Iran is not unlike an inverted soup-plate. We were now crawling over the rim—the foothills. Those mountains ahead were its steep and formidable sides, and beyond we would be on the base of the plate and out on to the great Iranian Plateau. . . .

Our road ran under the shadow of Elburz. In the middle of the blank emptiness we found a shop—a coal shop. The mountains are coal-bearing, and in front of a shaft-head a man was sitting by a table. We could have bought a sack or two over the counter and driven it away ourselves. Of course it doesn't pay. Transport is too difficult; but the coal will be convenient one day to the All-Iranian Railway. . . .

We entered Tehran by the Kasvin Gate, one of twelve gates set in the walls of the capital. We drove in under a huge arch with guard-houses on either side; it was crowned with six minarets, and the whole building was tiled. These Iranian tiles must be seen to be believed. The colours are mainly blue—turquoise, saxe and royal; the Arabic lettering is orange, green, brown and white. They looked absolutely perfect. They even made the rain cheerful. . . .

Resht is a fine modern town with boulevards in every direction, and a main square boasting a fountain and a band-stand, and on one side a town hall and a great hotel where we found excellent accommodation.

Cairo to Persia and back, by OWEN TWEEDY

212. In and Around Isfahan

(*a*) From Tehran we went south to Qum. The emptiness begins almost at once. . . . Bleaker and more desolate the vast stretches of land became; snow lit up the peaks of the mountains that every twenty miles barred the way. And then the lifeless miles began to liven up with strips of green, processions of thin poplars began, there were long ditches of water, and at last the full, fresh green of Isfahan. To the dust-choked traveller the sight of the green valley and the brown roofs of Isfahan through the curtains of trees is a delight.

How do you see Isfahan? In one way it is as western as Salisbury, Oxford, or Chichester, with mosques for churches; in another it is totally oriental. It is a poem; it is a tourist resort, a hardware shop, a textile town. They say society is as stuffy there as in any cathedral town in Trollope.

V. S. PRITCHETT, in *The Listener*

(*b*) As we drove from Shiraz, past Persepolis of immortal memory, and reached Isfahan in the evening dusk, the fading light was caught and held by the white petals of fields upon fields of poppies. The various industries arising from this culti-vation constitute some of the most fruitful products of the Iranian uplands. . . . The peasants living around Isfahan claim that the opium produced by their poppies is the finest in the world. The white flowers are held to give the best opium, and are the

M

earliest to flower, and thus are the most often cultivated. . . .
Oil is extracted from the seeds, which are crushed into pulp
beneath the grindstone of a mill propelled by a camel.

SIDNEY RALLI, in the *Sunday Statesman,* Calcutta

213.   Abadan — Oil Show-Place

"Abadan?" said the taxi-driver looking at my luggage-tag:
"Never 'eard of it." "Middle East," I told him. "Oil, you know."
"One o' them dumps eh? Send us a drop o' juice for the
old bus."

Seventeen hours later I was in Abadan, in South-West
Persia. It is anything but a dump. When the Anglo-Iranian Oil
Company made it the receiving end for some of the world's
biggest oil-fields they also made it one of the show-places of the
Middle East. I realized this when I climbed out of a B.O.A.C.
Argonaut to be told that what had been the oil company's
landing strip a few years ago had now achieved recognition
as an international airport used daily by the world's biggest
airlines. . . .

Since the first British oil-man arrived in Persia in the first
decade of this century, and pitched his tent on a stretch of palm-
fringed desert, Abadan has grown steadily and magnificently,
and it is now a modern town of 130,000[18] inhabitants, with
tree-lined boulevards, lush lawns, English gardens, lovely villas
and stylish flats. The place has a Continental air and a Hollywood
look.

There is a sense of orderliness and well-being in Abadan. . . .
All levels of the company's mixed team of British and Persians
share the general high standard of living and amenities. Native
artisans and their families have smart bungalows, with "mod-
cons.", receive paid holidays, qualify for pensions and send
their children to schools built by the company and to the
Abadan Technical Institute, which is not far short of university
status. . . .

From Haft Kel, Agha Jari . . . Masjid-I-Sulaiman and other
fields in the foothills of the Zagros Mountains run 1,600 miles
of pipe-line, bringing as much as a million gallons of oil an

[18]The population in 1967 was 339,121.

hour to Abadan. The company's tankers do not have to wait for
it, and do not dawdle when they have got it.

J. R. DIBB, in the *Yorkshire Post*, Leeds

Note. The oil industry in Iran is now nationalized, the State being a
partner in the ownership with private investors.

214. Pearling in the Persian Gulf

(*a*) It may be said that the pearling industry forms the support
of the Arabs on the western shore of the Persian Gulf; the
number of boats employed has been variously estimated at from
3,000 to 5,000, and the number of men at from 27,000 to
40,000. The richest banks are in the proximity of the Islands
of Bahrain, which send 2,500 boats to the fishery. The divers
descend by means of a heavy stone attached to a rope, and
begin at once to collect the oysters and put them in a bag,
basket or net, suspended from the waist or neck; they are able
to pick up from eight to fifteen oysters, and on jerking the rope
are hauled up to the boat. As soon as the boat is full of oysters
the captain sails to a sandy islet where the oysters are exposed
in the sun until they rot, when the pearls are gathered from
the shell.

The Countries and Tribes of the Persian Gulf, by s. b. MILES

(*b*) Many of the divers are brought up unconscious, and often
cannot be brought to life. Deafness, caused by the enormous
pressure of the water at such depths, is common among divers.
Rheumatism and neuralgia are universal, and the pearl-fishers
are the great exception among the Arabs in not possessing
beautiful teeth. On the shore the pearls are classified by the
merchants, according to weight, shape, colour and brilliancy.
There are button-pearls, pendants, roundish, oval, flat, and
perfect pearls. . . . I have seen a pendant-pearl the size of a
hazelnut, worth a few thousand rupees.

Arabia: The Cradle of Islam, by SAMUEL M. ZWEMER

215. Bahrain — From Pearls to Oil

Bahrain, now known to have been the fabulous Dilmun of
Assyrian times, is in fact an archipelago of eight islands lying
between Saudi Arabia and the Qatar peninsula; the name is,

however, more usually applied only to the largest of the group and it derives from the Arabic word for "sea"—in this case in its dual plural form, meaning "TWO SEAS"....

For centuries the wealth of Bahrain depended greatly on the pearling industry; and, although the industry continues on a diminished scale, the methods used in the tenth century, as recorded by the Arab historian, Abu Zaid Hassan, show little change even today. But the introduction of Japanese cultured pearls greatly undermined the natural pearl market in the 1930's and it was fortuitous that a new and even more valuable industry emerged at the same time and saved Bahrain's economy.

A New Zealander, Major Frank Holmes, was largely instrumental in obtaining the concession which led to the discovery of oil in May 1932, and its first commercial production in 1935. By 1954 the Refinery was processing 10 million tons of oil a year—much of it imported by submarine pipeline from Saudi Arabia—and income from oil royalties had risen to £4 million a year.[19] In recent years the State income has further increased and has allowed of major undertakings such as the construction of the deep water free port of Mina Suleman and the residential model town named after the present Ruler (Issa bin Suleman al Khalifah).

"Nomad", in *Gibbons Stamp Monthly*

216. Basra for Dates

From earliest times the date has been the staple food of Iraq, formerly Mesopotamia, "Land Between the Two Rivers". The soil is easily irrigable and amazingly fertile, being capable of raising three crops a year. This is one of the reasons why the date flourishes exceedingly, and it is cultivated particularly in the tidal riverine region of the south.

Basra is the chief port of the Middle East for the shipment of dates.... There are busy scenes at the height of the season, when the fruit is being rushed to the European and New World markets. Day and night, the winches whine as they lower the boxes into the holds, and, as Arabs invariably sing while working,

[19]Now much more. The profits are divided equally between the sheikhdom and the oil companies.

the sounds of melancholy quarter-tones and half-tones drift monotonously across the muddy Shatt-al-Arab. . . .

Every season as many as 20,000 women make their way to Basra, or Bussorah, the port of Sindbad the Sailor, as it was called in the romantic days of old. Daughters and husbands come too, but the latter prefer to leave the women to do the work. . . . The women packers of Basra take home—though "home" is usually nothing more than a reed hut by one of the ramifications of the Shatt-al-Arab upon which the port stands —a basketful of dates at night, and by the light of their charcoal fires squat round and eat them with great "flapjacks" of unleavened bread and handfuls of rice.

RICHARD C. STONE, in *Chambers's Journal*, Edinburgh

217. The Real Baghdad

I think to most people the name Baghdad conjures up pictures of the Arabian Nights, the Forty Thieves, and Harun-al-Rashid listening to the tales of a glamorous Scheherazade. It is a romantic picture, so I was a little surprised to find that the real Baghdad is a bustling, modern town of 900,000[20] people, larger than Liverpool, with an airport, at least one skyscraper, and the same car-parking and traffic congestion problem as we have in London.

The first city of Baghdad was built by Harun-al-Rashid's grandfather in A.D. 762. The city was circular and was called the Abode of Peace, a most inappropriate name as it turned out. The modern town is more than ten miles long on both banks of the Tigris, and is surrounded by dykes, called bunds, to prevent the annual floods from entering the city. There are few really old buildings in Baghdad. Most are of the nineteenth century or later, in the Persian or Turkish style, flat-roofed, of yellow brick, with overhanging balconies, pillared courtyards, and carved doorways. The narrow, winding streets are often no more than five feet wide. . . . You might see a Kurd in turban and baggy trousers, a porter carrying an immense wardrobe by a

[20]This figure evidently refers to the province of Baghdad. The city of that name had 552,000 in 1960 (the estimated population of Liverpool in 1967 was 705,000). The city of Baghdad is now much larger.

strap around his forehead, or a Baghdadi leading a horse. You would see few women completely veiled.

Baghdad mosques, with their Persian tiled minarets and golden or turquoise domes, are most attractive. Another typically eastern feature is the bazaar—a network of narrow lanes where each guild has its own street and where you can watch the craftsmen making gold bangles, shoes, or copper jugs.

ANTHONY MINOPRIO, in *The Listener*

218. Iraq Pipe-Line

When the late King Ghazi of Iraq turned the lever that opened the Mosul-Mediterranean oil pipe-line, early in 1935, he declared that a new prosperity, which would continue indefinitely, had been brought to the people of Iraq.... The main wells are at Kirkuk, 150 miles north of Baghdad.... Experts regard this as among the richest oil-fields in the world.... Most of the yield is of the heavy type from which lubricating oil is derived. Drilling is comparatively simple, and each well has taken an average of only three months to complete....

The construction of that gigantic snake of steel, the pipe-line, is one of the great romances of modern engineering.... Since it is buried throughout its course and there is little along its route to indicate its existence, it needs some imagination for the layman to realize the immensity of the grasp and resolution which designed it, and the human endurance which fashioned it....

From Kirkuk the line crosses the beds of the Tigris and Euphrates and travels on to Haditha, which is the point of division. There it bifurcates, one line going 532 miles to Tripoli, and the other 620 miles to Haifa. Its course to Haifa is followed closely by the Haifa-Baghdad highway....

The pipe-line is soaked as much in history as it is with crude oil. It traverses the great regions of Biblical and classical lore—Iraq, Syria, Lebanon, Transjordan and Palestine; crosses the Tigris, Euphrates, Orontes and Jordan Rivers; skirts the mountains of Moab, Nazareth and Carmel. It passes by Turkish villager and shepherd, Arab cultivator, Bedouin nomad, Transjordan peasant and Jewish settler of Palestine.

HARRY LEVIN, in the *Bulawayo Chronicle*

Note. Other oil pipe-lines now cross the desert from the Persian Gulf oilfields.

219. Progress in Armenia

The establishment of the Armenian Republic in the Caucasus under the protection of the U.S.S.R., and the subsequent progress and prosperity of the Armenian population, is one of the most interesting of modern developments; it has opened out a new life and a new hope for a martyred people. . . .

Armenia is a small country, about half the size of Scotland, but it is a land of beauty, historic interest and romance. . . . It is a region of great contrasts, with scorched arid wastes, wide level plains, fertile valleys, rugged mountainous areas of Alpine beauty, and towering volcanoes. . . .

The most up-to-date methods in agriculture are now being used, and farms are largely mechanized. This has resulted in an increased yield over a greatly extended area, and the abundance of fruit and vegetables has given rise to large fruit and vegetable canning industries. The fertile and rich pastures of the uplands provide food for scores of livestock and dairy farms. The building of an efficient irrigation system has made the desert blossom. A dense network of canals supersedes the primitive system of former days, and has transformed the parched plateau and low-lying desert lands into thriving regions producing cereals and crops of cotton, hemp, flax, tobacco and rice. . . . Owing to abundant water-power from Lake Sevan, and numerous rapid mountain streams, Armenia has been supplied with cheap electricity. . . .

The Armenians are the children of an ancient civilization, and naturally intellectual and artistic. With the coming of material prosperity their thoughts turned to the improvement of education, and the development of their national culture. . . . Armenian musicians, artists, actors, architects and sculptors now take their place beside the best in the U.S.S.R. Erevan, the capital, shows the most striking changes. From a provincial town of 30,000 inhabitants, with irregular streets, low shabby clay huts, little shops and clouds of dust, it has been transformed into a garden city, embowered in trees.[21]

A. C. BURT, in the *British Weekly*

Note. Since 1936, Armenia has been a constituent republic of the U.S.S.R.

[21]It now has well over 600,000 inhabitants, and is known as Yerevan.

220. "Noah's Ark Mountain"

Ararat, or more correctly, Airarat, "the plain of the Aryans", is the name given from time immemorial to the high land on the middle course of the River Araxes, and when it is stated in the Book of Genesis, chapter 8, v. 4, that Noah's Ark rested on Ararat, this high land is really meant, and the name has been in Europe improperly transferred to the mountain. Ararat is an almost isolated volcanic cone, consisting of trachite, slag and lapilli, and it attains to a height of 16,916 feet. There is no crater at the very top; near it stand two small subsidiary summits which only look like inequalities on the regular surface of the cone, and the latest eruptions of lava, which probably occurred in prehistoric times, forced their way out below the snow limit. The mountain was climbed as long ago as 1829 by Parrot, and many explorers have ascended it since then, and subjected it to a thorough investigation.

Overland to India, by SVEN HEDIN

221. Changing Arabia

Where we landed [in November 1935] from a sailing-boat on the edge of the virgin dunes of the [Arabia's] east coast is now an American industrial town, the centre of the oilfield of the Arabian-American Oil Company. There are quays, derricks, rigs, sheds, pipe-lines, telegraph-lines, power-plants, rushing motors, and hurrying gangs of workmen, with everything which goes to make up a modern oil-working. So sudden, complete, and limited is the contrast that it is as if gods playing jigsaw had in error fitted into the Arab set a piece from quite a different game: the American one. A hooded Bedouin, from his distant camp in the bare hills, rides on his camel through the blazing heat past a camp where drillers from Texas and California have ice-cooled drinks in air-conditioned rooms. To his "Peace upon you" they reply "O.K., boy". He has his pride, pride in his ancient lineage, in his religion and political independence, and they have theirs in industrial achievement and practical success in life. . . .

Four services of the British Overseas airline call weekly at Jedda. Aircraft have landed at Al Bowart, an hour by car from

Riyadh [the capital city].... There are over 15,000 miles of regularly used car-tracks in Arabia. Huge six-wheeled lorries rumble along them [well-metalled roads]—the noise of their motors echoing through the wadis—to Mecca, driven by strapping Nigerians who, formerly earning a precariously low wage at the pilgrim port of Jedda, are now competent regular chauffeurs.... All the more fertile valleys and the great oases are now reached by cars, and it would today be possible to motor from Aden to Baghdad, 3,400 kilometres, along existing tracks.

Arabia Phoenix, by GERALD DE GAURY

222. Locusts in Eastern Arabia

Locusts in Eastern Arabia are an article of food, nay, a dainty, and a good swarm of them is begged of heaven in Arabia no less fervently than it would be deprecated in India or in Syria. This difference of sentiment is grounded on several reasons; a main one lies in the diversity of the insects themselves. Those of Syria are small, of a pale green colour, and resemble not a little our own ordinary grasshoppers. The locust of Arabia is a reddish-brown insect, twice or three times the size of its northern homonym, resembling a large prawn in appearance, and as long as a man's little finger, which it equals also in thickness. This locust when boiled or fried is said to be delicious, and boiled or fried accordingly they are to an incredible extent.

Narrative of a Year's Journey through Central and Eastern Arabia, by W. G. PALGRAVE

223. Southern Arabia

We were now in the Rub-el-Khali, that huge high desert which extends across the whole of the eastern side of the Arabian peninsula, from Yemen in the south to the Persian Gulf in the north. On the map of Arabia, it is a great blank space, unknown and unexplored.[22] It is the "Empty Quarter", ruled by no prince, a no-man's land, a boundless sea of sand and stone,

[22]This statement now requires some modification.

but for all that not uninhabited. Wherever there is the smallest prospect of existence—especially where the country is undulating and Nature provides just enough moisture for the cattle to find some sort of grazing and for a little corn to be grown—there are human settlements. . . .

In Hadramaut we saw that almost every peak had its village perched high on the summit. The villages consisted of houses of three to five stories, built very close together, which from afar looked like a single, stoutly-built citadel. They were reached by a single goat-path, hard to find. All the doors and windows of these houses looked towards the interior of the village; on the outside only bare walls were to be seen. . . .

The incredible endurance and toughness of the Bedouins are responsible for the maintenance of a goods traffic between the coast and the high plateau. And these Bedouins always seem to be in a good temper. To encourage their camels they shout and sing to them, and this plan actually seems to make the animals step out.

Land without Shade, by HANS HELFRITZ

224.   The Coast of Southern Arabia

Makalla, which is 230 miles from Aden, is the only spot between Aden and Muscat which has any pretensions to the name of port. The name itself means "Harbour". Immediately behind the town rise grim, arid mountains of a reddish hue, and the town is plastered against this rich-tinged background. By the shore, like a lighthouse, stands the white minaret of the mosque. Not far from this rises the huge palace where the Sultan dwells. . . .

Between Aden and the Persian Gulf, Muscat is the only harbour where ships of any size can find anchorage, and it may, in fact, be said to play much the same part with respect to the Persian Gulf that Aden does to the Red Sea. In many other ways the places are strikingly similar. They are both constructed on arid, volcanic rocks, which produce the smallest amount of verdure and reflect the greatest amount of heat; water in both of them is the scarcest of commodities.

Southern Arabia, by THEODORE BENT

225. The Jordan Valley — East and West

The most striking feature of the country (Palestine) is the valley of the Jordan. The river is formed by the confluence of three streams at a point where it is a little above sea level. Within a short distance it drops to nearly 700 feet below sea level at the Lake of Galilee, and when it reaches the Dead Sea it is nearly 1,300 feet below sea level. This deep cleft in the earth cuts Western Palestine off from the desert, and has thus made possible its independent political and cultural development. Though the river can be forded in several places, the Jordan Valley constitutes a formidable barrier to invasion from the eastern side. Wild beasts infest it, guerilla bands can operate in it, the heat is tropical, the descent into it steep and difficult. On the east of it a fairly continuous though not unbroken range of mountains stretches from Hermon to the mountains of Moab. But Western Palestine is much more important. A range of mountains runs along the edge of the Jordan Valley from north to south, falling abruptly towards the Jordan, but shading off into the lower range of hills known as the Shephelah and then down to the Maritime Plain bounded by the sea.

But the mountains are interrupted by the Plain of Esdraelon, which cuts right across the country from Carmel to the Jordan Valley and permits important trade routes to run from east to west. This plain has been the battle-ground on which contending powers have fought for the control of Palestine. At the southern end of the country there is the Negeb (parched land), a desolate region thinly populated by nomads, which forms the transition between the cultivated land and the desert.

Tiny though the country is, it exhibits a marvellous range of variety in climate, soil, scenery and level. In its plains movement is easy for the traveller, the trade caravan, or the army. The soil in some districts is amazingly fertile. In other parts it is rugged and difficult to traverse, fitted for the rearing of sheep rather than the bearing of crops. Unlike Babylonia or Egypt or the sterile Arabia, its fertility is greatly conditioned by rain, and its failure may mean famine. Owing to the broken character of the surface there are fertile areas in the more mountainous districts. But the deep indentations in the surface make communication over a considerable part of the country far from easy; and this feature has had a profound influence upon political development.[23]

An Outline of Christianity, ed. A. S. PEAKE and R. G. PARSONS

226. The Extraordinary Dead Sea

I motored down to the Dead Sea one February morning. The road, after leaving Jerusalem's immediate surroundings, passes under the lee of the Mount of Olives and through the picturesque village of Bethany. Then it descends, by a series of steep, giddy loops, down the 2,500-ft. mountain upon which the Holy City stands. At the bottom of the mountain there is a signboard that says "Sea Level". And past that the road goes on down again for another 1,300 feet. Vegetation practically ceases to exist somewhere down that mountain-side. Here and there the road gives you a glimpse of a wild, rocky wadi, and humpy barren hills lend a weird, nightmarish aspect to the landscape. A fork to the left leads to Allenby Bridge and across into Transjordan. The right fork leads to the Dead Sea. A gleam of silver tells where it lies. . . .

I bathed in the Dead Sea before I left. The water is so strongly salt that it is, quite literally, impossible to sink in it. To float effortlessly, partly submerged in warm water, is one of the strangest sensations I have ever experienced. People really do go and sit there, and read. It is like riding on a cloud, and swimming is a tiring, profitless business.

In this density of the water lies its wealth. Among the salts that go to make up its brine are the potash and the bromine that the works extract. . . . February 1931 saw the first small plant installed at the north end of the Dead Sea. It produced bromine at first. . . . By the end of 1931 the first potash was also on its way to Britain. . . . Since then a much larger plant has been installed at the south end of the sea, on the actual site of ancient Sodom and Gomorrah.

CAPT. PARRY MARSHALL, in the *Contemporary Review*

[23]Since Palestine became a "National Home" for the Jewish people, following the Balfour Declaration of 1917, there have been a number of political changes.

227. Jerusalem

(*a*) As the train climbs and winds into the hills towards the mountain capital of Jerusalem, you are aware of something fierce and cruel in the air. You have the same feeling in Spain when the train crosses the Sierra de Guadarrama towards the mountain capital of Madrid. But Judea is fiercer than anything in Europe. It is a striped, tigerish country, crouched in the sun, tense with a terrific vitality and sullen and dispassionate with age.

The fierceness of the parched gullies, the harshness of the barren hill-tops, the passion of the caked earth where lizards dart and flash, and the burning cruelty of waterless valleys, are concentrated and made visible upon the highest of the hills. And the name of this materialization is Jerusalem.

In the Steps of the Master, by H. V. MORTON

(*b*) The City of Jerusalem is a twofold city consisting of the old and the new town. The old town is surrounded by high walls and intersected by narrow streets, often roofed in and frequently constructed in stairways, which limits the use of wheeled traffic to the south-west corner of the city and the Via Dolorosa. It is dark, hot in summer and rather unhealthy. . . .

It is, moreover, completely surrounded and commanded by the New City and could never resist any serious attempt at encroachment from without.

The area of the Old City is only 215 acres—less than two-thirds of the area of Hyde Park. The inhabitants of the Old City number, in normal times, about 18,000, of whom about four-fifths are Muslims (Arabs) and Christians and the re-mainder Jews. In the New City ... there are considerably more Jews than Arabs, but the actual area of Arab property, with all the spacious quarters on the south of the city, must be about equal to that owned by Jews.

R. M. GRAVES, in a letter to *The Times*

(*c*) Jerusalem is not only a city of 160,000 men and women[24] and the centre of three great religious faiths, but one of the most beautiful and historic monuments of man. Here, within the ancient walls of the Old City, is a fascinating jumble of

[24]Estimated in 1967 to be 266,300.

domes and minarets, Byzantine, Romanesque and Saracenic, courtyards and narrow streets decorated with balconies and oriels of stone, and pierced with gates and windows defended by iron grilles.

Not many of these buildings, perhaps, are of supreme architectural beauty—the seventh-century Dome of the Rock with its great dome and decoration added by Suleiman the Magnificent is outstanding—but in variety, in detail and historic interest they form an incomparable whole.

Manchester Guardian

(*d*) A few years ago the Old City *was* Jerusalem, and the few straggling houses outside the walls were nothing but a most apologetic suburb. Now all that is changed. Jerusalem is a gawky, commercially brazen, brand-new town of garish, gaudy, self-assertive buildings. The Old City is now nothing but an appendage to this brand-new town.

Palestine Picture, by DOUGLAS DUFFY

Note. In the war of June 1967, Israel annexed the Old City from Jordan.

228. Israel — Country of Hope

Israel has now established herself so firmly that when one is there, it is difficult to believe it is not a century old at least. . . . Everything cannot be done at once, but the general feeling one gets of confidence, of happiness, of dignity, is not only pleasing but reassuring.

The three main cities, Haifa, Tel Aviv and Jerusalem have grown enormously, and smaller places are taking on a new lease of life. Haifa has spread its residential area right up Mount Carmel. It is pleasantly planned, with plenty of gardens and trees. It is a lovely town, if somewhat staider than Tel Aviv, and the bay, as beautiful as ever, is dotted with ships and the docks are very busy. . . . Tel Aviv is a busy, bustling jolly place. It is far from beautiful, but its new residential areas are quite delightful with wide tree-shaded roads and pleasant enough buildings. . . .

The adjacent Jaffa, which was almost entirely Arab, saw a

lot of fighting and is now being cleaned up. A little headland
with a few old abandoned mosques and little gardens and
trees is gradually being turned into a charming area with converted studios and little houses for painters, sculptors and
writers to live in. Jerusalem, in spite of the sadness of its wired-
off Old City, is flourishing. It is the seat of Government, and
the new Hebrew University is splendidly sited and placed on
a hillside. . . .

Probably the most exciting and thrilling visit I paid was to
Ailat on the Gulf of Aqaba. There is an excellent, though
small, internal air-service sending regular planes from Tel Aviv
to this new port and back. They fly over the Negev[25]—about
a third of the whole of Israel—a great spectacular mountainous
and rocky desert. In Ailat[26] itself, still a raw little town, there
is a communal centre, a furniture factory and a little marine
museum.

HELEN KAPP, in the *Yorkshire Post*, Leeds

229. The Jewish "Kvutzah"

Bleak hillsides, barren plains and malarial swamps are laboratories for a unique social experiment. From these backgrounds
have emerged the collective farm settlements of Palestine—
practical workers' communities which embody the essence of
communalism, untainted by political pressure, and entirely free
from personal compulsion.

This form of collective living was started by the first labour
Zionists who came to Palestine. With their body-breaking task
of reclaiming a national homeland from a barren, impoverished
country, they combined the equally daring experiment of blazing a trail for a new social existence—a workers' world, in
which everyone shared according to his needs. In this new
society, the children were to become the proud responsibility
of the community, not of the parents alone. The present system
of collective living (such a settlement is called a "kvutzah"[27]
in Hebrew) grew from their practical needs, the result of trial
and error, and is still in a state of development and re-adjust-
ment. . . .

[25]Or Negeb.　　[26]Or Eilat.
[27]Or Kibbutz.

The "kvutzah" resembles a large working family with an absolutely equal standard of living for all its members. Every settlement has a communal kitchen (the huge dining-room also serves as the community room); a commissary which keeps in order and issues all supplies for members; and a collective children's home.

Settlements have anywhere from fifty to 1,000 members, but the system is the same throughout. Everyone does the amount of work he is able to do (when a member is ill, he naturally is not expected to work), but all alike receive their requirements.

ANITA ENGLE, in the *New Statesman*

Note. Residents in the *kibbutzim* (plural of *kibbutz*) are called *kibbutzniks*. They number slightly less than 4 per cent of the population of Israel.

230. Lebanon — Ancient and Modern

Lebanon has been a name to conjure with ever since the days of Solomon. The perfume of the great 2,000-year-old trees which now stand in a lonely protected clump on the snow line at the head of the great Qadisha gorge has come down across the turbulent centuries of history as an evocation of wealth and luxury.... The great cedars which once covered most of the Lebanese mountains are being slowly replanted, along with pines and other conifers, after 5,000 years of plunder....

Wealth and luxury are still the stock-in-trade of this tiny eastern Mediterranean country, only thirty-five miles wide and 120 long. Today Lebanon is a republic with not merely a reafforestation programme but a flourishing tourist trade.... Beirut, the capital, is a modern city with a sea front esplanade of new skyscraper blocks of flats built on huge concrete stilts, and suave international hotels ... (but) on the fringes of the town where the lemon and orange groves press into the city, Arab refugees from Israel live in shacks built of old petrol tins....

Dramatic though the cedars and their settings are, they are challenged as the most breathtaking sight in Lebanon by the great Roman temples at Baalbek in the plain of Bekaa, 3,000 feet up in the mountains. Built on the vast stones of an even more ancient temple to Baal, the great columns of the temple of Jupiter soar 120 feet above the plain into the cloudless blue

sky. Only slightly smaller are the better-preserved temple to
Bacchus nearby ... and a subsidiary temple to Venus.

IAIN CRAWFORD, in *Homes and Gardens*

231. Lebanon and Syria Compared

The first thing I had to understand was the substantial difference between the Lebanon and Syria. Under the French
mandate we grew accustomed to think of them as one country.
Since the dawn of independence they have fallen apart, and
now there are customs barriers and passport controls at the
frontier on all the main roads—to the great inconvenience of
the traveller. This difference goes far back into history. The
Lebanon was the old Phoenicia, where Hiram, King of Tyre, and
his predecessors ruled over a great commercial nation, based
on a narrow strip of fertile coast. Syria recalls Ben-hadad of
Damascus; it is an immense country, still largely feudal in social
structure, with Damascus set like a green jewel in the dun-
coloured desert. The Lebanon is about fifty per cent Christian
while Syria is Muslim; and it is open to the sea and to the West,
as Syria is open to the desert and the East.

The great tree-clad hills of the Lebanon and the more rugged
hills of the Anti-Lebanon enclose a fertile valley which is the
beginning of that strange cleft in the earth's surface which
runs southwards through the lakes of Huleh and Galilee, the
Jordan Valley and the Dead Sea to the Red Sea and the Nile.
At the head of this valley, where the two ranges draw together,
stands Baalbek. ... Here the roads met which carried merchants and armies to Aleppo in the north-west, Nineveh or
Babylon in the east, or Egypt in the south. The Syrian Desert
stretches away towards Iraq, and Palmyra stands near the
border to remind us of the ancient gods.

REV. ERIC FENN, in *The Bible in the World*

232. Glimpses of Syria

(*a*) Between Beirut and Damascus we climbed a steep mountain that towered above us sheer as a cliff, by a road that zig-
zagged across its face. On every side the hilltops and ridges

N

were covered with villages and gardens full of fruit trees, and there was an abundance of water. The hillsides were covered with a myriad of little fields, each terraced up to prevent it slipping down into the ravines.

Turkey and Syria reborn, by H. ARMSTRONG

(b)   Descending the slopes of Hermon, we see in a haze the white city (Damascus) embosomed in green, an island in the brown desert tints; and after riding over the barren plain, suddenly find ourselves in the most marvellous and unbroken series of orchards which it is possible to imagine. Almond and apricot trees in full flower, interrupted only by low mud walls dividing the gardens and by the narrow lanes between them, encompass the town with a ring of blossom and verdure so thick that to traverse it and to reach the beginnings of the city itself was the matter of an hour.

The Fringe of the East, by HENRY LUKACH

233. By Desert Bus to Baghdad

From Damascus, a remarkable oasis some twenty miles by ten to fifteen miles, we took a 600-mile journey by bus, only 200 miles of which are over properly made roads. The service crosses the Syrian Desert to Baghdad in twenty-four hours. The bus consists of a Diesel tractor and a stainless steel trailer with sleeping accommodation for fourteen passengers, air-conditioned by day and warmed during the night. Because of the sand storms prevalent on the route, all joints in the body-work are soldered, cemented and painted so that they cannot possibly let in dust. . . .

In the villages the people of Iraq live in little mud huts with palm thatching ten to fourteen feet wide. If they are rich enough to own a sheep or goat, that goes in first, then the husband and the children. Wives go in last of all. There is great wealth among the few on the one hand and abject poverty on the other, for about 95 per cent of the land is owned by about 5 per cent of the population. . . .

There is a deep belief in destiny and the will of Allah, by which the rich and poor alike accept their destiny and are satisfied with it. . . . Dates are the great export of Iraq; also

95 per cent of the world's liquorice comes from there, by far the greater part going directly to America for the curing of American tobacco.

REV. J. A. FIGURES, in the Ilkley Gazette

234. Dramatic Turkey

I take to Turkey greatly because it is as dramatic a land as I have ever visited. It is dramatic in its variability.

It is at once infinitely old and startlingly new, at once pure East and sheer West. It has everything; it is all possibility and all fulfilment, repose and restlessness, candour and sphinx-like secrecy, kindness and (I suspect) cruelty.

It is dramatic, no less, in its contrasts of landscape. Between Istanbul and Ankara you see strange lion-coloured hills brooding above rapid grey-pink streams, like nothing in Europe. And then around Izmir you would think you were among the Galloway hills of South-West Scotland until the illusion is abruptly dispelled by a string of camels on the road.

ALAN DENT, in the News Chronicle

235. Seen in Turkey

Malatya lies about thirty-five miles to the west of the Euphrates. Its valley is here extremely broad, irrigated by countless small tributaries, and is one of the most fertile regions of Turkey. For more than twenty-five miles stretches the green and yellow belt of orchards and fields of maize, wheat and melons, and only the flat-ridged, red mountains glow barren in the sun. . . .

Slowly we passed along the shore, bay after bay opening in wide or narrow curves, hemmed in by the steep walls of the mountains. We stopped at many villages, white houses stretching along the sandy beach, over-towered by poplars and minarets. Giresun owes her riches to hazelnuts, one of the most important export articles of Turkey; hardly anything is cultivated but nuts. For miles and miles they grow on every square inch of land. . . .

Samsun is the most important and the biggest of the Black

Sea towns. The streets are wide and clean and planted with trees.

Allah Dethroned, by LILO LINKE

236.   Istanbul: Star of the Bosporus

Istanbul is divided by water into three main parts—old Constantinople, which is separated from Galata and Beyoglu to the north by the Golden Horn; the more up-to-date business and residential districts north of the old city; and the vast spreading suburbs on the Asiatic shore.... Today, most people live in Beyoglu on the European side, or in one of the suburbs, but in the summer, which is long and very hot, many of the city's inhabitants move to houses along the Bosporus, which winds its way north for about seventeen miles to the Black Sea.

Moda on the Asiatic shore is a delightful place, but the treasures and beauties of the Ottoman Empire are nearly all in the old city.... There are three architectural wonders that should not be missed—the Mosque of Sultan Ahmet, which is more commonly known as the Blue Mosque, since its interior is completely covered with wonderful blue tiles; the Santa Sophia, a priceless museum; and the Topkapu Palace, the home of the Sultans until the middle of the nineteenth century. The latter houses the jewelled furniture, embroidered clothes, porcelain, gold plate and many other things used by them. It was the Dolma-Bahce, built in 1853, which later became the residence of the Sultan, and today official receptions are held there....

Istanbul, like most Oriental cities, turns out its lights very late. Soon after sunrise, however, the street vendors can be heard crying out their wares in melodious accents. Their trays are not only piled up with all kinds of fruit and vegetables, but even with bottled spring water, for no Turk will drink from the tap.

BARBARA TREACHER, in *Homes and Gardens*

237.   Cyprus — Colour and Contrast

(a) We had to negotiate a great deal of foam as we landed in a tiny unstable boat at the southern port of Limassol, but neither this nor the continuing rain could depress my friend. As we drove in a far too swift taxi towards Nicosia, the capital, he assured me as we rushed through that indistinguishable country that the colours of Cyprus are superb. He was perfectly right, for in a few days I had seen the golden walls and green gardens of Famagusta, that legendary, war-scarred city which has the one good harbour of the island, I had seen the strings of tawny-coloured camels and the priestly salutation of the camel-driver as he meets you on the road, I had seen the red cliffs of the pointed Carpas peninsula extended across the blue waters to the Syrian coast, I had seen the white ruins of ancient Salamis smothered with lizards and white anemones, I had seen the range of arid, orange mountains in the North, gleaming unbroken in the glaring sun, and the steel-blue rows of olive trees.

Leaves in the Wind, by HENRY BAERLEIN

(*b*) In spite of the many changes that have taken place on the island in recent years, the climate is the same—cool and pleasant from November until about June, and then too hot for comfort. When water in flower vases dries up several times a day and children refuse food, it is time, if possible, to take them to the mountain station, Troödos, and its cool, bracing air.... Our young Greek cook-boy rose at dawn to fetch us fruits and vegetables a size or two larger than any seen in England, other food being brought to us in panniers slung on donkeys. Melons would often yield as much as a pint of juice. Pine-clad mountains are everywhere one looks on Troödos, and the delicious scent of warm sunshine on pines is always in the air. Sometimes this rarefied air at 5,000 feet may cause noses to bleed, or an ivory handle to split.

ANGELA BOWIE, in *Homes and Gardens*

Africa

238. Egypt — Land of the Lily

(a) Egypt has been called the "Land of the Lily", but this has nothing to do—as is sometimes supposed—with the lotus flower that is common in the country. Seven hundred miles long, and rarely more than ten miles wide, Egypt is, in fact, shaped like a lily.[1] The Valley of the Nile, a ravine scooped out by the famous river, varying from one to ten miles in width, is the stalk. The Delta is the flower. A little to the west is the bud, called the Fayoum, a depression made fertile by the introduction of the Nile waters. On either side of the "stalk" rise barren, sun-scorched hills. Behind these lie the eternal sands. No other country in the world is so hard to defend, to conquer, or to govern, on account of this peculiar shape. . . .

The Delta, the flower of the lily, is known as Lower Egypt. The long thin stalk of the Nile Valley is Upper Egypt. . . . Entering Lower Egypt from the Mediterranean one sees only a vast alluvial plain, stretching away to an horizon as flat as the horizon of a sea. This is perhaps the most fertile area of land on earth, for it is the accumulated deposit brought down by the Nile through untold ages.

Proceeding southwards, this scene persists for a hundred miles, when it gives way to something utterly different—Upper Egypt. The plain shrinks to a narrow valley, with the view on either hand blocked out by gaunt mountains that would almost seem to have been put there for the express purpose of cutting off the river from the rest of the world. You may now proceed for 700 miles along the river and see no change.

These, then, are the two Egypts. Both depend for life upon the river. If the Nile dried up Egypt would cease to exist; the land would become as the deserts on either side. So really

[1]The Nile Valley, the "effective" Egypt, is evidently referred to here, not the political entity called "Egypt". It has been said, figuratively, "The Nile is Egypt".

Egypt is the Nile. Apart from making the land fertile, the river serves another vital purpose. It forms a main highway through the country—a highway that never needs repair. . . .

In the matter of square miles the real Egypt is a small country, but as size is secondary to productiveness, the land has always flourished. Producing three harvests a year, in the time of the Pharaohs it was the granary of the world. The first crop is grain, wheat that yields a hundredfold. Then come flax and rice; then the vegetables. There is no winter, no autumn, only an ever-recurring cycle of spring and summer. Spring is from October to May. By February the fruit trees are in flower. Crops ripen in March and are gathered in April. Snow and frost are unknown. Fog and rain are rare.

W. E. JOHNS, in the Air Training Corps Gazette

(*b*) The houses of the "fellahin" (Egyptian peasants) are square, low, and almost windowless. Above the roofs, usually covered with "dhurra" (millet) stalks, untidily heaped, rise domed pigeon-cots. The mud-ovens lie outside the houses, little mounds of beaten mud like large, lop-sided bee-hives. Piles of "dhurra", strolling goats, tumbling dirty babies, and thin hens and chickens, heap themselves about the doorway. Yet most of the inhabitants smile through the dirt and appear to be happy and gay. . . . The huts of the village are merely used as sleeping rooms, and for store cupboards for the limited possessions—the sleeping rugs, the cooking pots, and such simple odds and ends. In most places there are nearly 360 fine days in the year, and all the life of the "fellah" and his family is lived out of doors.

The Egypt of the Sojourner, by GLADYS PETO

239. Cairo Contrasts

(*a*) Of all the capitals of the earth none offers to the traveller from the West such a fullness of fresh impressions or such a variety of picturesque scenes brilliantly contrasted as does Cairo, the city of the Caliphs. West jostles East at every hand. The luxury and elegance of a European capital are seen against a sky-line of minarets and pinnacles and waving palm trees. Within view of the clanging trams and rushing motor cars of the Opera Square the public letter-writers, each squatted before his low desk, wait for custom along the railings outside the big modern post office; and in the shaded alleys of the bazaar, not five minutes' walk from the terrace of Shepheard's Hotel,[2] the unchanging life of the Orient unfolds itself in a series of scenes that have scarcely altered since the days of Haroun Al Raschid.

Countries of the World, ed. by SIR JOHN HAMMERTON

(b) At first I was bewildered. The noise, dirt and confusion beggared description. Skyscrapers jostle single-story slums and luxury cohabits with squalor. . . . Some images of Cairo are so vivid they will stay in my imagination for ever. How, for instance, on one of those hot days in July or August, when the very earth seems to pant with the heat and your shirt sticks to you like a postage stamp, suddenly the sherbet seller comes down the street clashing his metal cups and shouting "Drink, O ye thirsty ones". The heat of the day finds its compensation in the extraordinary softness of the Egyptian night, a quality I have never experienced elsewhere.

JAMES DICKIE, in *The Listener*

240. Ethiopia in Brief

(a) Ethiopia, is practically a series of extensive plateaux, rising one from the other from the south and east, and culminating in the high mountains of Simien in the north, which are over 16,000 feet above sea-level. These plateaux are separated by deep rifts or canyons, the valleys of rivers which carry off the large annual rainfall.

In the Land of Sheba, by E. J. BARTLEET

(b) For agricultural purposes Ethiopia is divided into three definite zones according to altitude. In the lower plateau between sea-level and about 3,000 feet, the temperature is high and the rainfall low, while the country consists of steppes, marshes and jungle; the vegetation is tropical. In the regions between the high mountains and the low plateau from 3,000

[2]Shepheard's Hotel has since been destroyed by fire.

to 7,500 feet, the temperature is moderate and the rainfall high; the country consists of fertile valleys, rolling plains and hills, interspersed with forest and jungle; fig trees, cactus and coffee grow wild, while many varieties of European fruits, flowers and vegetables increase rapidly once they are introduced. The mountainous regions over 7,500 feet have low temperatures and frequent night frosts; prairie grass and woods are characteristic of the vegetation.

The New Abyssinia, by E. W. POLSON NEWMAN

Note. The Danakil Depression is one of the hottest spots on earth. Temperatures up to 134°F. (56°C.) have been recorded there. The Great Salt Desert is a block of salt 140 miles long, 20 miles wide, and half a mile thick.

241. By Rail to the Nile

There is no better approach to the Sudan than through Port Sudan. Here, as the ship touches the quay, one glance takes in the primitive and the new.

Substantial commercial buildings fringe the spacious harbour, its waters alive with strange fish and flashing with the hues of coral rocks. On the quayside huge negroes, sweltering under a relentless tropical sun, display the wares they have to sell—walking sticks of rhinoceros hide, rudely carved elephants in ebony wood from the dense forests of the Southern Sudan, baskets of fibre, little idols sculptured from ivory and strangely suggestive of much of modern art—all telling of crafts that may have survived through thousands of years. Fifty yards away waits a train with saloon carriages, with native Customs officers in attendance and half a dozen motor cars standing by.

That train, on its 3 ft. 6 in. gauge, will carry the traveller along the edge of the Nubian Desert to Atbara on the Nile, and thence north to Wadi Halfa or south to Khartoum, or branching south at Haiya will pass through Kassala till it reaches the Blue Nile at Sennar.... Along much the same routes as the railways traverse must have come the invading Arabs of the seventh and eighth centuries who were to impose their rule on the land, bringing with them that peculiarly fanatical aspect of the Islamic faith which has coloured so much of the history of the Sudan.... Cotton growing and transport have been the salvation of the Sudan. Today much of the finest long staple cotton the world produces is grown in the lands lying between the White and the Blue Nile before the streams unite, and round Kassala.

The *Daily Telegraph*

242. The Sudan: Contrasts and Cattle

(*a*) The Sudan is a country of unbelievable contrasts. Within this vast territory dwell six and a half million people,[3] infinitely various, and still very little known. Here you find a score of races, and dozens of religions and creeds, many of them unique. In this million square miles of burning desert or turgid swamp, of arid rock or teeming jungle, you can travel by one of the most luxurious trains in the world, or on a raft of three logs roughly lashed together.

Khartoum in the north, sometimes called the air-crossroads of Africa, is a fine modern capital, its wide thoroughfares and impressive government buildings contrasting strangely with its twin city across the Nile, Omdurman—epitome of the East, where you can wander through colourful narrow streets and see displayed before low mud hovels the finest examples of native craftsmanship. . . .

The southern Sudan contrasts sharply with the north, much of it being swampland and forest, haunt of lions, hippos and elephants. It is far more backward than the north. This is partly due to its inaccessibility, for the swamp of the Sudd (i.e. barrier) makes travel extremely slow, and in some places quite impossible. . . .

Perhaps the best-known of the southern tribes are the Shilluks, glossy, black-skinned, all of them over six feet tall. . . . Then there are the Dinkas, also extremely tall, but physically inferior to the Shilluks. . . .

N. M. WOODALL, in *Chambers's Journal*, Edinburgh

(*b*) Every night the Dinka man makes a heap of wood ashes beside the post which anchors his favourite bull or cow, and sleeps within touch of his beloved one. The care and endearing

[3]Now over 14 millions.

terms he lavishes on his cattle are beyond belief, and never bestowed on his womenkind.

A cow is never killed, but carefully tended if ill. Only those which die from some cause are eaten. At the loss of a cow the bereaved owner will sit for days in a state of melancholy, as if his misfortunes were too great to be endured, and will even refuse to partake of the meat of the dead beast.

Far Away up the Nile, by J. G. MILLAIS

243. Among the Bedouin of North Africa

The nomad tribes of North Africa, variously called Bedouin or Berbers, and divided into scores of groups each one with their own customs and costumes, stretch from Libya to Morocco. I had caught tantalizing glimpses of them on the edge of the desert and longed to share their hard life, even for just a few days, to find out what nomad life entails for all concerned. I got my chance at last when an urbanized Berber from Tripoli introduced me to a friend, Ahmed, a motor mechanic, who had only recently given up the nomad life himself—attracted by city glamour and the mechanized life. He laughed uncontrollably when he was told that I wanted to take a leap into the primitive past of camel-riding life.

I was doubly in luck because Ahmed's tribe should, he said, after some consultation of the calendar, be approaching the coast. They do this several times during the summer, to give their camels a cool wash-down in the sea and spruce themselves up before attending one of the great annual tribal courts that are held in tents in the desert, to settle the many disputes that arise between the various tribes. . . .

We came across Ahmed's tribe about a quarter of a mile away: a string of camels, large and small, surrounded by flocks of goats and sheep and about thirty people—men, women and children. . . . They were making for a well about a mile distant, where they had decided to pitch their tents for the night. . . . At last we reached the camp site by the water-well. It was a stone well that had been built by the Romans, for all this territory used to belong to the great Roman empire. . . .

It was time for the Muslim evening prayer. The men of the tribe slipped off their camels and bowed to the sand in the direction of Mecca. The barefoot women quietly started to make fires for the evening meal, using dry camel dung as fuel. In the meantime the younger men, helped by the children, put up the tents made of long strips of cloth woven from goat and camel hair. These were quickly "furnished" with camel bags and saddles, waterskins hung on poles, a few bright rugs and blankets.

The tents were pitched opening inwards in a square, and the central space was used as a fold for the animals. Then the encampment was surrounded by a hedge of thorny branches— there were plenty of them around in the sand. Savage-looking dogs kept watch over the tents—large white sheepdogs.

NINA EPTON, in *Home and Country*

244. Old and New Tripoli

Tripoli is a brand new city . . . except for the Arab quarter, a Roman arch, and a Moorish fort which is now the governor's residence. At sunset every night they fire a cannon from the fort and everybody stands to attention. The modern buildings are mostly white and flat-roofed. There is a cathedral. And there are the usual attractions for tourists: hotels, a casino and the great motor-racing track. The Italians wanted Tripoli to oust Cairo as a winter resort. It hasn't any pyramids, like Cairo, but it has two superb Roman sites. The sand has ruined the soil in North Africa, which in Roman times was extremely fertile, but it has preserved the monuments. These sites are Sabratha and Leptis Magna, which is about seventy miles from Tripoli. Leptis is near Homs: 2,000 years ago it was a vast city with 200,000 inhabitants. Today the sand has been cleared, and you can walk about the old streets, the forum and basilica, and see the market, the harbour and the vast underground water-storage tanks. . . .

It is a good drive from Tripoli to Homs along Mussolini's road, taking a couple of hours. You leave the oasis of Tripoli itself and plunge into the desert. You pass many of the new agricultural settlements, and extraordinarily interesting they are. They first plant Australian wattle to stop the movement of sand and start a humus; after that, pines or olives, though it is seventeen years before the olives bear properly. Or they plant rye and plough it in for the first year or two. It is a long time before they begin to see any return. And all the time they have got to live—on money borrowed from the state. One day they, or their sons, will have to repay it; not a very cheerful prospect.

BRUCE BALSDON, in *The Listener*

245. Water in the Desert

When one is wading knee deep in burning sand, it is disconcerting to be told, "We are walking on water." That is what the French scientists say. For one thing, they have established, by borings, the existence of a vast fresh-water lake under the Sahara. For another, they say the dunes under rainless skies are great sponges dripping with water. In these regions of extreme heat and cold, the dew condenses out of the atmosphere in the night, and before the sun evaporates it again, the dunes have absorbed it and stored it out of reach of the heat. ... The great underground lake has been reached at considerable depths at Zelfana in the Algerian Sahara; and it is within shallower reach at Gabes, in Tunisia....

In Tunisia, we saw the birth of a new oasis. It was south of Gafsa, reputedly the Garden of the Hesperides of Greek legend. Between Tozeur, a honeymoon oasis and tourist centre, and De Gache, another old oasis, the new oasis will spread and link them both. Castilia is man-made. An artesian well has been sunk to a great depth, and the water was bubbling up at the rate of three gallons a second into a reservoir, from which is fed a network of concrete irrigation canals. The plots were already planted with annual crops and with infant date palms, which will one day form a huge palmery.

The problem of water is linked with afforestation.... It is essential not only to reclothe the mountains of the rainy north, but to spread trees over the shifting dunes. In the first instance, reafforestation will prevent further erosion and the run-off which squanders water which ought to be feeding springs and recreating oases far away in the desert. In the second instance, trees, with other vegetation, can anchor the dunes and act as windbreaks, preventing the wind-erosion which builds up into those terrifying dust-storms.

(NOW LORD) RITCHIE CALDER, in *Picture Post*

246. A Brief View of Algeria

(a) During our stay we motored more than 1,600 miles throughout the central part of Algeria, from the coast to the mountains further south, and even as far south as the Sahara— where it rained! Algeria is a large and beautiful country, and we were lucky to be there when the wild flowers were at their best. The colours had to be seen to be believed.

This was my first visit to a Moslem country, and it was strange to see the veiled women in a country whose towns are largely of modern French buildings, side by side with older Arab buildings, Roman remains, primitive shacks and, in the interior, nomad tents. . . .

The Province of Orleansville covers a large area, west of Algiers, stretching from the coast far south into the mountains. The Provincial Government centre is in the town of Orleans-ville itself. The town is a modern one, which was almost entirely rebuilt after being destroyed by an earthquake some years ago.

N. JEAN ADAMS, in *The World's Children*

(b) Algeria is two countries: the narrow coastal plain is heavy with the scent of orange groves, a vegetable grower's paradise, the one time "granary of the Roman Empire"; but drive through the spectacular passes in the Atlas Mountains and you are in the land of the High Plateau, where tracts of potato fields end in patches of Nomad Corn fighting a losing battle with the sand, scrub and rocks of the sub-desert.

VALENTINE RYLANDS, in *The World's Children*

247. Saharan Trek

We left Laghouat on the third day, after making some minor repairs, and crossed arid, flat land interspersed with oases of jujube and pistachio trees on the way to Ghardaia. Soon the road became a bumpy track, which so shook the trucks that it seemed as though they must fall to pieces. On more than one occasion the track was so bad that the driver left it and drove along the open desert. The Shebka, as this part of the Desert is called, is a reminder that the bulk of the Sahara is not sand, but a desolate extent of rocks and waste stony land. . . . Ghardaia is a town of some 12,000 inhabitants[4]—quite an important trading centre, watered by about 3,000 deep wells—a great feat of ingenuity and initiative. . . .

The warm embrace of the sun became a biting, blistering heat as we passed from the rocky Shebka region to the monotonous "Erg" area, a flat stretch of unbroken, loose grey gravel. There was no landmark of any kind, not a hint of vegetation. We travelled for six hours before we sighted the golden sand so well-beloved of the film-makers. . . .

For the last sixty kilometres to El Golea we raced against a sandstorm, which we had been warned to expect. In the sky was not a hint of a storm as sunset approached. . . . Then, just as the sun was about to set, a change came over the scene. A sudden draught cut sharply across the Desert, followed by short gusts of wind that drove the sand along the track like a tidal-wave. . . . By the time we sighted El Golea, sand was being churned up in waterspout fashion all around us, filling our hair and nostrils, choking our ears and smarting our eyes. El Golea was a welcome sight that night. . . . Desolation for hundreds of miles, then this lovely garden-village, sheltered by luxuriant trees and garlanded with flowers of all descriptions.

G. D. K. MCCORMICK, in *Chambers's Journal*, Edinburgh

248. Morocco is Poor but Happy

Bigger than England in size, Morocco barely supports a population of seven millions[5] . . . largely because of its lack of water. There are no considerable rivers, and until you come to the Atlas Mountains there are no wild trees at all, except in a few areas where the French started reafforestation. . . . There are some 200,000 Europeans in Morocco, French or Frenchified Spanish. The seaport of Casablanca has a white proletariat of perhaps 70,000.[6] Of the rest of the population, about five millions would be Arabs, 100,000 Jews, and the rest chiefly

---

[4]58,327 in 1960.
[5]14,580,000 in 1968 (estimated).
[6]Casablanca had a total population of 965,000 in 1960. Now over a million.

Chleuh, a rather primitive Berber people inhabiting the Atlas.
. . . The Arabs, the vast majority of whom are small peasants,
cultivate a dried-up, treeless soil on which they grow barley,
lucerne, and various fruits and vegetables. They live chiefly
on barley and the milk of miserable goats which graze on
cacti, and whose daily yield is a quarter of a pint per head. . . .

Except for Casablanca the big towns are really enormous
villages where the peasants come to sell their beasts and buy
cooking pots, nails, etc. Everything is made by hand with tools
which have not altered since Biblical times. The Moroccan
handicrafts, especially the pottery and the blankets, are some
of the finest in the world, and have held their own against
European or Japanese imports because of the miserable wages
paid to the people who make them. . . .

One saw everywhere the most shocking destitution and drud-
gery, but also, on the whole, one saw happy faces and magnificent bodies. The Chleuh, even poorer than the Arabs of the
plains, were one of the most debonair peoples I have seen.

GEORGE ORWELL, in *Tribune*

Note. There are now important exports of phosphates and oil.

249.　The Seaport of Mogador

Mogador is a Portuguese word, though the Portuguese stayed
there for only a few years at the beginning of the sixteenth
century. Now the town, which is 100-odd miles west of Marrakesh, is called by its Arabic name, Essaouira. . . .

It certainly is a pretty place. A large sandy bay curves round
to the north to make a natural harbour, and opposite the
shore lie several islands which act as wind- and sea-breaks.
Behind the town are scrub-covered hills. A few years ago they
were sand-dunes, but the French persuaded various trees to
grow, including arganias, fascinating prickly things up which
goats climb to nibble the leaves. Perched on the edge of the
sea, Mogador looks, as one approaches along the beach, like
any little Moroccan port, with the usual minarets and houses
painted white, and a typical high wall surrounding the town.
As one gets closer, however, one sees that it is not typical at
all. Unlike any other Arab town in Morocco, the buildings all

have two or three storeys. Passing through one of the gates one finds, to one's astonishment, that the streets are straight. . . .

Mogador is none the less in all other respects a wholly Arab town, with its bustling markets, its perpetually crowded streets, and its separate Jewish quarters. Many Moroccan towns have a compulsory colour-scheme for all buildings—Marrakesh, for instance, is terracotta—and Mogador is white, with all doors and windows charmingly picked out in blue.

JULIAN MITCHELL, in *The Listener*

Note. Mogador (Essaouira) had a population of 26,392 in 1960.

250. Saharan Oasis

(*a*) Beside narrow paths, leading to all parts of the oasis, were irrigation ditches through which clear water flowed. Vines clambered over the white walls of the houses, while a variety of flowers and ripening fruit—orange, mandarin, apricot—made splashes of colour more vivid for the rich bowering green about them. Overhead, the fronds of unnumbered date-palms sighed and rustled in the cooling wind; beneath them, flecked with light and shade, grew barley, oats, wheat and rye, covering the ground with bright-green carpets; and in a later season other greens to come—legumes, lentils, tuberous herbs, the fruit of roots, and vines of vegetables.

Desert Winds, by "Hafsa"

(*b*) I mentioned market-places. A few days later I saw one—they are called "souks"—outside a Moroccan oasis beyond the Atlas Mountains, where I lived in a mud-built kasbah. (It looked as gorgeous as a castle, but they are apt to crumble every few years, when they are abandoned, and a new one is built nearby.)

For six days of the week we were isolated among the kasbahs and the palm trees. But on the seventh day—market day—everything changed. Rickety buses came groaning and spluttering from miles away, bringing traders from the nearest town, loaded with goods and gossip. They stayed for twenty-four

hours and then went back again on the same buses with our
messages and mail for the outside world.

NINA EPTON, in *Home and Country*

251.   Sierra Leone: "White Man's Grave"?

My feelings on appointment to Freetown, Sierra Leone, were
not of the happiest. Memories of books and articles describing
the hardships and diseases of this country were no more encouraging than the repeated warnings of my friends. A brief
glance at the encyclopedia completed my discomfort. All this
pessimism proved to be unfounded. Instead of life in a mud
hut swarming with bugs, I was installed in a concrete block-
house with mosquito-proof netting on all the windows. The
malaria bogey had, to a large extent, been laid by the energies
of the Malarial Control, who supervise the filling-in of all
likely malarial swamps. Comparatively few Europeans sicken
with this illness since the use of mepacrine commenced, while
a new drug, at present under experiment, is expected to have
even greater success.

Freetown, the capital of Sierra Leone, is an interesting if
not very beautiful town. Enclosed as it is by a wooded range
of hills—from which is derived the colony's name, Lion Mountain or Sierra Leone—its appearance from the harbour is striking. The old Imperial Garrison on Tower Hill scowls down on
the town sprawling untidily to all sides. As we travel from the
harbour to Tower Hill, the strange juxtaposition of modern
concrete buildings looking down on wretched tin shacks—
some of them built from discarded petrol-cans—the old Cotton
Tree, at the base of which the slaves were liberated, the aggres-
sive edifice of the Law Courts, the humble dwellings of wood
and corrugated iron, and the stately Government House, home
of the Governor, make up a picture of violent contrast.

C. H. JOHNSTON, in *Chambers's Journal*, Edinburgh

252.   I Live in Kumasi

My home is in Kumasi, the capital of Ashanti, where the garden
seems to change overnight, so quickly do the young plants grow.

Today Kumasi, which lies on the fringe of the Ashanti forest in Ghana, has many well-built modern stores and a hospital with an up-to-date training school for nurses, yet in 1900 it was just an isolated fortress in the bush. . . .

For most of the year the climate is humid and so hot that sleep does not come readily. Yet, as I write, we are in the midst of the "Harmattan", a cool, sand-laden breeze which comes from the Sahara. . . .

Unlike the coastal regions, where cultivation is made difficult because of lack of water for months on end, Ashanti has a plentiful supply, and even in the dry season I have known heaven-sent showers revive many a weary garden. . . .

Occasionally, as a diversion from tending the garden, my husband and I motor a few miles along the red laterite road that leads to the arid lands of the Northern Territories, where the most important export is labour. We seldom fail to meet men and boys flocking south to work on the cocoa farms and in the gold mines, so as to earn a few pounds a year and be provided with food and clothing.

Another familiar sight is the drovers with their flocks of cattle. They come down on trek for some 300 dusty miles because south of the Northern Territories is the tsetse belt, where the tsetse fly attacks and kills the cattle. Each drover carries a hurricane lamp which he hangs on a tree beside him at night to keep the cattle nearby.

FREDA SADLER, in *Homes and Gardens*

253. Christmas in Nigeria

Christmas in Nigeria comes in the middle of the dry season. At that time of the year a cool wind, called the Harmattan, blows down the country from the Sahara from midnight to mid-day, bringing with it clouds of finest dust. The air is full of it like a haze. The sun rises as a copper ball. The temperature is still much higher than on a British summer morning, but the African feels it cold. Arms hug shoulders over chests. Little fires of leaves and sticks appear among the huts, each with its group of men and boys with backs turned to the feeble blaze. Sweaters and even Balaclavas are the wear for the day, if you are lucky enough to possess such. The crowds at church are well-covered, if only because of the nip in the air. . . .

With the spreading of churches, Christmas has nowadays taken its place alongside the New Year as a major festival of the year. It is a day of mixed services and feasting and jollity. . . . Women boil busily their pots and cauldrons preparing the peppery, oily soups and stews the African loves. Children, frantic with excitement, race about getting in everybody's way. . . . The merriment of the day gets into feet and legs. The afternoon, fiercely hot after the Harmattan has dropped, passes on to dusk with dust rising in choking clouds from dancing feet. And so the starry night comes, with tired, happy people finding their way through the dark paths beneath the trees to their huts and sleeping mats.

British Weekly

254. Lagos

Across the door, in a barely perceptible wind, the bead curtains are clicking like false teeth: the fan in the ceiling has been turning all day. In the street, dark-faced men in white gowns are strolling very slowly past the stalls that sell combs and mangoes. There is little noise of traffic, only that ancient noise a city makes in the sun, the murmur in unison of thousands of voices, the sudden sound of a man shouting in anger behind a wall, dogs barking and cocks crowing, the steady "thud, thud" from women grinding millet in a wooden bowl.

This city is neither old nor beautiful. Time has not treated it gently, but seems to have torn at it with nails as it passed by. The pavements are broken, the shutters hang crooked, electric wires make a careless web across the front of buildings, the mean houses peer over each other's shoulders without plan or grace.

Beyond the city there is a wide lagoon crossed by an iron bridge, and little boats, like willow leaves on the water, are waiting for fish.

PATRICK O'DONOVAN, in *The Observer*

255. An African Jungle

(*a*) There is the strong African teak, the camwood, the

African mahogany, the everlasting iron-wood, the no less hard yellow wood by the riverside, infinitely harder than an oak, the ebony, the copal-wood tree with its glossy and burnished foliage, the arborescent wild mango, the small-leaved wild orange, the silver-boled wild fig, the butter tree, the acacia tribes, and the thousands of wild fruit-trees, most of which are unknown to me. Therefore, to understand what this truly tropical forest is like, you must imagine all these confusedly mixed together, and lashed together by millions of vines, creepers, and giant convolvuli, until a perfect tangle has been formed, and sunshine quite cut out, except a little flickering dust of light here and there to tell you that the sun is out in the sky like a burning lustrous orb.

In Darkest Africa, by SIR HENRY STANLEY

(*b*) Congo is to a great extent covered by these thick forests. But the Belgian Government cut tens of thousands of miles of road through the jungles, and brought new conditions right into the very heart of this great land. Huts, which some ten to twenty years ago were hundreds of miles away from the road, are now passed by huge lorries, and news is spread rapidly by radio and newspaper. Large firms are busy advertising their sales of products like bicycles, sewing machines, radios and kerosene lamps. One therefore finds many Africans in a city like Leopoldville[7] who are comparatively wealthy. Motor cars, motor bicycles, scooters and large modern buses are not uncommon in the big centres.

REV. A. W. MARTHINSON, in *The Bible in the World*

256. The Pygmies

(*a*) These people live in the thick, damp, tropical forests of the Congo basin of Central Africa, in an area about five degrees north and south of the equator. This region of huge trees and massed undergrowth, where the temperature is seldom below 80 degrees fahrenheit, is still largely unexplored, and many of the pygmies have never seen a white man. ... They

[7]Leopoldville is now called Kinshasa. It is the capital of the Democratic Republic of the Congo (formerly Belgian Congo), and in 1964 had 403,000 people. In the next five years it more than doubled in size.

are very small—about 4 ft. 4 in. to 4 ft. 9 in. in height—with chocolate-coloured skins, black curly hair, broad noses, and wide mouths. . . .

The pygmies live by hunting and food-gathering. They collect fruits, roots and nuts, and trap small animals. For large animals they use bows with poisoned arrows. . . . They are clever at climbing trees to collect honey. Some of the honey and game they trade for agricultural products, such as maize, with their Bantu neighbours.

The Oxford Junior Encyclopaedia, ed. LAURA E. SALT and
GEOFFREY BOUMPHREY

(b)   Much of the barter is by "silent trade". The pygmy, after a successful hunt, will go to a neighbouring village in the dead of night and place a chunk of meat outside the door of a hut. In the morning the occupant, seeing this, knows only too well its meaning. He must, without fail, place a full equivalent of bananas, flour, or other foodstuffs in the same place. The pygmy has a good idea of comparative values. If he is not satisfied when he steals round next night, the occupant of the hut may have a rude awakening.

Tramping through Africa, by W. J. W. ROOME

257. The Face of East Africa

East Africa consists of a great block of country which lies between the Great Lakes of Central Africa and the Indian Ocean. The three territories of Kenya, Tanganyika and Uganda with the small island of Zanzibar cover an area of 642,728 square miles of land (more than twelve times the area of England) as well as 38,901 square miles of water.[8] The tremendous fresh water lake of Victoria Nyanza, which is as large in area as Scotland, has had a profound effect on the life of scores of tribes which inhabit its shores.

There are nearly nineteen million[9] people of three main races: African, European and Asian. Of these 98.5 per cent

[8]Tanzania (comprising Tanganyika and Zanzibar), Kenya, and Uganda are now all Republics but members of the British Commonwealth.
[9]Now about 30 millions.

are African divided into seventy main tribes and at least 150
minor ones. Each of these has its own language or dialect.
This complicated linguistic pattern is only partially simplified
by the fact that there is a remarkable "lingua franca" called
Swahili, a living relic of the Arab slave-traders, which is understood by most of the tribes of Kenya and Tanganyika. . . .

East Africa contains every contrast of climate and vegetation,
from arid deserts to that snow-capped giant Mount Kilimanjaro, which dominates the border between Kenya and Tanganyika and is the highest mountain in the whole of Africa.

REV. F. J. BEDFORD, in *The Bible in the World*

258. Some Golf Hazards in East Africa

There are no doubt some unusual golf-courses in different parts
of the world, but the members of the club at northern Lake
Rudolf are probably not far wrong in believing that theirs is
really the strangest course of all. The lake runs from the
extreme north-west corner of Kenya to the Abyssinian border,
and when the golf course was opened there in 1939 it consisted only of two holes. The first ran from the Abyssinian
frontier to the Lakitaung Boma, a distance of twenty-seven
miles, and the second a distance of about eight miles along the
gorge through which the Lakitaung River occasionally runs.
Among the rules in this club are: (*a*) that if a leopard is seen
approaching, the game may be postponed indefinitely; (*b*) that
if a goat should eat a golf-ball another ball may be dropped
without penalty; (*c*) that camels, goats, and all other species
of livestock may be treated as casual hazards and may be removed before playing the ball.

We come across something reminiscent of all this, but rather
more orthodox, in the rules of the Jinja Golf Club, Uganda.
(At Jinja, Lake Victoria narrows to a bay and, pouring over
the low Ripon Falls, becomes the first link in the long series
of waterways that form the source of the Nile.) One rule is to
the effect: "On the green a ball lying in a hippo footmark may
be lifted and placed not nearer the hole without penalty."
Probably no other golf-club has a rule to equal this.

W. L. SPEIGHT, in *Chambers's Journal*, Edinburgh

259.   A Garden in Kenya

In Kenya we always spell rain with a capital "R", for it is the
life blood of the country, and when it fails to come, which it
does only too often, our crops fail too, and our gardens wither
and die under our frustrated noses.

But when the Rains do come, at their due season in April
or May, the great dusty khaki plains where the game roams
develop a faint green bloom overnight, and in a few days are
ankle deep in grass and flowers, while our lawns, which for
months past have merged into the earth paths, suddenly become defined tracks of comforting, soft, fresh green. . . .

Beyond his own house, Warki our under-gardener has a
"Shamba" on our land, in which maize grows eight feet high,
and beans and red peppers and sweet potatoes flourish in its
shade A split bamboo fence, beautifully made, keeps out the
zebra and the deer, and a deep narrow trench frustrates the
porcupines, whose nightly invasions of *our* garden cause such
havoc amongst the vegetables. . . .

Hyenas sometimes visit us at night, and the jackal's melancholy voice is often heard. When the plains are dry and dusty,
the zebra file up over the hill and past the houses to browse on
our land. . . .

From our garden, which is near Nairobi and more than
5,500 feet above sea level, we can sometimes see Mt Kenya's
white crest rising to 17,000 feet a hundred miles away, and
there are few nights in a year when it is warm enough to sit
out of doors to enjoy the brilliant moonlight.

ELSPETH HUXLEY, in *Homes and Gardens*

260.   Street-Corner in Mombasa

Let us say that you station yourself at a busy corner in one of
the African east coast ports—Mombasa, perhaps, the gateway
into Kenya and Uganda—and accost the first half-dozen
passers-by who take your fancy.

First comes a bearded Arab, dressed in the long white
cotton robe traditional to his race, with a brocaded waistcoat
and a red sash round the middle. His dark face wears an
arrogant look, even though all cause for arrogance, Arab dominion and Arab wealth, has crumbled. . . .

You might choose to speak next to a man of the present rather than the past. A clean-shaven, alert-looking young Englishman, walking down the street with the assurance of a ruler, clad in newly laundered and uncreased white ducks and a white topee shining like a daisy in a sunlit field, black tie trimly in position—you could not take him for anyone but an officer of the Administration.[10]. . . .

The next man whom you may choose to address also comes from another continent, but he was born in East Africa, and in East Africa he expects to die. He is an Indian, perhaps a Hindu with relations in Bombay. . . . His face is plump and round and dark-brown, his nature peaceful, and his mind—outside the cares of his religion and his wives and numerous children—is wholly devoted to the interests of trade. . . .

The man you next select for cross-examination may be a hulking stalwart with short woolly hair and broad Negro features, and teeth of amazing whiteness. A dock labourer, you discover, working on a six months' contract loading and unloading the cargoes of ships. . . . The next, by contrast, may be a tall, turbaned Somali from the north, with thin aquiline features, slim wrists and ankles, a coppery complexion. He will be polite, but frigid and reserved: a Moslem, cherishing the traditional Moslem contempt for Christians.

East Africa, by ELSPETH HUXLEY
published in the "Britain in Pictures" series in 1941 by Collins.

261. Tanganyika Illustrates East Africa's Problems

It is the vast conglomerate which is Tanganyika that best focuses the real issues in East Africa. Typically, today and in any conceivable state of internal communications, even a geographically more central capital than Dar-es-Salaam is bound to be inaccessible to most of the vast domain it has to administer. Its one highway, the Central Railway, gives access, mostly through bush, only to the country between the two great lakes, where a large cattle-keeping population fights a doubtful battle with the tsetse-fly, though the people also grow some good

[10]Kenya is now an independent republic.

cotton. The most highly developed Province lies north, where a lesser railway runs from Tanga to the truly delectable lower slopes of Kilimanjaro, and of that other great mountain, 15,000 foot Meru.

Here Wachagga peasants thrive by growing coffee on fabulously rich volcanic soil; and here also some scores of European farmers of many nationalities (and a few Asians) add variety by their respectable economic activity, and some complications by their political demands. Rather farther on the other side of Dar-es-Salaam, the Southern Province has obvious possibilities, permanent water, and as yet unexploited coal. Meantime much of it is utterly out of reach (except on foot) for six months in the year. The neighbouring Southern Highlands (a scene of small-scale white settlement) is more likely to be linked presently by railway developments to Rhodesia and the south. . . .

To complete the picture, sketch in vast blocks of country in which very untouched and ill-nourished tribes still war ineffectively with disease and pests, and recurring drought and famine.

w. m. MACMILLAN, in *The Listener*

Note. Tanganyika, with Zanzibar, now forms the United Republic of Tanzania.

262. Wild Life in Northern Rhodesia
(now Zambia)

(*a*) Apart from the Copper Belt there are very few white folk throughout Northern Rhodesia. One may travel for hours at a time on the highways without meeting a fellow traveller. In five hours and over 100 miles through the escarpment of the Great East Road that leads from Lusaka into Nyasaland (now Malawi) we met no other vehicle—fortunate that, for one rounds sharp bends, drops down steep declines, crosses over narrow bridges with the constant thought in mind: what would happen if a lion or an elephant suddenly appeared around one of those bends? At a Government rest-house that evening we commented on the fact that we had seen practically no wild life. The reply was not reassuring—for we learned that lions and elephants were all around us, but the grass by the side of the road was so high that we could not see them. We did see families of baboons and creatures that looked like foxes. It was reported that the lions had roared near where we slept at nights, and we were regaled with accounts of encounters with lions and the dangerous spotted hyena, while Mission stations lamented the damage done to their gardens and banana crops by marauding elephant herds.

REV. M. W. BOOTH, in The Bible in the World

(b) The wild life of Africa is resilient in its own habitat and in my opinion has quite extraordinary powers of persistence and regeneration, and of spread-back into areas where there has been extermination. The toll of wild life by the rural African might well be possible to maintain if the animals did not live in a wasting habitat and were purely for consumption within the family. Unfortunately this is not so. The industrialization of the Copper Belt has brought together large numbers of rural Africans for mining work of one sort and another. These people are constantly meat-hungry and high prices are paid, even by European standards, for meat in a condition which Europeans would not touch.... What is certain is that the sale of game meat is a highly profitable business; the bigger African fish operators have not taken part in it until recently, but the bicycle men, weaving through the bush unseen and unchecked, use the fish trade as cover for selling illegally killed game....

It is certain that as sporting pursuit of wild life declines, the aesthetic pleasure and comfort of the human spirit to be gained by contemplation of wild life in its unspoiled habitats of swamp, flood plain, bush, forest and high plateau will be more positively sought. The tourist value of wild life is already considerable and has every expectation of increasing. The present rather irritating regimentation within national parks and reserves is necessary at the moment, but in a possible future the need may pass.

Wild Life in an African Territory, by F. FRASER DARLING

263. Down the Zambesi

Last year three of us followed the Zambesi from its birth in the heart of Africa to its death in the Indian Ocean. On its way it winds through three countries, Zambia, Angola, and Mozambique, and forms the frontier of a fourth, Rhodesia. It boasts at least two superlatives—the largest curtain of falling water in the world, the Victoria Falls, and Kariba, the biggest of all man-made lakes. But it also produces other wonders that do not depend on mere statistics to make you feel they are unparalleled. Like every river it is the focus of all life, animal and human, and in Africa both are spectacular and dramatic.

Herds of elephant wade through its shallows. Giraffe, zebra, and rare antelope come down to drink from it. Hippopotamus lounge and grunt in its backwaters. In the swamps of its estuary, lungfish cocoon themselves in holes during the dry season and manage to survive for months, breathing air and starving, while the mud around them is baked brick-hard by the ferocious sun.

Stone Age men camped beside its gorges and left behind them thousands of flint tools strewn among the gravel. Four hundred years ago Portuguese explorers sailed up it, pursuing the legend of a golden city—a legend that sprang, perhaps, from the mysterious ruins of Zimbabwe down in the south. And Livingstone travelled along most of its course, the first European to do so, when he crossed Africa in one of the most heroic and astounding journeys in the history of exploration.

DAVID ATTENBOROUGH, in *Radio Times*

264. Rhodesia and Tobacco

Southern Rhodesia (now called Rhodesia), 150,000 square miles in extent and the homeland of the Matabele and Mashona tribes, is land-locked between the Zambesi and Limpopo rivers. Her outlets to the sea are the Portuguese East African port of Beira and the South African ports of Cape Town, Durban and Port Elizabeth. . . . The country's economy has been based on her primary industries of agriculture and mining; tobacco, maize and cattle; gold, chromium, asbestos and coal. Most of the tobacco crop and the whole of the mineral production is exported. . . .

The land at present developed for tobacco cultivation lies mostly within a 100-mile radius of Salisbury, the capital, in the north-eastern quarter of the territory. The area under tobacco each year on an average holding is about 100 acres, and the growers are, for the most part, men of the British farmer type. . . .

The tobacco-grower has to accept certain risks—very serious risks—which are no part of the hazard of ordinary farming. This is because he sells, not his crop, but the finished, or at least the processed, product. He sows the seed in September, transplants from November to the New Year, reaps from February to May. The auctions start in April, but between the reaping and the fateful journey to Salisbury there is the curing, which could easily lose the farmer fifty per cent of his earnings, and the grading, in which each individual leaf has to be classified by at least five different qualities—colour, length, stretch, etc.

Scope

Note. Following Rhodesia's unilateral declaration of independence, the farmer has found it difficult to sell his tobacco, owing to Sanctions.

265. Here is South Africa

Cape Town, called by sailormen the "Tavern of the Seas", lies on the lower slopes of Table Mountain with its doorstep washed by the South Atlantic. One thousand miles away are the sky-scrapers of Johannesburg, rising incongruously from the bare South African veld which is 6,000 feet above sea-level. South-east, down from the high, central plateau, four hundred miles farther on is Durban, sunning itself among the sugar-cane beside the warm Indian Ocean. It is a matter of twelve hundred miles or more, north to south, from where the crocodiles bask in the lazy Limpopo to Port Elizabeth, swept by winds from a sea which extends unbroken to the South Polar ice-cap.

Here is South Africa, as excitingly varied as those Little Karroo sunsets which etch the harsh mountain ramparts against the riotous backcloth of blood-red, purple and gold. A land, this, where the existence of problems is itself witness to the immense vitality infusing it, where nearly three million Europeans, about nine million Bantus, one-and-a-quarter million Coloureds and half-a-million Indians are working out their destinies in the modern age.[11] Here is a land where drought and fertility rub

[11]Now 3,779,650 whites, 14,893,000 Bantus, and 1,996,089 Coloureds. There are also over half a million Asians, mostly Indians.

shoulders; where gold, uranium, diamonds, abundance of iron
and coal, with the secondary industries which accompany
them, are quickly transforming an agricultural country into a
complicated, industrialized State.

REV. T. HAWTHORN, in *The Bible in the World*

266. On the High Veld

One hundred and seventy-six miles north of Pretoria is the
quiet little town of Pietersburg. The road goes straight across
the veld, and you drive down it at 65 miles an hour, and it is
like driving down an air-strip in a 'plane that never quite takes-
off. There are only two big streets in P'burg, and two cinemas
and a few shops ... in the hotels in the town they are selling
the morning papers from Johannesburg at three in the
afternoon. ...
   The Mamabola people live twenty miles north-west of P'burg,
in little thatched rondavels clustered together in the lee of the
hills, and grouped among the great cactus trees on the hill-tops.
They are farming people, keeping cattle and goats and cultivat-
ing small patches of mealies, their staple food. Nearly every
family has at least one absent member, a husband, a wife, a
daughter, working in Jo'burg or in Pretoria, and sending money
home each month to help to support the children and the old
folk. ...
   Half an hour out of P'burg, the car turns off the main road
and begins to climb slowly along the rough track up between
the hills. On either side of the track the high veld grass rises,
burned brown in the winter sunshine and moving in the wind
like water. On the long, broad slope of the hills, the cactus trees
grow thick and tall, and there are great outcrops of smooth,
yellow rock thrusting up two hundred feet into the sky.

STUART B. JACKMAN, in the *British Missionary*

267. Johannesburg: The city built on gold

About the year 1890 Johannesburg had some fifty inhabitants;
in fifty years the population had grown to over 500,000.[12]

[12]In 1970 it was 1,407,963, including 482,589 whites.

The result is that its streets have all the vulgarity of a successful American city and its suburbs all the luxury of those of New York. The pedestrian is treated with greater contempt than in any other place I have visited. . . .

In many ways, then, Johannesburg is not an attractive city. But the history of no other city illustrates better the basic rivalry between the two sections of South Africa's Whites, the Dutch and the English. For the first inhabitants of the Witwatersrand, the ridge of hills that is now the greatest goldfield in the world, were Boer farmers who had taken part in the Great Trek from Cape Colony in order to find solitude and freedom from the interferences and fiscal impositions of the English. . . .

And not much more than a generation after they had settled on the great, treeless, lonely plain of the High Veld, prospectors struck gold almost in their farmyards. The like of the Johannesburg gold rush had never been known, for, unlike the Klondike, the Witwatersrand was land that had been already settled. The newcomers built their saloons, their stores and their gaming dens along dusty waggon tracks that a few months before had been grazing land and a few years later were to become the streets of Johannesburg. . . .

There are, then, causes of friction in South Africa not only between Europeans and natives, Europeans and coloureds, and Europeans and Indians, but also between the sixty per cent of Europeans who speak Afrikaans and the forty per cent who speak English.

VERNON BARTLETT, in the *News Chronicle*

268. From Johannesburg to Durban

Johannesburg is the largest city in the world not on a coast or on a river,[13] and the second largest in the Southern Hemisphere. At night when the stars hang low in the blue-black sky and the neon signs flare to life on the city's buildings, Johannesburg is all fun and gaiety. . . . From Johannesburg we travelled the following morning to Pretoria, the administrative capital of the Union,[14] where the Union Buildings with their magnificent

[13]In view of the world-wide trend towards agglomeration in cities, this statement may no longer be correct.
[14]Now a Republic and not now a member of the Commonwealth.

gardens dominate the jacaranda-lined streets, a haze of mauve
and blue. The atmosphere is different here, quieter and more
stately, as befits a seat of government and the home of one of
the South African universities.

And so to Durban, focal point of a 300-mile-long holiday
coast, which spreads on either side of the city along the shores
of the Indian Ocean. Durban has a year-round season, but
perhaps the most popular time for visitors is during the winter
(June and July) when visitors from the Cape especially, which
lies in a winter rainfall area, are drawn by the dry, warm climate
and by the attractions which this premier holiday city offers. . . .

We were enchanted by Durban. The Indian Market with
its long rows of spice, silver and silk-laden stalls, and the Native
Market with its pots, beads and carved souvenirs proved
wonderful sources of gifts to take to relations and friends at
home, and the long golden beaches, washed by the warm sea,
are a constant invitation to relax and stay longer.

FRANCES M. A. ROBERTSON,
in *Yorkshire Life Illustrated*, Bradford

269. The Scenery of Natal

(*a*) It was beautiful on this last stretch of the High Veld
whose edge is the mighty wall of the Drakensburg that over-
hangs Natal. Here were great kopjes and boulders and pinnacles
of rock with grass and plentiful water between and, since it was
October, flowers everywhere. Retief and the lasses delighted to
gather them, especially the big red ones they had never seen
before. Suddenly, at a bend in the track, there was nothing
ahead; a little farther still and the panorama of west central
Natal opened out hundreds of feet below. The mountain-side
dropped downward in great rounded knees and jagged rocky
krantzes, while below, green, blue and grey in the last distance,
was a tumbled sea of rounded hills that faded out in the haze of
the horizon. . . .

At last the blue line of the sea showed through a gap in the
hills. Cornfields and kraals of beehive huts set round with thorn-
bush palisades broke the alternating monotony of bush and forest
and grass high as a man's head, and then the huts of the English
on the very edge of the land-locked lagoon set with islets

that was Port Natal. A lovely land and the best harbour on all
the coast from Table to Delagoa Bay. Here surely was journey's
end.

The Great Trek, by ERIC ANDERSON WALKER

(*b*) We were bound for Pietermaritzburg, and as the train
climbed and spiralled its way through the lovely hills towards
this charming and peaceful city, 3,000 feet above Durban, our
conversation almost ceased so that we might the better admire
the scenery. Past pineapple and the mealie fields, past sudden
waterfalls and through the famous Valley of a Thousand Hills,
past country stations and lonely dorps, native kraals and kopjes
we went. . . .

Yorkshire Post, Leeds

270. Zulu Life

(*a*) On dismounting in the dark at a kraal we come to the
small door of the hut, which is about two feet high, and, kneeling down, signify our presence by a grunt. Being told to
come in, we find it easier said than done. Crawling "on all
fours", we push our head into the hut, and then draw it back,
feeling as if we had been struck in the face: this is caused by
the dense smoke—thick enough to be cut with a knife—and the
Kaffir odour. It is far worse than a good London pea-soup fog
of the most virulent type. . . . The fire is placed near the centre
of the floor; the smoke rises into the hut and escapes as best
it may, causing the roof to have the appearance of the deepest
jet-black polished ebony.

The Essential Kaffir, by DUDLEY KIDD

(*b*) The simple life of the kraal still lingers, in spite of the
steady northward advance of civilization and the increasing
tendency of the men to seek work for a period at the mining
centres or in the towns. Many changes are taking place—and
not all of them for the better. European clothing is becoming
generally worn, especially by the men. Cheap novelties,
purchased in Johannesburg or Pietermaritzburg or Durban,
find their way to the kraals when the wanderers return, and
P

too often vices learned from the white man are reproduced in places where he has never been.

Africa and her Peoples, by F. DEAVILLE WALKER

271. Soil-Conservation in Basutoland[15]

In spite of my arrival in the rain, the first day in Basutoland was fine, and I was given a bird's eye view of the country by the Chief Soil Conservation Officer while flying over it in a light aeroplane. Below us at first was the Caledon River, tributary of the Orange, and boundary between Basutoland and the Orange Free State.

The river itself marked a complete change in landscape: on the Free State side, a country of wide European farms, fairly well wooded; on the Basutoland side, the most intensely farmed land in Africa, a patchwork of little fields, over-ploughed, completely treeless, and showing the ugly gashes of soil erosion. Yet as we looked down there were clear signs of action to improve the soil, for spread over all this patchwork of fields were the superimposed marks of the Soil Conservation Team.

In the first areas we crossed the ploughing was already following the lines of the contours, and the farms had taken a new geometric shape. Further to the south, the interval contours recently ploughed by the Team showed as lines running across the pattern of the fields; it will be the next ploughing season before the farmers' ploughs follow the lines which will prevent their soil being washed down into the Orange River.... The next stage will be the rehabilitation of the soil through planned rotation and improved animal husbandry.

REV. T. A. BEETHAM, in the *Methodist Recorder*

272. Cape Town

Cape Town is the capital of the biggest of the four Provinces of South Africa, and the area where White settlement has had almost three centuries to mature. With its unique back-cloth of Table Mountain, the Mother City has a setting not inferior to

[15]Now called Lesotho (an independent state).

the famed peaks surrounding Rio de Janeiro. And hidden among the fertile, vine-clad valleys of the massive mountain series of the immediate interior are little towns like Paarl, Worcester, Stellenbosch, Tulbagh, Ceres and Robertson, with their thatched roofs and white Dutch gables to remind passers-by of the traditions which have gone to the building of the South African nation.

Cape Town lies spreadeagled around the mighty plinth of Table Mountain and its outlying masses. At the foot are the Houses of Parliament. Upon the slopes of the Mountain stand out the University buildings, and in the direction of Devil's Peak is Groote Schuur—"Big Barn"—the residence given by Cecil Rhodes to South African Prime Ministers in perpetuity, and the best-known monument to Rhodes himself. Cape Town is not well planned, but it has individuality in a big way.... Adderley Street, the former Dutch Heerengracht, is the main thoroughfare.

A few miles inland are Paarl and Stellenbosch; the former is the hub of the wine industry; the latter, a university town with musical furrows, handsome gables and teak-shuttered windows. It is the quintessence of amiability and grace in the historical Cape.

The *Commonwealth and Empire Review*

273. From Cape Town to Port Elizabeth

The journey took us the better part of a week. It was through the most varied scenery—a diversity of hill and plain, forest, river, deep precipitous gorge and mountains. Caledon was interesting. It is a hot spring station which people frequent for various ills. It is delightfully situated in a fruitful region ringed with trees, with long views over the undulating landscape. There was Swellendam, too, which interested me as centre of a big agricultural district. Some monster wheat fields were passed with the stubble still in the ground....

On the road we met the ox-waggon everywhere with the "voor-looper" in front leading the way with a piece of rope attached to the first pair. The post is always held by a youngster, who wears a piece of sacking round his nakedness, tied with a string. He is mostly a friendly little soul who beams upon the passer-by. A negro of larger growth acts as driver and switches a great whip with extraordinary dexterity. He knows exactly where to hit the great, patient, soft-eyed beasts, who are drawing logs, perhaps, or bags of flour over the eternal grasslands. . . .

The amazing loneliness of it impresses one—miles without a living soul. Cattle and sheep in their thousands are there, but the country is so vast that we hardly remark them unless they come down upon our path, and we have to slow down because of them. . . . We have reached stony ground, and now ostriches are seen, running wildly at the sight of our car. One young one gets in front and for half a mile lopes away from us with the most ridiculous stride. . . . We spent the night at Mossel Bay . . . then came the glorious region of Knysna, with gigantic trees of yellow wood. . . . And now to Port Elizabeth, trim and prosperous looking, whence a train rumbles me to Pretoria.

My South African Year, by CHARLES DAWBARN

274. The Diamond Road

They call it the "Diamond Road" nowadays, but it was a treasure trail centuries before the first diamond was found in South Africa. It is the road that leads northwards from Cape Town, never very far from the coast, for five hundred miles through the hot wastes of Namaqualand to its end on the banks of the mighty Orange River. When I first went that way, in 1925, there were rumours of diamonds on the Namaqualand coast, but Kimberley was still without a rival. . . .

The road starts near the edge of Table Bay and passes almost immediately into the wheat belt, the Swartland which supplies all South Africa with bread. In the spring it is like travelling through a vast, undulating green sea. . . . The plains of wheat end a hundred miles from Cape Town, and the road climbs steeply over the Grey's Pass gap in the Olifants Mountains. Over the pass the Diamond Road crosses the Olifants River and runs northwards through a sweltering valley of oranges. Some of the oldest orange-trees in the world grow in this valley. I know a hospitable farm, owned by one family for more than two centuries, where a few of the original trees are still bearing. . . .

Entering dismal, often fog-covered dune country near the coast, the Diamond Road skirts the depressing settlement of

Port Nolloth, and turns northward again on the last lap.... Our journey ends when a barbed-wire fence appears, with a gate across the road. It is fifty miles from Port Nolloth to the end of the road at Alexander Bay diamond diggings, but the ordinary traveller may drive only a few miles up this road. In the forbidden zone ahead, almost warlike precautions are taken.

LAWRENCE G. GREEN, in *Chambers's Journal*, Edinburgh

275. Karroo and Veld

(*a*) THE KARROOS. Now we were pounding along a desert of brown, dried-up land, ringed with distant mountains, and without a blade of grass or anything else that was green within view. The scanty herbage was sage-grey; it seemed to have no more life in it than the stony soil it grew upon.... The river beds, when not mere pebbly tracks, dry as high roads, had only a few muddy pebbles, or a thin trickle of water, brown and thick, to hint that occasional bridges across them may positively be required.

South Africa Calling, by A. LOWTH

(*b*) THE VELD. Once beyond the barrier ranges, the undulating plains spread on every side desolate and illimitable. The surface of the earth is broken only by rounded and flat-topped masses....

There is neither tree nor shrub, homestead nor boundary, to arrest the eye. At most, a line of mimosa bushes mark the barren tract of the periodic water-course, and the brown earth at our feet is studded here and there by stunted bushes. Such is the veld, and such is the characteristic landscape of settled South Africa.

The Union of South Africa, by E. O. WORSFOLD

276. The Great Karroo: This is Drought

Each morning dawn breaks sparkling and exhilarating on the Great Karroo. Miles and miles of sun-baked earth, with not a green blade to be seen. The unbroken stretch of barren country lies unfurled like the drab, worn carpet of some great giant.

Pebbles glitter like glass. Clumps of dolomite, "jewels of the Karroo", lie in purple masses shining almost as if wet with rain that never falls. And overhead incessantly blazes a pitiless, burning sky.

At midday, regular as clockwork, a hot wind springs up from the Kalahari, scorching and blistering everything in its wake. The veld is shrouded in a cloud of golden-red dust.

On one occasion we travelled for 130 miles through the most stricken area—a valley of desolation. Tiny, mud-coloured houses were dotted about the veld, like small islands on a grey sea. All were deserted, the pathetic little patches of gardens dry and untended. The empty dam resembled a huge brown basin. Near the dam wall lay the bodies of starved animals, which had persisted in their last desperate search for water.

The last small cottage was still occupied. A weary man and a hopeless-looking woman were making a final, gallant stand. Their eyes bore a strained look of waiting. Round the house some scraggy goats and sheep nosed about among the tins and stones, searching for some fragments of food or trace of moisture. We were invited to enter the house, in the friendly South African fashion. Coffee made of acorns was all they had to offer.... The only spot of green was a pepper tree waving its dusty leaves against the window. Their food—goat's meat and mealie-meal. Their pleasures—none. Their only relaxation was church in the dorp each Sabbath Day....

ROSALIND MALAN, in the *Cape Argus*, Cape Town

277. De Aar Junction

De Aar is a railway junction on the Northern Karroo, in the heart of the old Cape Colony, and in 1905 it wasn't much else.... But Aunt Olive[16] said that there was one great thing about living at De Aar, and that was the knowledge that you could always get away, that you could take a train any day, and go North to the Transvaal, or South to Cape Town. And the other inhabitants must have had this same feeling, for they made the station their rendezvous, the hub of their social life, and turned out regularly to walk up and down the platform,

[16]Olive Schreiner, author of *Story of an African Farm*.

morning or evening, when the mail trains arrived and halted to take in water and coal. . . .

Around lay the ironstone kopjes, only dear to those born beside them; stark and red, with scattered boulders on top, they strew the landscape to its farthest horizon, and at sunset are at their worst (and most beautiful), black and threatening in their infinite monotony. Walking there of an evening, with my uncle, I wanted to lift up my head and howl like a dog. The only set walks outside the village were to the golf links or to the Animal Cemetery. There was a certain thrill to be got from the golf greens, since they were covered with "Kimberley blue", which contained a sprinkling of garnets, none big enough to be worth cutting—but there was always hope of a lucky find. . . . The Animal Cemetery, reached by its own special road over the bare veld, was made during the Boer War, when many ailing horses and mules had to be shot at the Remount Depot of De Aar.

LYNDALL GREGG, in *Chambers's Journal*, Edinburgh

Australia and New Zealand

278. "Empty" Australia

Australia is too often advertised in glowing and misleading phrases. It has open spaces, but they are not rich. "Watering the inland" is a glorious phantasy, but an Australian source of water adequate for the purpose has not yet been found.[1] A study of the distribution maps of our population, wheat, agriculture generally, dairying, cattle and sheep, must make all thoughtful people hesitate before clamouring for rapid increases of millions of population.

It is time we told the world the reason why so much of Australia is empty. The narrow strip reaching about 200 miles inland along the east and south-east, and on the south-west of the continent may, through industrialization and intensive settlement, carry a much greater population than at present, but much planning and development work is required before that can eventuate.

We Australians as a whole are on our guard against any people markedly different from ourselves. If, for example, a group coming from south-eastern Europe settles in apparently useless country and, working long hours, denying themselves amenities and pleasures, make a success of their location, we become suspicious of them and are apt to resent their success. Australians also have a strong colour prejudice. We react with horror when we hear of the marriage of one of ourselves to a coloured spouse.

PROF. A. P. ELKIN, in the *Australian Quarterly*, Sydney

279. The Trees of Australia

(a) Probably the greater part of the Queenslander's "open

[1] Through the Hume Reservoir and the Snowy Mountain Project (1950–75) large additional areas of the Riverina are being irrigated, with increased wheat and fruit growing.

forest" would be described as grassland more or less lightly sprinkled with trees. Most of the trees are species of the great genus "eucalyptus", which in Australia completely dominates arboreal society. The eucalypts do not bear edible fruit, but, usually at intervals of two or three years, they bear lavish crops of petal-less flowers. The blossoms, though little more than tufts of stamens, happen to be very rich in nectar, and when a big gum tree is in flower it is thronged from dawn to dark by flocks of honey-eating birds.

Flying Fox and Drifting Sand, by FRANCIS RATCLIFFE

(b) The trees of Australia nearly all belong to one family (the foliage is scanty and of a rather peculiar light green tint—it is not periodically shed), and have the surface of their leaves placed in a vertical instead of, as in Europe, a horizontal position. This fact, and their scantiness, makes the woods light and shadowless; although under the scorching sun of the summer this is a loss of comfort, it is of importance to the farmer, as it allows grass to grow where it otherwise could not. The greater number of the trees, with the exception of some of the Blue Gums, do not attain a large size, but they grow tall and tolerably straight and stand well apart. It is singular that the bark of some kinds annually falls, or hangs dead in long shreds, which swing about with the wind; and hence the woods appear desolate and untidy.

Diary of the Voyage of H.M.S. Beagle, by CHARLES DARWIN,
ed. N. BARLOW

280. Some Native Animals of Australia

(a) How far the absence from Australia of the higher animals, such as were capable of domestication, is to be associated with the present backward state of the aborigines, can only, of course, be a matter of speculation; but it is, at all events, a significant fact that the Australian fauna contains no large-sized animals suitable for domestication either as beast of burden or as food supply. . . .

During the dry season there is very little animal life to be seen on the steppe lands, except for interminable numbers of ants and, at certain seasons, locusts or grasshoppers. Every now and then a few large red kangaroos will bound away; and perhaps an emu or two, after gazing curiously at the travellers, will think it best to beat a hasty retreat. In good seasons, and in certain parts of the scrub-covered plains where the food is good, kangaroos may be fairly plentiful, but they suffer severely in time of drought.

Across Australia, by B. SPENCER and F. J. GILLEN

(*b*) This curious bird (laughing jackass) was remarkably common near the Ranges, and I once counted no less than half a dozen perched together on one small tree. He is a favourite everywhere. He is also useful as a vermin destroyer, and I believe it is a most interesting and instructive experience to watch one of these birds tackle and kill a large and poisonous snake. His uncanny cackling laughter, gradually rising from a low satirical chuckle to a prolonged raucous, "Hoo! hoo! hoo!" of diabolical mirth, used to ring through the oppressive silence of the Bush with startling vigour at the most unexpected moments. . . .

The dingo, or wild dog of Australia, is a tall fine member of the canine race, with a yellow coat, bright yellow eyes, and tall prick ears, an attractive but not easily tameable animal. For long it was considered that the dingo was the descendant of domestic dogs imported into Australia, but scientific discoveries of recent years have gone to prove that perhaps the much-detested dingo is the most ancient inhabitant of the continent, for this animal's fossilized bones have been unearthed in caves and in strata of the soil of immense geological antiquity.

An Australian Wander Year, by H. M. VAUGHAN

(*c*) Koalas are on view at any hour of the day. You will see half a dozen small grey forms tucked securely into the forks of the trees, peacefully asleep. You have met the most lovable toy of your childhood come to life. The same big bushy ears, the same trusting little face, the same absurd black button of a nose.

Cobbers, by THOMAS WOOD

281. Some Towns and Cities of Australia

No country today offers so much space and scope for men to build cities as Australia. The coastal capitals developed as outlets for the products of the fertile interior. The inland cities were invariably built around rich mineral deposits. Thus there is Kalgoorlie, gold city of Western Australia; Broken Hill, silver city of New South Wales; Whyalla, iron ore city of South Australia; Yallourn, Victoria's brown coal city, built on the Empire's largest brown coalfield. Heavyweight of the industrial cities is Newcastle, the Australian Birmingham. Outside the mineral cities and the six State capitals there are what might be called the irrigation cities....

Most Australian cities and towns have the usual land titles permitting private ownership of land. But the national capital, Canberra, is a Commonwealth Government concern, as Darwin will be. Land will be available only on lease. Canberra is a fourteen million pound city, built on what was formerly an immense sheep station, seventy-five miles inland from the east coast and 2,000 feet up in the highlands. In summer the surrounding hills shimmer with heat haze—in winter they glisten snow-white. Darwin is a tropical port on the north coast, with an excellent climate in the dry season from April to September. The temperature ranges from sixty-five degrees in July to ninety-one degrees in December.... It may develop along lines different architecturally from Canberra, but its general scheme of administration will probably follow the national capital[2]....

Other planned living areas in Australia are worth mentioning. There is Whyalla, on the western shore of Spencer's Gulf in South Australia, built less than forty miles from a veritable mountain of 100 million tons of iron ore which stands above the landscape.... Instead of the usual makeshift town, sprawling around factories, Whyalla was built with broad streets, ample parks and gardens. A desert settlement became one of the busiest industrial centres, with thriving shipbuilding yards and a blast furnace. A pipeline, 223 miles long, brings water from the River Murray—Australia's Mississippi.

Yallourn, in Victoria, stands on twenty-seven million tons of brown coal, obtained not by tunnel mining, but by open cut. It is a model township, set on the slopes of wooded hills and

[2]By 1966, Canberra had 92,199 people, and Darwin 20,261.

looking out over plain and undulating country. . . . Of Yallourn it has been said : "Here indeed the townsman enjoys all that the heart of man may desire."

JOHN BRIEARS in the *Commonwealth and Empire Review*

282. Australian Homes

Homes in the bigger capital cities of Australia do not differ greatly from those in big cities in England, but the country (or "bush" as we call it) Australian home is very unlike its English counterpart. The solidly-built house of stone or brick, with tiled roof, so familiar in English country towns and villages, is almost completely absent in Australia, where corrugated iron roofs and weatherboard walls are general.

In the days of the early settlers, the typical home had a verandah around as much of the house as the owner could afford. With the growth of the family, extra rooms were added without any idea of design and usually sloping, at varying heights, from the back. Many houses in the country are still improvised in this fashion, and the lack of planning brings many inconveniences. The drumming of rain, when it comes, on the iron roof, and the scampering of 'possums over it at night are familiar sounds in most country homes. . . . Water is usually collected from the roof and stored in 1,000- or 2,000-gallon tanks of galvanized iron, and generally has to be sparingly used.

The original verandah-type designs were used in some of the larger sheep-station homes, where greater expenditure and care in planning have produced some charming houses. . . .

The greatest trial of every Australian housewife is the dust, often blown hundreds of miles from the central plains.

CLARA WELLS, in *Homes and Gardens*

283. Australia's Daring Mailmen

Delivering mails throughout Australia's roughly 3,000,000 square miles provides one of the many romantic stories that can be told about the Australian bush—a story of courage, daring and devotion to duty scarcely equalled. . . . The mailmen are carriers of foodstuffs, newspapers, and other bulkier items.

Whether he is a long-distance packhorse or motor mailman, or only has a short motor run in a farming area, this factotum is general messenger and newsman for everyone along his route.

In tropical North Queensland ... he traverses some of the roughest and wildest country in Australia on a faint track that winds through rugged ranges, vast eucalypt forests, through almost impenetrable jungle and across a score of crocodile-infested rivers. . . . Two mailmen use camels. One route is from Horseshoe Bend on the Alice Springs railway to Hermannsburg Mission Station on the edge of the Great Inland Desert—a distance of 160 miles. The other camel mail also operates in desert country. It runs from Windorah to Birdsville in south-west Queensland and is the longest run: 930 miles across sand-hills, gibber plains, and dried-up river beds and salt lakes. . . . There are mail routes in the more closely-settled pastoral country ... that are still horse mails (packhorse and buggy). . . .

The mailman who drives a five-ton truck from Birdsville to Marree, a distance of 325 miles across the Great Stony Desert, has installed a pedal radio set in his truck. Miniature transmitting and receiving sets have saved hundreds of lives in the "Outback". . . . The bush people know that, whatever happens, the mailman is prepared to risk his life in order that the mails may "get through to the blokes who want it".

GLENVILLE PIKE, in *Chambers's Journal*, Edinburgh

284. Australian Aborigines

For many thousands of years, indeed, since the invention of husbandry, mankind has lived chiefly by manipulating the environment, by actively and practically entering into the business of producing the essentials of survival. Not so the Australian aborigine. He took what nature provided and co-operated only to the extent of attempting to stimulate natural processes by ritual acts. He gathered and ate seeds, but did not go the further step and sow those seeds; in fact, it is said that he did not even comprehend that the plant and its fruit develop from seed. Similarly, he hunted for animal food with spear or boomerang or club or trap, but made no attempt to capture animals and then breed them for increase. Actually the aborigine's lack of progress in husbandry is not surprising: even the modern British inhabitants of Australia have not succeeded in developing any indigenous species to practical food uses.

Nowhere in Australia was the food supply plentiful enough to permit the parasitic natives to live sedentary lives; they had to hunt and gather their food over wide areas, temporarily exhausting resources in one place and moving on to the next. But this nomadism was somewhat circumscribed: groups usually returned to the same places year after year, and the wide territory over which each group moved was identified with it alone. In more fertile regions this territory may be thought of as having been continuous; but in desert regions it consisted of several fertile places connected by paths, with all the intervening economically useless country ignored and not identified with any group.

The Pacific Islands, by DOUGLAS L. OLIVER

285.   Rain in Northern Australia

In Darwin and the coastal belt the annual rainfall is round about five or six feet, all of which descends in the four months from December to the following March. The year is sharply divided into two seasons, the "wet" and the "dry". The "wet" is a great feature of Darwin to those who know the sweep and the howl of the nor'-wester when the monsoon roars across the sea from up the equator. As a result overnight the local world changes with dramatic suddenness. From a dry parched land there springs a wonderfully beautiful tinge of green. "The grass has started", someone will exclaim delightedly as the annual miracle of Nature takes place once more. Then the real deluge commences, and day and night, to the accompaniment of deep rolling thunder and terrific lightning the rain, with brief spells, teems down. Heat and rain combine to force up a prolific growth of vegetation.

North Australia, by C. P. CONIGRAVE

286.   Overland Patrol

"A beat as big as Belgium" might describe the area administered by Australia's Northern Territory Police, men who live and work beyond the pavement's end. In this astonishing land, six times the size of Great Britain, where stark desert contrasts with tropical jungle, there are cattle stations like principalities, tiny townships, uranium mines, huge ricefields . . . and the lost shacks of lonely men.

The Northern Territory policeman is a colourful survivor of a frontier tradition. His home often serves as police station, post office and first-aid post. Among other things, he is Stock and Brands Inspector, Registrar of Births, Deaths, Dogs and Motor-vehicles, Census-taker and Assistant Bailiff. In his "manor" are cattlemen who use aeroplanes like taxis, as well as Territory "old hands"—die-hard prospectors, crocodile-hunters, dingo-shooters, and Afghan camel-drivers. He is father-protector to the aboriginal tribesmen, and still uses his personal "black-tracker" as a sort of super magnifying-glass. He works with radio, planes and cars, and yet on his long, lonely patrols he often travels by horseback. Always, the country itself is the ultimate enemy. . . . It is a strange, beautiful, and implacable land.

MAURICE TRAVERS and ANTHONY SCOTT VEITCH, in *Radio Times*

287. The Northern Territory and its Future

I thought that the Northern Territory presented the most formidable problems, and perhaps the richest opportunities. Here are some of the far-flung cattle stations which look so vast to European eyes. I motored all morning over one, 1,300 square miles in extent. We failed to find the owner and he failed to find us. No unusual occurrence, and despite our experienced guide, we were ourselves for a few minutes "bushed", which merely meant that we took the wrong turning where there are no turnings.

Yet by no means all this territory is desolate. We were fortunate enough to see the area round Alice Springs soon after the rain. The rolling country, the trees and shrubs and flights of parrots were beautiful to look upon, and the transient green freshness of pasture bore no resemblance to the popular conception of the dead heart of Australia.

But in reality life in much of this Northern Territory is pretty tough and solitary. Nothing has done more to alleviate danger and loneliness in the Outback than the Flying Doctor Service. This has been an inestimable boon.... Any one of the Outback stations can call up its base on the pedal wireless and consult the Flying Doctor, who will prescribe treatment, or if necessary, fly to it and bring back the sick or the injured to hospital. There are now seven Flying Doctors. There is even one Flying Dentist....

I came across men who know the Northern Territory and who are convinced of the substantial contribution it can one day make to the world's supply of meat, and of the decisive part that it can play in Australia's future.

RIGHT HON. ANTHONY EDEN (now Lord Avon) in the
Yorkshire Post, Leeds

288. The Great Barrier Reef

(a) The Great Barrier Reef is the greatest coral reef in the world. It is approximately 1,250 miles long and encloses an area of about 80,000 square miles, consisting of an intricate maze of coral reefs, islets, and shoals. The distance of its outer edge from the coast varies from about ten to 150 miles.... The Reef produces fish not only of rare beauty, but of a flavour and consistency unsurpassed anywhere on the Australian coast. Prominent on every pool, however, and conspicuous for their ugliness rather than their beauty, are long, drab bêche-de-mer, or sea-slugs, great, sluggishly-animated sausages. Their colours vary from pale cream through mottled browns to black; one that is particularly prevalent throughout the Reef is black on the upper surface and a bright crimson below. In size they range from a few inches to about eighteen inches in length.

Wonders of the Great Barrier Reef, by T. C. ROUGHLEY

(b) Every stretch of coast on every island we saw near the Great Barrier Reef, if it was formed of mud, was fringed with mangroves. The mangrove lives in the sea. At high tide, offshore, you notice giant bushes apparently afloat. The tide drops. Trunks emerge, and branches, interlaced; then roots, higher than your head, which stretch up from the mud, twist themselves, curve down again, and are lost in loops and coils of other roots.

Cobbers, by THOMAS WOOD

Note. One-quarter of the Great Barrier Reef is now dead and at least thirteen Pacific island reefs are dying. The "Crown of Thorns" starfish has "exploded" into herds that graze and kill the coral.

289. The Coast of South Queensland

Eudlo (near Ilkley) is fifty-eight miles north of Brisbane, Queensland, on the North Coast line. It is a small farming community of perhaps 150 people all told, though the centre of a district that extends westward toward the Blackall Range and eastward to the coast. Ilkley is one of the smaller communities of which there are a number in the district, and is about five miles from the railway at Eudlo and seven miles from the coast.... At one time it was on the road to Brisbane, but the new Bruce Highway by-passes it.

Industries are still of a primary nature: dairying, timber getting, fruit growing and general farming. Cream is sent to a butter factory about thirty miles away, timber goes to the sawmill by bullock wagon, and each township along the railway has a sawmill. Some of the eighty-foot-long turpentine and stringy-bark piles that went into the new wharves at Liverpool before the war, came from the Ilkley district. Fruit grown consists of bananas, pineapples, strawberries and citrus. General farming includes potatoes, maize, pumpkins, and some small crops like beans and peas. Sugar cane is grown in a small way, taken to Eudlo by motor vehicle, thence to a sugar mill five miles away.

Ilkley Gazette, Ilkley, Yorkshire

Note. Fruits of the kinds named above are grown along the coast northwards to about Rockhampton and southward over the N.S.W. border to Grafton. Sugar cane is chiefly important round Bowen and Mackay.

290. Storm at Brisbane

Towards four o'clock the skies in the west grew dark, and when

Q

Hammond and Yardley came from the pavilion after tea to continue their magnificent partnership there was an immediate and expected appeal against the light. . . . The players wandered from the field. Five minutes later they would have been washed from it. First came the lightning, streaking the sky with electric blue and silently without thunder; then followed urgent raindrops, definite and big and menacing, and thereafter came chaos to the earth.

A cold wind swept across the ground and lifted the litter into swirling towers. The raindrops became hailstones, marble-sized, that bounced upon the grass and were collected by the small boys who still maintained the freedom of the open. "This," we said, "is certainly a storm." It had not begun.

Without further warning the wind became a tempest, howling and shrieking through the rafters of the stands, tearing down flags and flagpoles, hurling a sight screen upon its back and lifting the weighted tarpaulin from the wicket as though it were a handkerchief. . . .

Thunder joined the incessant lightning and tumult ruled the world. In fifteen minutes the whole playing area was under water; there was not a blade of grass to be seen, not one, and the stumps, which had been left lying near the wicket, drifted to and fro upon the tides. When some dim light returned the floods were seen to be collecting. . . . Half the ground was a mighty lake, deep enough to drown the wheels and struts of the one standing sight screen and to cover three feet of the boundary pickets. . . . Reports of damage in Brisbane's city will be heard for weeks to come.

Yorkshire Post, Leeds

291.   Charters Towers — Dying but not Dead

The town of Charters Towers was founded in 1871, when a prospector stood alone in the Australian bush, staring at the yellow, the authentic gold. . . . The rocks were torn up to reach the gold, the scrub was cut down and the wooden town slung together.

Within a few months Charters Towers had 20,000 inhabitants: two years later it had forty thousand. They called their town The World. Today most of it lies rotting and empty in the hot sun. The gold reef that might with luck have run half the hundred miles to Brisbane, sank, hesitated and was swallowed by the harder rock; the miners dwindled, lingered, then abruptly turned away. Four thousand people still linger on in Charters Towers[3], languidly watching the town fall down around them. . . .

Today it is enervated, depopulated, but not yet dead. As a town it has no competitor for a hundred miles, and to the cattle and sheep station men it is still a town with twenty-five different places where a man can get a drink. It has shops, schools, a railway station, a racecourse and an undertaker; it will probably survive in its state of arrested senility for years. There is still one mine, the Black Jack, working in Charters Towers, but the inhabitants are now so indifferent to gold that it struggles against labour shortage. . . . The other 499 mines are dead. . . .

The town is still the sporting centre of the district, but some of the old sports, like cock-fighting, have died out, and the women no longer play croquet, which was their relaxation in the womanly days. It is still, of course, a horseback town, but no one now drives six in hand.

Lilliput

292. On a Queensland Sheep Station

Mr Alan Campbell was my new boss. I had met him just by chance, and we talked together in the main street of Roma, a typically Australian country town, away in the Queensland bush 400 miles north-west of Brisbane. . . . That first evening Mr Campbell drove me out thirty miles to Dalmally, our trip punctuated by the opening and shutting of gates across the unfenced track. . . . He owned the freehold of three properties, Dalmally, Cooinda and Merino Downs, adjoining and worked as one. His 30,000 acres supported 10,000 sheep, 460 cattle and fifty horses—plus the uneconomic emu and kangaroo. On this dry country with its average rainfall of twenty-two inches—most of it in the four summer months from November to February —all the sheep were hardy Merino. . . .

I was taken on as an extra man for the shearing. Two of us

[3]The 1966 population figure was 7,533. This is the latest available.

would ride out through 1,500-acre paddocks, among the sandal-wood and ironbark trees, and muster some "woollies". It was grand work, free and exciting, as our galloping horses swung here and there about the creeks and through the trees, racing to cut off the wayward sheep. But generally, heavy with their load of wool, the sheep preferred to come quietly in the great heat.

So we would bring them back and hold them for a time in the home paddock until the shearers were ready, then put them through to the yards by the sheds. Drafting the lambs from the ewes was hot work, dusty and smelly, with plenty of fun— and some bad language—as they bunched and jammed in the narrow races.... The shearers worked four shifts daily, each of two hours, with a break between for "smoke-o" or dinner.... There were six of them, and together they did nearly 900 a day.

STEWART HARRIS, in the *Yorkshire Post*, Leeds

293. The Prickly Pear of Queensland

The prickly pear is a very serious problem for Queensland. Thousands of acres in the state are so thickly covered with it that it is impossible to walk through them, and beneath the pear no vegetation grows. Most of us had had enough acquaintance with the prickly pear to have decided studiously to avoid it; but a professor, whose acquaintance with it had been made at the botanical gardens, had not learned to treat it with such respect. He brushed casually against it, and was soon in agony with sheaves of the little pointed barbs boring their way into his arms and legs. Human beings are not the only ones to suffer from this plant pest, for we found that the little barbs had penetrated the skins and even the bones of some of the animals we caught, and had lodged beneath the feathers of some of the birds.

Undiscovered Australia, by SIR G. H. WILKINS

Note. The prickly pear spread alarmingly for nearly a century, but about 1930 a moth whose larvae fed on the cactus was imported into Australia. Within a relatively short time most of the prickly pear was wiped out.

294. Sydney — And Westwards

(*a*)   Sydney is a city of contrasts. No place that I have ever been
to provided me with more contradictory first impressions. It is
extremely friendly, extremely hospitable. And yet you have the
sensation of being an unwanted stranger. It is extremely modern,
but you are conscious, at every turn, of history. . . . It is the
seventh largest city in the world. But its inhabitants lead an
outdoor country life. Every week-end they are on the beaches
—Manly, Coogee, Bondi—stretched out on the sand under
the sun in the intervals of surf-riding. Very many of them bathe
every day before going to their work. It is a city without pasty
faces. No one who has been to Sydney could call Paris the city
of lovely women. It is one of the chief ports of the world. Japan
and China are contiguous. But there are no slums. . . . Sydney
is the first site for a city in the world, . . . yet from the sea
Sydney is not beautiful; and there are times when you walk
down its streets that you wonder whether there is an uglier city
upon earth. A moment later you are wondering if there is
one lovelier. For you have turned a corner and there in front
of you at the end of the avenue of houses is the harbour, in all
the beauty of its blue distances.

Hot Countries (first published as *The Coloured Countries*), by
                                                            ALEC WAUGH

Note. Of Sydney, a writer in 1969 said ". . . one of the world's most
rapidly developing places. . . . Here some $2\frac{1}{2}$ million people are on the
move both materially and culturally . . . people from many lands."

(*b*)   The sublimest spectacle of the entire flight from London
to our journey's end was to burst upon us when we arrived
over Sydney and its wonderful harbour. Like a mighty fern-leaf,
ramifying and studded with islets, this glorious waterway unfolded below. The city and its environs, massed along the
water-front and extending into the hinter-lands, flanked by the
Blue Mountains, compose a spectacle of exquisite charm and
beauty.

14,000 *Miles through the Air,* by SIR ROSS SMITH

(*c*)   We reach the slope of the Blue Mountains behind Sydney.
The ascent is not steep, the road having been cut with much

care, on the side of the sandstone cliffs; at no great elevation we come to a tolerably level plain, which almost imperceptibly rises to westward, till at last its height exceeds 3,000 feet. By the term Blue Mountains, and hearing of their absolute elevation, I had expected to see a bold chain crossing the country; instead of this, a sloping plain presents merely an inconsiderable front to the low country.

Diary of the Voyage of H.M.S. Beagle, by CHARLES DARWIN, ed. N. BARLOW

295. Hydro-Electric Projects in the East

To most people Australia means, first of all, wool; then meat and wheat, timber, eggs and butter. This will always be true in essentials, for she will remain one of the greatest agricultural and pastoral countries in the world. But Australia is already emerging as a nation with a big industrial future. . . .

One great drawback has been the lack of water and of electric power in some areas. Water will always be a difficulty, though new schemes plan to treble the 800,000 acres already served by irrigation, and a country which can build the Hume dam, the largest in the Southern Hemisphere, will continue to develop these schemes to the utmost. As for electricity, there are two projects under consideration: one of them proposes to harness either the Snowy River in Victoria or the Shoalhaven River, which flows through the southern part of New South Wales.[4] The other project, which will use the Clarence River to the north of this State, is more than a proposition. The site has been chosen and the engineering problems worked out. It will supply cheap industrial and domestic power to the towns and countryside of northern New South Wales and South Queensland. It will not only encourage rural industries in these areas: it will open up the possibilities of rich stores of such metals as gold and copper and zirconium which lie almost untouched. . . . Aluminium is also to be produced in Australia, where bauxite is available.

A. L. MILNE, in the *British Australian, New Zealand and Pacific Weekly*

[4]See note to No. 278.

296. Around Port Phillip Bay

Situated in Corio Bay, quite a sizable inlet within the great
sixty-five-mile-wide Port Phillip Bay, Geelong is the leading
provincial city of Victoria, second only to the capital, Melbourne.
It has grown rapidly during the last fifty years, introducing
industries and doubling its population so that today its people
number nearly 100,000.[5]
Among the various industrial enterprises there are both BP
and Shell Oil Refineries, a Ford chassis factory and a Pilkington's
glass works. All the works are housed in giant modern buildings
on the city's outskirts.... The streets of Geelong itself,
however, show no signs of its industrial activities. They are
clean and wide ... flanked by both giant stores and smaller
shops. . . .
Geelong is an important seaport for the products of the
western plains of Victoria. Cargo ships constantly put into
harbour to deliver goods and load up. Wheat is the chief export,
a good proportion of it going to China, and on the quayside
are great chutes which feed the ships with grain. And in the
distance across the bay there are enormous storage silos.
Geelong is fast becoming a tourist centre, too. Lawns and
gardens flank the roads by the sea-front. There is a swimming
pool in the bay—a special pool this. Sharks in the open sea
are only too eager to bite off human arms and legs whenever
possible, and so the pool is finely netted all round the edge to
protect bathers—a very necessary precaution.... Beyond the
road inland, there are vast stretches of agricultural and grazing
lands, together with grey-green clumps of tall gum trees, and in
the far distance the range of hills known as the You Yangs.

A. L. LAISHLEY, in the *Yorkshire Post,* Leeds

297. By Rail to the Heart of Australia

The starting point from the south is Port Augusta, the junction
on the east-west transcontinental railway. From Port Augusta the
Central Australia Express leaves for Alice Springs, whence the
motor highway runs to Birdum, the railhead for Pine Creek and
Darwin.
Our little train was quite comfortable and had a good dining

[5] In 1966 almost 105,000.

car. It was already late in the afternoon when we started towards the north. Dairy cattle in small paddocks told of the richness of this southern earth. But the small paddocks soon gave way to larger paddocks and the cows were succeeded by sheep. It's very pleasant the whole first day; green grass and canary yellow wattle trees all over. Towards the end of the day the yellow increases. The wattle trees climb in large groups uphill; you see nothing but an orgy in ochre ... until the night kills any living colour under the skies.

At Marree the country was dead. Marree is the terminus of several beef highways, stock routes where the cattle from the semi-arid inland gather to catch a train for the abattoirs of Adelaide. Three black drovers who brought stock from Queensland to Marree a few days before were the first Black-fellows I had seen. At Marree you see nothing but desolate gibber plains. The face of the bleak soil is covered with small and great shiny red-brown lumps polished by wind-blown sand.... I was surprised to learn that this desolate country between Marree and Oodnadatta was taken up at all.... But this is hopeless land for now and for ever. The rainfall is five inches or less a year and irrigation is impossible.

Crossing into Central Australia we travelled through some-what better land. It was pretty to the eye, anyway. The sandy soil was attractive, varying in colour from pink to terracotta. The red sand looked wet and fresh as if after yesterday's rain, though it had not rained for months and may not rain for years— perhaps. The soil owes its wet appearance to the large quantity of salt it contains.

Enormous pin-cushions of the platinum-blonde bull spinifex grow in little silvery islands on the terracotta plain. They help to bind the sand drifts.... Also in little round colonies we see the opulent Parakelia. This violet-blossoming desert water reser-voir is a highly nutritious herbage and so succulent that stock do not require water when feeding on it....

Nearing the Macdonnell Ranges, more trees appear. But I miss the animals.... In the late afternoon of the third day a tobacco-brown, flat-roofed mountain chain blocked the plains from the north, and we rushed through a narrow gap in the Ranges into the balmy valley of the Alice, where the warm sun shines constantly, summer and winter, from the cloudless sky.

EDGAR LAYTHA, in *Walkabout*, Melbourne

298. Underground Water in Central Australia

(*a*) The stocking of cattle in central and western Queensland, where the rivers are bone-dry for most of the year, is only possible by reason of the under-ground water supply known as the Great Artesian Basin. This vast basin covers an area of over 600,000 square miles. Of Australia's three million square miles of territory close on one million is artesian water-bearing. A bore in north-west Australia only 300 feet deep produced a flow of nearly three million gallons a day.

We find Australia, by CHARLES H. HOLMES

(*b*) On the western side of Lake Eyre, and extending as far as some miles north of Oodnadatta, the country is dotted over with what, from their usual form, are called mound springs. They vary much in size, from little heaps to great rounded mounds which may be as much as fifty feet in height. Each one has a stream of water, bubbling up into a pool on its summit, which may be cool or warm or even hot, according to the depth from which it rises. The temperature of the water in springs quite close to one another will often vary to a large extent.

Across Australia, by B. SPENCER and F. J. GILLEN

299. Areas of Unpredictable Rainfall

(*a*) The rainfall in Central Australia occurs at rare and irregular intervals, generally in the warmer months, and is often associated with thunderstorms. I have started out, under apparently normal weather conditions, in the arid regions east of Lake Torrens—where not a drop of rain has fallen for nearly a year—and within half an hour I have been driven back by a tremendous rainstorm which flooded all the creeks and covered the whole district with a sheet of water.

Australia, by GRIFFITH TAYLOR

(*b*) Many of the rivers of Western Australia are dry beds most of the year, with a decent-sized pool or two; but when the rains come.... I was in the car once, coming this way home, and just as I got to the bank she started to flow. Only a trickle. I thought I'd risk it. The bed is half a mile across, but she nearly got me. That night she was running a banker, with sheep, trees— oh, anything like—coming down, and the water a mile wide.

Cobbers, by THOMAS WOOD

300. Western Australia

Perth normally contains a disproportionate share of the State population. Just now[6] something like seventy-five per cent of the people of an area equalling half Europe are concentrated within a square mile or two. Thus is emphasised not only the attraction of Perth but also the vast emptiness of Western Australia, whose total population has just reached 500,000.[7]

Much of the region will never be peopled, for inland the desert stretches its enormous distances, bare and brown and uninviting, with only the rich rewards of such mineral resources as the gold fields of Kalgoorlie to stimulate settlement.

But a great deal of Western Australia is far from desert. The coastal lands at least can offer almost everything the determined adventurer could demand. Adequately cultivated and irrigated, the sandy soil will grow almost anything, and water by rainfall or from underground stores is available, while cultivation is a matter of harrowing rather than deep ploughing.

Natural resources are considerable. In the south-west the giant forests of Jarrah and Karri provide hardwoods unrivalled in the world. Wheatlands, sheeplands and mixed farms fill the temperate regions from the sea coast for 100 miles inland, and in the north the sub-tropical vegetation and mineral wealth send out their call to settlers.

This is not immigration propaganda.... I speak only as a traveller who is beneath a spell of fascination for a lovely land with a charming people.

Yorkshire Post, Leeds

301. Australia's Market Garden

The people of Tasmania are friendly folk. It is, of course,

[6]This temporary concentration was due to a Royal Visit.
[7]In 1968, Western Australia was estimated to have 930,756 people, Perth and Fremantle accounting for 600,000 of these.

partly their business to be friendly, for the tourist traffic is a major industry. Tasmania has mountains to be climbed (mainly by motor-coach, for he is an eccentric Australian who walks for pleasure), rivers to be fished and harbours to be sailed. . . . Once we asked if there happened to be any Yorkshiremen in the neighbourhood.

"No," came the studied reply. "Drought and rabbits are the main troubles round here."

Tasmania has more than tourists for its trade. It is Australia's market-garden, supplying the mainland with most of its potatoes and a good many of its strawberries, raspberries and apples. There are dairy pastures and fields of hay.

Hobart's glory is the harbour made by the estuary of the River Derwent—a harbour dwarfing Sydney's harbour to the stature of a creek, a harbour where the greatest ships of the world can tie up alongside the Ocean Pier and wherein the fleets of the world could not only be accommodated but very nearly carry out manoeuvres as well. . . .

Hobart as a city is unimpressive; Hobart has a setting unforgettable. The buildings are nothing, but the mountains and the waters are magnificent.

Yorkshire Post, Leeds

302. Western Tasmania and its Minerals

Tasmania's chief mineral-bearing country occupies nearly two-thirds of the island, and includes practically the whole of the south-west, the west coast and the north-east. For a large part it is clothed with dense forests, and in the west and south-west the land is very mountainous, the gullies being filled with rain-forest trees while the ground is covered with great ferns and tangled scrub. In places there are few tracks, and the miner or wandering prospector is compelled to carry all his food and essential supplies on his back. There are no pack-horses. Frequently he is forced to slash his path through the vegetation. There are streams to be forded and hills to be climbed, with dense scrub on the lower slopes and stark gleaming quartzite rock above; and even high on the ranges marshy bogs make his way one of great discomfort and labour.

This is the type of country which has yielded gold, silver,

copper, tin and other precious metals, a country that personi-
fies all that is inhospitable. Osmiridium was found in commercial quantities in 1925, in a remote district of the central
south. The little valley is hedged about by mountains, and
through it run two rivers, one named Adam, the other Eve.
A village of small rude slab-hewn huts and tents, where the
miners and their families live, sprawls untidily along the edge
of the streams and the green darkness of the forest.... The
miners christened the village Adamsfield; and close by runs the
Adam river, the waters of which have helped to unearth the
field's richest treasures.

M. S. R. SHARLAND, in *Walkabout*, Melbourne

303. Life in New Zealand

Many people in New Zealand live in isolated places, up among
the hills, in dim green forests, or on the long, lonely stretches
of rocky shores. This does not mean that it is a primitive
country: there are the four modern cities[8] besides other large
centres where the population gathers together and lives in
much the same way as in other parts of the world, hurrying
in cars and buses to a variety of activities.

But New Zealand is regarded, quite rightly, as an agricultural
country. Do we not receive from her large supplies of lamb
and mutton, butter and cheese, and wool? It is a land of wide
spaces, and many families spend their lives far away from the
rush and bustle of modern life, too far away to benefit by the
many advantages which in the cities are taken for granted.
Often large families grow up without the possibility of going to
school even by the school buses which make long rounds each
day to collect children from outlying places. The government
education department provides for such children by sending
correspondence courses; they are required to carry out their
lessons as regularly as if they were in an ordinary school.

E. A. DOWNS, in the *British Missionary*

[8]Auckland, Christchurch, Wellington (the capital), Dunedin.

304. Kauri Gum

Dairy farming is bringing a stable population and a settled appearance to some of the desolate, lonely scrub-land of the far north of New Zealand, but there are still thousands of acres up there where the only sign that men have passed that way is the pitting and scarring left by hordes of itinerant com- munities who came as diggers when Kauri gum was an im- portant New Zealand export. The gum is now not in sufficient quantities for the industry ever to become important again, but gum is fetching a good price at present, and those few men who have a taste for the unconventional existence of the gum-digger are making good money.

It sometimes happens that a man travelling in the seemingly empty, silent country of the far northern gum-fields comes surprisingly upon the sudden staccato sound of an oil engine, apparently secreted somewhere in the scrub or out of sight in the bed of a gully. It is the sound of one of New Zealand's strangest industries—gum washing, i.e. washing gum out of the surface soil of old Kauri forests.

Walkabout, Melbourne

305. The Rotorua Thermal Region

(*a*) In this region is a hole several feet across, with its lip almost touching the path, and it is filled nearly to the brim with boiling mud. A dirty brown in colour, it heaves and surges, and vast bubbles rise up in it to burst with the loud plopping sounds we heard. The mud exactly resembles cooking por- ridge. I went out to the Maori village, which lies on the shores of the lake on the other side of Rotorua. This is quite a large village where, at each street corner, is the communal cooking- place, which is a steaming hole in which have been placed large stones. I have never seen so much steam as in that village. Everything steamed: the lakeside, the small stream, pools, paths, walls and even grass plots; but no one took any notice.

In Asia's Arms, by s. e. g. PONDER

(*b*) In one place there is a lake upon which pennies and stones will float. There are multi-coloured trout in the cold pools, and about the edge of the hot pools there are ferns and flowers, oblivious of the gases which rise from the boiling mud and water. You may find valleys in which the cliffs are made of alum and brilliant yellow sulphur, and plateaux where the earth hisses under your feet. There are places where you may sit on the ground, catch a fish from a stream on one side of you, and, swinging your line over, cook it in a hot pool on the other side.

The New Zealanders, by H. BOLITHO

(c) When a pound of soap is inserted in the Lady Knox Geyser, it plays a stream of superheated water 70 feet into the air, and continues playing for about an hour. It is soaped at 10 A.M. daily. This beautiful geyser is notable for the fact that it never performs without soaping and never fails to perform when soaped. It is believed that many of the geysers now extinct have failed through excessive soaping, and that is why the Lady Knox is asked to perform only once daily.

Touring in New Zealand, by A. J. HARROP

306. Ruapehu: A Young Volcano

Mt Ruapehu, in the North Island of New Zealand, is a comparatively young volcano.[9] After one or two earlier ejections of mud and water, real activity began in 1945, when dense smoke and steam were emitted, with showers of ash and jets of flame. This rose to a crescendo in six months, and there has been a low grumbling ever since. At one point the crater held a big lake, and although the mountain is usually coated with snow, the water at one side of the lake or the other was warm enough to steam. Yet on one occasion it was frozen over.

Ruapehu might break out again with great violence, but so far it has only been a nuisance. Its volcanic ash and dust drifted with the wind and caused vegetable gardeners annoyance when crisp lettuces were spoilt by a thin powdering, whilst housewives were vexed as washing hung out to dry absorbed a grey film of ash.

Shell Magazine

[9] 9,175 feet high.

307. Windy Wellington, N.Z.

Outside Wellington[10] we drove up the Rimitakas, a little more than 1,800 feet above sea level, and as we curved into a kind of bay at this height we were warned "CAUTION", and underneath this arresting word appeared in large letters "BE-WARE OF THE WIND".

Here the wind slapped against the side of the car, making it shudder. There seemed to be a funnel there, caused by a depression. A palisade of wood was built across where we had to take a bend over it, to prevent the wind getting underneath cars. We peeped over and looked down to a beautiful fertile valley and to a town down in the colourful haze, looking calm and peaceful. It might have been the Valley of Jordan and this the Hill of Temptation. The wind screamed and came in great gusts that nearly blew us off our feet, and tore my scarf from my clenched hand. HASTE! SPEED! said the wind. "BE-WARE OF THE WIND" warn the signs, both coming and going, on this high curve of the rugged Rimitakas.

Walkabout, Melbourne

308. The Kiwi

Suddenly from the thickest clump of ferns ran a brown shape, about the size of a fowl, and looking like a ball of feathers rounded at the back, where usually birds display a tail. The long slender beak sniffed at the ground as the kiwi searched for his evening meal. He crossed the open space, and then a second bird, larger and lighter in colour, emerged from the undergrowth and, with a plaintive piping note, followed her mate into the deepest shadows of the bush. Such was my first glimpse of the kiwi in his native haunt. New Zealand has no stranger bird alive today, a queer survival from dim far-distant days when moas, taller than elephants, might be seen stalking abroad.

The kiwi is an anomaly. Its head seems borrowed from the long-billed waders, its legs from the domestic fowl, and its

[10]Wellington is a city and seaport of about 300,000 people, with a university and iron foundries, and manufactures of soap, candles and footwear.

wings, tiny as they are, from flightless birds, such as the emu and cassowary. Shy and retiring by nature, defenceless against its enemies, the kiwi is slowly disappearing from localities where once it flourished. Its home is in the most secluded parts of the bush, which as the tides of civilization sweep relentlessly on, is steadily decreased, until finally it is no more. . . .

Four or five species of kiwi inhabit New Zealand, but the brown kiwi is the only one found in the North Island. . . . This differs from the other species in that at first sight he appears to have stiff hairs or bristles, because his feathers are harsh to the touch and unlike the soft feathers of the greyish-brown kiwi of the South Island. . . . Once on the west coast of Otago a beautiful and very rare specimen of an albino kiwi was seen, the plumage being snow-white, with the tips of the feathers a faint yellowish tint.

LILIAN B. TOMLINSON, in *Chambers's Journal*, Edinburgh

309. The Maoris

The Maoris are a fine race. The men are of medium height, broad, strong, and well-proportioned. Their skin is a light brown in colour, and their hair is usually dark brown or black, and straight or wavy. In feature they are remarkably like Europeans. The native dress consists of a kilt known as the piu piu. The men wear them from the waist down to the knee, the women wear a bodice attached and held by shoulder straps, and the skirt reaches to a little above the ankle. These kilts are made from the leaves of the flax. A Maori village consists of a collection of small huts dotted about irregularly. These are built of wood or reeds, and are oblong in shape with overhanging eaves. Usually there is one door and one window. Most of them are beautifully carved, especially at the edges of the roof in front. Whenever possible native villages are built near hot pools, which are utilized for cooking and washing purposes.

New Zealand, by ELLEN ROBERTS

310. The Maori Renaissance

Last century, it was believed that the Maoris would die out, exhausted and defeated after the long wars against the white invaders. In our time, the Maori population has increased so much that the natives now number one in twenty of the entire population of the Dominion.[11] The Maori renaissance is at hand.

New Zealand was the last place in the world to be inhabited by man. Isolated in thundering seas, the long lonely islands were first discovered by Polynesian sailors who navigated their open canoes across a vast uncharted ocean centuries before the Vikings had ventured from home. The Pacific is the size of the moon, while hardly a horizon separates Norway from Britain. The enterprise of the ancestors of the Maoris is commemorated in the annual gathering or "marae"....

There is no colour-bar in New Zealand. Maori university graduates, professional men and musicians are too numerous to excite comment. There is no public feeling against mixed marriages.... Maoris are distinguishing themselves in the most complex phases of modern city life, and white poets and writers in New Zealand are beginning to look to their own land and people for inspiration instead of to England.

Amongst both peoples, there is an abundance of goodwill. The Maori, after a century—his Dark Age—of suffering and purgation, has earned the right to fair treatment. The Maori renaissance may yet reveal a people as entertaining and cultured as those who first dared to sail from mythical Hawaiki to the last and loveliest of the remote places of the earth.

DARRY MCCARTHY, in *Chambers's Journal*, Edinburgh

311. The Canterbury District of South Island

(*a*) New Zealand lives primarily on her grass. Soil and climate together produce wonderful pasture.... Run out 30 to 40 miles from most cities and you will find monster hills inhabited by sheep and cattle alone. New Zealand meat is generally known in London as Canterbury Lamb. This is because the farmers of Canterbury, the South Island provincial

---

[11]In 1966 the Maoris were 7.5 per cent of the total, and the proportion is still increasing.

R

district of which Christchurch is the centre,[12] for many years held pride of place among the meat producers of New Zealand.

New Zealand from Within, by DONALD COWIE

(*b*) Christchurch, the capital of Canterbury, is a beautiful city, set in the great Canterbury Plains, looking west to the panorama of the Southern Alps and south to the Cashmere Hills. The streets are laid out at right angles to each other, but any suggestion of monotony is avoided by the windings of the River Avon which flows placidly through the city. Christchurch owes the excellence of its lay-out to the fact that it was founded by the Canterbury Association according to the principles of systematic colonization.

Touring in New Zealand, by A. J. HARROP

312.   The Southern Alps and the "Sounds"

That sublime range of mountains, the Southern Alps, runs for over 300 miles westward through the South Island of New Zealand, dominating with their superb ice-peaks and snow-domes the great Canterbury plains, whose mighty and swift rivers are fed at their glaciers, and whose blue ice-lakes are nursed in their arms, their dazzling summits silver and purple and blue, their lower ranges densely clothed with forest and fringed with flowers....

Mount Cook, or Aorangi, is the highest of a magnificent group of peaks and sierras, "a glorious galaxy of snowy heights". ... To right and left, above and below, a stainless paradise of glittering beauty; and below the slopes, where the avalanches fall from the upper icefields, in a valley rich with mountain flora, is the Hooker River, one of those white, turbulent, foaming mountain streams that have their origins in the glaciers.... Proceeding down the lower Hooker Valley, a magnificent view of the Tasman Glacier is seen, the most famous glacier of the Southern Alps....

Numerous ice-cascades descend into the Tasman Valley from its neighbouring glaciers and glittering domes. The

[12]Christchurch has large exports of lamb, wool, and grain, and has varied industries. It is expanding its port facilities.

Hochstetter Ice-Fall of the Tasman Glacier has been described as a Niagara of frozen ice, a mile wide, falling 4,000 feet in waves of milky whiteness, plunging down a rugged mountain-side of more than 12,000 feet in height, a many-coloured, downward-rolling, frozen cataract. . . .

That wild and but half-explored vastness of magnificent mountains and deep fjords, known as the West Coast Sounds of New Zealand, is beyond description—an unpeopled wilderness of countless snow-domes and primeval forests whose silence of ages is scarce broken save by the echoes of falling fountains, the thunder of mighty waterfalls in majestic leap from the snow-capped towers, or by the foaming cascades dancing to swift snow rivers that roar their way through deep canyons to the Pacific Sea.

The crowning-point of this wonder-cruise is Milford Sound. It is the last of the fjords that, thirteen in number, stretch for hundreds of miles from mere beauty to a grandeur which culminates at this point. Bounded by gigantic granite cliffs that rise 5,000 feet sheer out of the water and dip a thousand feet beneath, Milford has been robbed of the glacial austerity of its origin by the wealth of the forests that climb over its shoulders and touch the snows. Seven miles from Milford are the Sutherland Falls. But the overland route to the falls from the head of Lake Te Anau, through thirty miles of scenery of the wildest and most beautiful description, is more popular. The way through inland Fjordland is for some distance beside the Clinton River, which cuts through the great valley-canyon mid scenes of gorgeous colouring. . . . In this scenic paradise of snow-capped peak and fairyland forest and stream, the Sutherland Fall bounds down its 1,900 feet in three great leaps . . . but it is in reality one fall, not a series of cascades.

Wonders of the World (Odhams Press)

North America, Central America and the West Indies

313. Alaska

A large portion of Alaska lies in the same latitude as Sweden, Norway and Finland; it has a much better climate, more fertile soil, and is larger than all three of these countries combined. ... Provided there is no haze, the Siberian coast may be seen from Cape Prince of Wales, Seward Peninsula, Alaska, with a strong glass. The distance between the two countries is about seventy-five miles.... Many portions of Alaska have never been trodden by the foot of a white man. The development of its resources is hardly yet begun, nor have all its possibilities been discovered....

Beneath the compact mass of timber seen from the ship grows a still denser mass of bushes, vines and berry plants of every description, and an underbrush that is strongly suggestive of the tropics. Moss, lichens, ferns, and millions of dainty white flowers are everywhere. The air along the coast is saturated with moisture from the Japan Current, and this vaporous atmosphere, combined with the vast amount of strong sunlight that prevails in the north during the summer, makes the vegetable and plant life grow quickly and with a luxuriance almost beyond belief....

Resting in the shadow of a dark frowning mountain lies Juneau, the present capital of Alaska. In the summer evening mists, Juneau looks like a Swiss village, on the shores of a lake. It has good hotels, and any number of thriving stores, at many of which hammered copper and silverware, baskets, furs, and other Alaskan products are offered for sale.

Alaska, by J. J. UNDERWOOD

Note. Alaska is now a state of the U.S.A. Gold, silver, oil, natural gas, etc. are worked.

314. The Volcanoes of Alaska

We were approaching the great crater glacier of Veniaminof, the second in size to Aniakchak, which is the world's largest active volcano. The last major eruption of the huge twenty-one-mile-round crater of Aniakchak was in 1931. It blew a three-mile hole out of the floor, raised lava ridges, opened huge steam vents, sending flames 7,000 feet into the air, and for twenty-five days rained ashes over hundreds of miles of surrounding country. The great Alaskan volcanic eruptions do not get world-wide publicity because they are not attended with loss of life. No one lives close enough to Alaskan volcanoes to get killed.

Cradle of the Storms, by BERNARD HUBBARD

Note. There was a severe earthquake in March 1964.

315. The Kicking Horse

The white shoulder of Mount Victoria's northern peak is grandly visible above the creek; right in front towers the north-eastern spur of the Cathedral Massif (whose topmost pinnacles were in full view on the Divide), and at the base of these splendid ramparts a deep, sombre chasm opens beyond the outlet of the lake. This is the famous Canyon of the Kicking Horse, and its passage on foot should be one of the most sacred duties of every visitor who enjoys majestic scenery. Ample time is thus given to appreciate the exquisite views that render every step of the way delightful, and though the train goes very slowly, occupying forty-five minutes for the seven miles, the artistic and nature-loving heart is always crying out for time to stop and revel in the grandeur of the succession of new and peerless visions. . . . Filling the narrow valley is a dense sea of spruce and pine woods, which struggle painfully up the lower slopes, dwindling and scattering as they find the rigours of the ascent too great for them. . . .

The engineering is of surpassing interest in itself. In the ascent three or four locomotives are usually employed, one being necessary for every three cars on the train; and even then it is a strenuous climb, spasmodic puffs and the futile whirls of wheels that cannot grip being by no means an infrequent variation from the steady powerful pant and throb of the giant engines.

In the Heart of the Canadian Rockies, by SIR JAMES OUTRAM

316. British Columbia: Rossland and Trail

I had two towns to visit: Trail, in the valley, and Rossland, 2,000 feet up the mountain side. Trail was packed into two streets, half a mile long, with five or six cross streets of about a quarter of a mile. That, with the Columbia River and a small fringe of town on the other side of it, was about all that could be squeezed into the valley. The mountains rose up all around it in precipitous humps. The original mining town was Rossland, now little more than a residential suburb of Trail. In the old days, before the railroad, gold had been discovered up there. The gold rush that followed gave Rossland a population of 20,000, living mostly in tents and huts. Trail was merely the point where the gold seekers landed, after a long voyage up the Columbia River, and took the trail up the mountains to the mines. Hence the name "Trail". With the exhaustion of the gold, Rossland had dwindled. But Trail had grown into a commercial centre, and had continued to prosper. Nowadays its huge smelting plant is its livelihood.[1] It handles all the ore from the mines round about, producing lead, zinc and silver.

A Cockney on Main Street, by HERBERT HODGE

317. Vancouver: Entertainment Capital

Vancouverites are very proud of the magnificent natural setting of their city. From the ski slopes of the North Shore mountains, across a huge natural harbour, to the rich farmland of the Fraser Valley, nature couldn't have done a better job. Some visitors feel we get a bit smug about our good fortune, but it is difficult to deny what so many people tell us: Vancouver is a beautiful city....

Anyone coming here will notice that Vancouver is a leisurely place. People don't stride along the sidewalks, they stroll. The motorist, even if he may get somewhat impatient, gives way to

[1] It is the largest in the British Commonwealth.

the pedestrian, jaywalking or not.... In fact we're so leisurely that people say we work a lot harder at our leisure than we do at our job. And I believe they're right. Those of us who came to Vancouver to live did so because there is so much to do here and so much longer to do it.

The golfer in the prairies has to put his clubs away in the winter. But in Vancouver golf can be played all year round. ... Meanwhile there are hundreds of boats out on the waters of the harbour and nearby fjords. Pacific salmon abound, and with so many boats you would expect it to be hard to catch them. But nearly everyone seems to catch salmon here and there is no need for contrived fish stories. There are also yacht races and dinghy sailing besides cruising. The islands off the coast offer plenty of shelter and delightful anchorages for the week-end sailor.

MIKE TYTHERLEIGH, in *Beautiful British Columbia,*
Victoria, B.C.

318. The Trees of the Western Mountains

The trees sometimes have a diameter of a dozen feet. The cedars, in particular, reach a vast girth, and in the valley was one with a circumference at the ground of sixty-three feet, and nearby was another that had a gothic arch cut through it affording easy passage for a person on horseback. Two hundred feet is a very moderate height, and some shoot up to above 300. The fall of one of these monsters, when the woodsmen have cut through its base, is something appalling. As the tree begins to give, the sawyers seek a safe distance. The creaking and snapping increase, and the tree sways slowly at first, but soon with tremendous rapidity, and crashes down through the forest to the earth. There is a flying of bark and broken branches, and the air is filled with slow-settling dust. The men climb on the prostrate giant and walk along the broad pathway of the trunk to see how it lies. What pigmies they seem amid the mighty trees around! Yet their persistency and ingenuity are irresistible, and the woodland is doomed.

Highways and Byways of the Pacific Coast, by
CLIFTON JOHNSON

319. The Snake River Basin

The Columbia Plateau, covered with enormous black lava sheets, 4,000 feet thick, extends over most of Idaho, Washington and Oregon. It has been dissected into tremendous canyons by the Snake River and its tributaries. The lava sheets have been pushed up the valleys, and the peaks rise above their surface like islands in a solid black sea.

The World We Live In, ed. GRAEME WILLIAMS,
in a chapter by R. J. Finch

Note. Between Weiser and Lewiston parts of the gorge formed by the Snake are 7900 feet deep (deeper than the Colorado Canyon). As the river emerges from the mountains, water, held back by dams, is led into canals and then into irrigation ditches. Potatoes, sugar-beet, alfalfa, and beans are grown. Seventy per cent of Idaho's people live within twenty-five miles of the Snake river.

320. Peaches by the Bushel

It's a long way to California. There is an ocean, a mountain-range, a desert, and a vast featureless plain dividing us from it; but the migration has always led westwards into the promised land of sunshine and blue skies—never eastwards. As soon as I landed on the eastern shores of America, I felt the call of the Pacific, as thousands before me must have felt it; and the call being strong enough I eventually reached the west coast and looked down with delight upon the blue bay of San Francisco and the delicate span of the Golden Gate bridge.

Not being an immigrant, however, it wasn't enough just to be there. I had to get home again, and to do that I needed a little more money; so I looked around to see what California had to offer in the way of employment—and the obvious answer seemed to be peach-picking. . . .

Before I had picked half a dozen boxes I was filthy. The mingled bloom from the peaches and the dust from the leaves and the ground was caked finely all over my face and hair and white cotton shirt. It had infiltrated into my pockets and the rolled-up bottoms of my trousers and clung like a little fringe along each separate hair of my arms. But I was happy. The sun glowed between the leaves, and the air was deliciously warm, and the dust felt good when I stepped in it and it spurted up in little fountains between my toes. . . .

Every time I finished my allotted group of trees I shouted: "Checker", and the little man appeared. I watched him jealously as he sorted over my picking, and we exchanged a few words before he clipped my card—one clip for each box—and I was free to move on to another set. . . . I never produced more than thirty-three boxes (some of the men did as many as eighty) and never made more than five dollars in a day.

MARION J. HUME, in *Chambers's Journal*, Edinburgh

321. Southern California: Sunshine and Fogs

The southern portion of California possesses an exquisitely clear sky for about 300 days in the year. Imagine a sky, as pure as the mind can conceive, that for 300 days every year sees never a cloud to mar its spotlessness. Yet there are certain meteorological conditions in this region that produce clouds and fog which are as interesting as they are peculiar.

For 250 miles southern California lies open to the Pacific. This allows free access of the breezes from the ocean, without any of the winds that are caused when a mountain barrier, with its passes, stands between the ocean and the land. This open region varies in width from a mile or two to fifty or even 100 miles, and is then arrested by a high mountain chain with peaks six, seven, eight or as much as twelve thousand feet high. Immediately on the other side of these towering heights the mountains decline rapidly to the sands of the Mohave, Colorado, Arizona, and Sonora deserts, some portions of which are below sea-level, and all of which contain little verdure above the hardy desert shrubs, such as the creosote bush, the salt bush, the yucca, cactus, etc.

Here, then, are wonderful conditions for the manufacture of climate that scarce exist anywhere else in the world. When the sun shines upon the sandy face of the barren desert the rapid ascent of the heated air causes a gentle current slowly to flow from the ocean. . . . Then, later in the day, the current is reversed and the land breeze comes gently over the slopes of the snow-clad mountains. Under certain conditions of barometric pressure these ocean and desert breezes come laden with moisture, which changes into clouds and fog.

Wonders of the World (Odhams Press)

Note. Los Angeles lies on the coast of this region. In 1960 the population of the city was nearly 2½ millions, and of Greater Los Angeles about 7 millions.

322. The Deserts of the U.S.A.

The lowest and the highest spots in the United States are practically across the street from each other. Death Valley, 280 feet below sea-level, lies only seventy miles distant from Mount Whitney, the loftiest and most spectacular snow-crowned peak in the High Sierra. . . .

There is the flat cactus; this bears the well-known prickly pear, as well as gorgeous flowers, bright red, with their edges tinted yellow. It is on this cactus that the minute and brilliant red insect, the cochineal, flourishes. The barrel cactus contains a sweetish water which the traveller can extract in sufficient quantities to drink; candy is also made from this juice. . . . The Imperial Valley Desert will not be at all like your preconceived ideas of desert land. They do not call it a desert any more since it has yielded so bountifully to irrigation. Fresh water has made that barren district blossom like the rose, and it will not be many years before there will be no desert visible to the eye. It will all be under cultivation.[2]

Trails through the Golden West, by ROBERT FROTHINGHAM

323. The Colorado Canyon

Having now reached the edge of the Grand Canyon, I must devote a few sentences to that unique wonder of the world. This gorge of the River Colorado is most accessible at the point to which a branch railroad has been built. Here the Canyon is 6,000 feet deep and about twelve miles wide from one edge to the other of the gulf which the swift torrent has excavated, cutting its way down through successive lines of

[2]Water is brought from the Colorado river by the Imperial and All-American canals.

horizontal strata—sandstones, white, yellow and red; lime-stones, grey and blue. Wonderful are the colours of these strata, superimposed one upon the other, and they stand strongly out, for in this dry air no mosses or lichens cling to their precipitous faces. Why this deep hole in the ground should inspire more wonder and awe than the loftiest snow mountain or the grandest waterfall I will not attempt to explain, but it does. One cannot leave off gazing and wondering. One descends by a very steep and winding footpath to the river at the bottom, and ascends again, seeing all there is to see, but the spell is the same when one emerges. The vastness and the changelessness create a sense of solemn silence.

Memories of Travel, by VISCOUNT BRYCE

324. Plains East of the Rockies

The landscape of the plains is full of life, full of charm—lonely indeed, but never wearisome. Now great rolling uplands of enormous sweep, now boundless grassy plains; there is all the grandeur of monotony, and yet continual change. Sometimes the distances are broken by blue buttes or ragged bluffs. Over all there is a sparkling atmosphere and never-failing breeze; the air is bracing even when most hot; the sky is cloudless, and no rain falls. A solitude which no words can paint, and the bound-less prairie swell, convey an idea of vastness which is the over-whelming feature of the plains.

Greater Britain, by SIR CHARLES DILKE

325. The Eskimos

(*a*) THE IGLOO. The snow hut of the Eskimo resembles the upper half of a sphere, slightly flattened at the top, with a diameter at floor level of about nine feet, and a maximum height slightly below six. A low platform covered with musk-ox and caribou robes takes up more than half the floor space; it serves as a bed by night and a place for sitting and working during the day. The entrance, which faces the middle of the platform, is simply a hole at the bottom of the wall, large enough for a person to crawl through on hands and knees; a single snow-block at night makes a satisfactory door. To the

right or left of the entrance is the saucer-shaped lamp for
burning seal-blubber; the stone cooking pot hangs over it, and
over the pot is a large tray or rack where boots and mittens
are spread out to dry.

The People of the Twilight, by DIAMOND JENNESS

(*b*) MODERN CHANGES. Since he now has to trap foxes
(for the white trader) during the time when he should be
catching seals and hunting caribou for food and clothing, he
must now go to the trader to procure these necessities. This
change from an exclusive meat and fish diet to badly cooked
bread, jams, tea and canned foods, and from his own sensible
skin apparel to the imported clothing of the white man has not
been beneficial to the Eskimo, and has lowered his health and
vitality, and left him with little resistance against the contagious
diseases that always follow the advance of civilization.

from a Canadian Government Report

326. Yellowknife

This little mining town is less than 300 miles from the Arctic
Circle. It lies on a pleasant bay on the northern shore of Great
Slave Lake. The rising sun pours into my window, waking
me about two o'clock every morning. It is never really dark;
there are only two or three hours of dim twilight.

Yellowknife's only reason for existence, its livelihood and its
passion, are all in the one word "gold". A solitary traveller
found gold here in 1897; serious prospecting started in 1934.
Now there are three big mines and several smaller ones in the
neighbourhood, all good producers with prospects for years to
come.... Permanent buildings—a school, a hospital, and a
cinema—now stand on a hill above the lake where a layer of
gravel gives hope of a sewage system.

The miscellaneous boats moored round the shore are almost
outnumbered by the aeroplanes. Small "bush" 'planes are the
common carriers of the North, using pontoons in summer and
skis in winter. There is always water or ice to land on. Mining
companies keep them to visit their remote claims, charter companies run them like taxis, and Canadian Pacific Airlines use
them to carry mail and freight and passengers to outlying

camps. C.P.A. flies a comfortable modern airliner daily from Edmonton, but heavy stores and mining and construction equipment have to come overland. . . .

The daily air service provides most of the amenities. Newspapers, vegetables, eggs, and meat come in this way. For the land is not productive. When it is not frozen solid, it is a mass of rock interspersed with gravel, growing only scrub and small trees.

MARTIN ROSS, in *The Scotsman*, Edinburgh

Note. From Pine Point Mine, near the Great Slave Lake, trains of the Canadian National freight railway carry iron ore south, roughly parallel with the Mackenzie Highway.

327. Moose and Wolves in Canada

The moose, the largest living member of the deer family, ranges over the whole forest country of Canada and Alaska. A big Alaskan bull-moose will stand well over seven feet at the shoulder, while his huge palmated antlers commonly have a span of six feet. Wolves are common in all parts of the North except in the neighbourhood of the lower Mackenzie River, where big game is scarce. All over the mountainous districts they follow the caribou herds, pulling down the stragglers. A timber wolf is undoubtedly the most formidable animal, but I am absolutely convinced that under no conditions, save those of absolute famine and self-defence, will wolves attack a human being. While hunting alone I have been followed by wolves, day after day; I believe it was partly curiosity and partly the hope of sharing the kill. I was sleeping in open camps night after night and allowed the fire to die down while I slept, but the wolves never approached nearer than fifty yards.

The Arctic Forests, by MICHAEL H. MASON

328. Prairie Wheat

(*a*) The wheat fields of the boundless prairies that send their supplies to the loading platforms and the elevators of various kinds, are among the most desirable sites in Canada, whether in the season when whole batteries of tractors break the rich soil of the farm, or when, months later, the wind sweeps over the fields, billowing the stalks until they look like a vast green sea, or when the harvest fields are alive with the men whom the railroads have brought from city and country in the east.

Seeing Canada, by J. T. FARIS

(*b*)   The agricultural barometer indicates the state of the city's business as accurately as it does that of the farm. As the time for harvest approaches the banker watches the weather as anxiously as the farmer. Railway companies and financial institutions send out an army of experts to keep them supplied with crop reports and estimates of the probable yield. Almost every business move depends on these reports. Let an adverse rumour appear and a spirit of retrenchment or economy permeates the air. But let a bumper crop be announced and everybody smiles. Railroads rush in empty cars on every siding in readiness to receive the golden grain, bankers work overtime changing money, and business everywhere booms. Implement dealers relax their anxious vigils, while the piano agent gets his opportunity to make a record sale.

The Province of Saskatchewan, by F. H. KITTO

329   "Prairie Cathedrals"

Gray, Saskatchewan, is a typical prairie village dominated by its grain elevators. It's about thirty miles south of Regina on a rich strip of dark soil that they call "gumbo". For fifteen or sixteen hours a day the farmers rode their combines round the fields. With the help of a hired man, or a stalwart son, each farmer harvested his half or his whole section—640 acres to a section.

Some of the grain was stored in their own barns. More went to the elevators on the first stage of its journey to your breakfast table. There are four elevators in Gray to serve the surrounding farms. Three are owned by private companies and the fourth by the Saskatchewan Wheat Pool, or farmers' co-operative. They stand alongside the single railway track that leads in a bee-line from Regina to the U.S.—through North Dakota to Minneapolis and eventually Chicago.

The "pool" elevator is the biggest at Gray, and its manager, Bert Crookes, is very proud of it. Bert is getting on in years and he can't tackle the heavy work like he used to. But it takes skill and knowledge to run an elevator and Bert has got that. His little giant stands 125 feet high and holds 30,000 bushels of wheat, divided into a couple of dozen bins (for the different grades).

These great wooden towers are the distinctive architecture of the mid-continental plain all the way from Hudson Bay to the Gulf of Mexico. They were well nicknamed "prairie cathedrals". They are the only landmarks for hundreds of miles and they dot the flat wheatlands wherever there is a railway track.

MICHAEL BARKWAY, in the *News Chronicle*

330. The Land of the Rancher

Always the sun seems to shine in this fair land that stretches 700 miles from the Arctic regions to the edge of the United States, and extends from 300 to 400 miles from Saskatchewan to the crest of the proud Rockies. This rolling land is well supplied with water by its rivers and lakes. Much of the land is arable, and much is covered with luxuriant grasses and merchantable timber. We are in the land of the rancher. About two million cattle, horses and sheep graze on the rich grasses of the prairie. The visitor who happens to be near a ranch toward the end of May will find a "round up" on the plains a most interesting sight. Parties of cowboys with boots and spurs, and the familiar slouch hat, can be observed in the distance scouting and driving in the cattle to the corral for branding and re-sorting, after which the cattle are sent to a market, or handed over to their respective owners, or turned loose on the plains again, as the case may be.

Things Seen in Canada, by J. E. RAY

331. Across Canada by Rail

Villages, towns and cities followed close upon the heels of the constructors of the railway. The forests were cleared away; the soil of the prairie was turned over; mines were opened; and even before the last rail was in its place, the completed sections were carrying on a large and profitable trade. . . .

The country from Montreal to, say, fifty miles eastward of Winnipeg, is very pretty, richly wooded, moderately hilly, and frequently interspersed with beautiful lakelets and rivers. From the fifty-mile point onward to Calgary, a distance of about 900 miles, the line runs through prairie land, with only a few good-sized trees to enliven the view. From Calgary, the scene changes rapidly as the Rockies, now very prominently in sight, are swiftly approached, but when their portal is passed, a completely new world is opened out. A world of splendour, and beauty, and rugged grandeur, and snowy peaks, and beautiful rivers, and awe-inspiring canyons, and ultimately, lovely plains fringed with receding mountains, until Vancouver is reached.

3,800 *Miles across Canada*, by J. W. C. HALDANE

332.   Across Canada on Horseback

The ride is over, but these are my possessions. Wherever I go from here these will go with me. Always for me there will be mountains running down to the Pacific, great trees and tiny trails and deer, and packers lighting fires and pitching tents. ... There will be rain and sun in the foothills, rivers and ranches, great fantastic western saddles on little lean bronchos, steers bucking at stampedes, ten-gallon hats and high-heeled boots and close-fitting overalls on bandy legs, horses milling in high corrals and little ranch-houses filling with unexpected guests. After that, sunset over the wheatfields and Northern Lights arching up the sky, and straight sandy roads which go on almost for ever, and elevators and cottonwood trees and the rare delight of river valleys.

Then Winnipeg and the wilderness beyond, and tameracks burning gold out of the blue swamps, naked rocks and lonely lakes shivering in the wind. Then the vast expanse of Lake Superior, and so winter on the farm—lamplight in the early morning kitchen—milking time in misty barns—teams labouring out of the bush—spring and syrup-boiling under budding maples, daisied hay standing high, and a boat floating down a river on the trail of a timber drive.... And always through everything the horses with me, tireless and kind, giving me their unbroken trust.

Remembering Canada, I remember, too, the majesty of Vancouver, standing between the mountains and the sea, Calgary and Winnipeg on the borders of the Prairies, Ottawa and the Parliament Houses standing upon their hill, and Montreal grouped round its royal mountain.

But when seas divide me from her, Canada will live for me, not in the memory of her cities, but of hip-roofed barns and snake fences and stout corrals, of the dark flash of a red-winged blackbird and the snort of a little branded bronco, of mountains and wheatfields and the wilderness. The soul of Canada is not in her cities.

For the soul of the world has fled from cities. And if it is ever to inhabit them again it is from mountains and wheat-fields and the sea that it must return.

Canada Ride, by MARY BOSANQUET

333. The River St Lawrence

In Cartier's time the St Lawrence flowed through thick forests. To-day most of them have been cleared. In some places it flows through cultivated land which extends right to the edge of the water; in other places, as at Quebec, it is in a cleft bounded by steeply rising rocky banks. In some stretches it is bordered by small villages with high-spired churches, at others by apple orchards and maple woods or pine forests, and at others it passes extensive modern factories. It is crossed by many fine bridges. One of them, the Victoria Jubilee Bridge at Montreal, is a mile and a quarter long and so wide that it has separate tracks for trains, trolley-buses, road vehicles and pedestrians.... For the greater part of its course it is a very broad river, capable of taking ocean-going liners to Montreal, a thousand miles from its mouth, and reaching a width of about ninety miles near the Gulf of St Lawrence....

The construction of canals has overcome such obstacles as cataracts and rapids, but the St Lawrence has a still greater drawback—every winter it freezes as far downstream as Quebec, about 150 miles from its mouth. This means that Montreal is usable as a port for only seven months of the year. However, the importance of the river has been emphasized by an agreement between the Governments of Canada and the U.S.A. (the St Lawrence is the boundary between the State of New York

s

and the Province of Ontario) which provides for the spending of £70,000,000 to improve it as a waterway to the Atlantic
Ocean.[3]

Vol. III of the *Oxford Junior Encyclopaedia*,
ed. LAURA E. SALT and GEOFFREY BOUMPHREY

334. Niagara Falls

(*a*) I was disappointed by my first view of the world-famous
falls, as seen from the train while traversing the great suspen-
sion bridge spanning the chasm; for so wide is the expanse of
this mighty cascade that its height of 154 feet seemed comparatively dwarfed. But this feeling soon faded away when we
had clambered about the islands and beautiful banks close to
the margin of the ledge over which this ceaseless avalanche of
water poured. Steaming about in the placid basin at the foot
of the falls in the little "Maid of the Mist", and looking upwards, finally banished my doubts as to whether Niagara was
an overrated wonder of Nature or not.

Some Rambles of a Sapper, by H. H. AUSTIN

(*b*) I never stirred in all that time from the Canadian side,
whither I had gone at first. I never crossed the river again; for I
knew there were people on the other shore, and in such a place
it is natural to shun strange company. To wander to and fro
all day, and see the cataracts from all points of view; to stand
upon the edge of the Great Horseshoe Fall, marking the
hurried water gathering strength as it approached the verge,
yet seeming, too, to pause before it shot into the gulf below;
to gaze from the river's level up at the torrent as it came
streaming down ... to have Niagara before me lighted by the
sun and by the moon, red in the day's decline, and grey as
evening slowly fell upon it ... this was enough.

The Uncommercial Traveller, by CHARLES DICKENS

335. The City of Quebec

(*a*) Quebec will always be remarkable for its historical associa-

---

[3]This improved waterway is now in use, and is called the St Lawrence
Seaway.

tions, and for the exquisite beauty of its scenery. On one side is the citadel in all its strength and grandeur. Immediately below, the majestic St Lawrence flows. To the north rise the bold heights of the Laurentian Range.

England and Canada, by SIR S. FLEMING

(b) Above the masts and wharves that shut out the lower town, sharp-gabled houses and the towers and spires of churches, monasteries, and public buildings, in a style for the most part quite alien to modern American civilization, and deeply suggestive of another age and another land, rise tier above tier up the steep slopes of the mighty rock to the batteries of the citadel which so fittingly crown its summit. Ranges of lofty but retiring hills surround the noble harbour, where ships of war and great liners lie side by side amid a swarm of smaller craft; while a continuous chain of leafy villages encircles the shores, and the falls of Montmorency, leaping from their wooded hills upon the extreme right, make a fitting background to one of the most inspiring tableaux in the world.

Canada in the Twentieth Century, by A. G. BRADLEY

336. Forests, Fruit, and Fun in Nova Scotia

The country is one of endless woods and forests, as far as the eye can see, and there are practically no clear spaces except those made by man. Lakes and rivers abound everywhere. The chief industry is in lumber, and New Ross turns out a large quantity of barrels for packing the apples which grow in profusion in the nearby Annapolis Valley, where the Gravenstein variety appears to be the most popular. Trucks may be seen leaving here with a load of 300 barrels on a special fitment, somewhat like the old hay-wains. There is also a very big and profitable business in supplying Christmas-trees for the American market....

The paved road from Halifax, which goes over several open railway crossings, runs for about fifty miles westward to Chester, alongside creeks and bays and inlets of the sea, so big that the open sea is not visible. Chester is very popular as a summer resort for rich Americans, who have beautiful homes there. They bring their yachts for sailing on the large and very lovely island-studded bay. The beaches of white sand and shallow water are popular for bathing. . . .

The most lasting impressions gained by one who visits Nova Scotia for any length of time are likely to be the very large families, the great kindness and help given willingly to each other in times of sickness or want, the vast extent of tree-covered hills, the abundance of game and fish, the undoubtedly enormous potential wealth in minerals and lumber, and the extreme beauty of the province as a whole.

F. G. LEVIEN, in *Chambers's Journal*, Edinburgh

337. Newfoundland Fishing

(*a*) Newfoundland, although only about the size of Ireland,[4] has a coastline of about 6,000 miles. In the past the country has depended on its well-known cod-fishery for work and wealth, and this is still, though declining, an industry of the Out-Ports. Owing to the falling-off in this industry, through movements away of fish, and the modern demand for fresh rather than salted fish, many of the Out-Port communities are poorly off, and some settlements have been abandoned and evacuated. This is particularly true of the south coast.

REV. B. P. MOHAN, in *The Bible in the World*

(*b*) I am standing close to the water's edge at Beachy Cove, about ten miles from St John's. As each wave breaks and rolls in, it carries with it countless glistening, squirming caplin, washing them right up on the beach. . . . Codfish and other species of ground fish follow the caplin, feeding on them as they move towards the shore, so that when the caplin season arrives,[5] large quantities of codfish are caught in the fisherman's traps and nets, and the dragger fleets get their share, too. Large numbers of seabirds also follow the caplin, feeding on them at will.

The caplin are from six to seven inches in length; they are silver in colour, with streaks of dark green. They have

[4]The island of Newfoundland, apart from Labrador, is somewhat larger than Ireland.
[5]About three weeks in July.

many uses. Besides attracting quantities of ground fish, they themselves make excellent fertilizer when spread on the ground; and the aroma of rotting caplin fills the country here for weeks after the season is over. Some of them are used as bait, but the most popular use is as a food delicacy.

DAVE GUNN, in *The Listener*

338. The Other England

Anyone who goes to America with the good old British prejudice that there is nothing like England is due for some pleasant shocks. No part of the world was so aptly named as New England, and I am not the first Englishman to have travelled through the lovely countryside of Massachusetts, Vermont and New Hampshire with a queer feeling of inverted homesickness. There is green, rich, altogether lovely country just north of Boston that continually reminded me of the best of England. The deep-wooded, shallow-streamed valleys of the White Mountains recalled the Valley of the Exe; the woods of Massachusetts are very like the woods of the English south country. But the real New England is probably in the villages: the white-painted eighteenth-century houses standing back from the streets behind green lawns and weeping New England elms, the lovely, severe white Unitarian churches, the village green where the band plays on summer evenings.

Apart from this placid and rather homely kind of countryside, extremely beautiful though it is, New England can offer a good deal more. The lakes with the dreamy Indian names are a sailing paradise; there is good climbing all along the Washington Range, where the mountains too are Indian-named, and in June there will still be ten or fifteen feet of snow in the famous Tuckermann Ravine.... But the best of the country is felt in its huge unspoilt expanse of natural beauty. Unlike the English countryside, very little of it is man-made. From the top of Mount Monadnock I looked down on a stretch of lake and forest that cannot have changed much in 200 years.

H. E. BATES, in *The Spectator*

339.   New York

(*a*)   Ages back, Nature cast up an island of solid rock between two rivers at a place we call New York. On that island, a city began to rise and it grew with time, and kept on growing. It could not cross the waters which bound it on either side, consequently it had to climb upward, and having rock for an impregnable base, it did so without fear of falling. Thus, out of Nature really, came the skyscraper of New York, which lends to it a dominant, and if you like, triumphant note.

Travels in Hope, by JAMES MILNE

(*b*)   The splendour and the luxury and the wealth of the East live again in this city of the West. No Oriental palace could be more fantastic than the Chrysler Building.... Caliphs as wealthy as Haroun drive about the streets. Jewels as rare as the Timur ruby are on sale in the bazaars. All the world meets in the new Baghdad. In an hour's walk you can see men of China and Japan, of Africa and the primeval jungle, of the Hebrews, of Europe and of Siberia.

A Visit to America, by A. G. MACDONELL

(*c*)   Widen old Father Thames by at least twenty miles, multiply the normal number of vessels passing up and down the river by about 10,000, and Londoners may obtain some idea of the traffic on the Hudson. Blaring sirens, screeching whistles, huge double-decker ferryboats, crammed with humanity, tearing slantways across the river from New Jersey to Manhattan and vice versa; tankers, barges, sailing ships, cattle boats, giant liners, fussy tugs; long, floating contraptions like gigantic rafts, transferring whole trains complete with engine, trucks and carriages from New York City to the mainland—these are just a few of the craft, and the scene of hustle, bustle and animation beggars description.

A Million Ocean Miles, by SIR EDGAR BRITTEN

Note. The population of New York City in 1960 was 7,782,000; that of Greater N.Y. in 1965 was 11,348,000.

340. Washington, D.C.

Over nine-million tourists a year visit Washington, District of Columbia, U.S.A. They come from many nations and must all agree that it is one of the world's most beautiful cities. This should not be surprising since it was built to order, on virgin soil, according to plans drawn up by Pierre l'Enfant. Although the original design was deserted in later stages, we still have the essential lay-out, with imposing buildings on the few natural hills, and most imaginative use being made of the water which is readily available. The scene is dominated by the gleaming marble dome of the Capitol which, although not ancient by our standards, is still older than our present Houses of Parliament. The White House, nearby, is open to the public (if one is prepared to wait for hours) and there are museums and galleries to cover every facet of knowledge and culture.

The original city clustered round this heart and consisted chiefly of solid houses, many with turrets reminiscent of the Loire Chateaux. A few remain as Society headquarters, others are adapted for multi-family occupation, while many have been torn down to make way for Apartment blocks. Ten years ago the area had gone very seriously downhill, being over-inhabited by the city's poor, who are mostly of the Negro race. Since then urban renewal has taken place, and although many Negroes still live here they are of the middle class.

PHYLLIS E. MOSSES, in *The Rostrum*, Liverpool

341. New York to St Louis by Bus

The first stage of the transcontinental run to Los Angeles is from New York to St Louis, a distance of about 1,100 miles, taking twenty-nine hours. Leaving at ten o'clock in the morning, the bus runs out through the Holland Tunnel to the suburbs, and away up the Pennsylvania Turnpike, climbing through the Appalachian Mountains to Harrisburg, old red-brick capital of Pennsylvania, with buildings darkened by age and industrial smoke, with the dome of the State Building looking green in the afternoon sun. . . . On it continues through the night to Columbus, Ohio. . . . Indianapolis is reached in the early morning in time for breakfast. The speed increases as the bus has passed out of the winding mountain-roads into the flat farmlands of Indiana. The capital has a pleasant appearance, with tree-lined streets, and factories that fit the landscape.

Beyond Indianapolis, and into more friendly farming country, where fields of Indian corn flash past in quick succession.... Through more neat farmlands to Effingham and Granite City, with tidy, well-painted wooden houses, on to East St Louis, and the Mississippi. This river is never disappointing, even when seen several times. The creamy-brown muddy waters whirl beneath the bridge leading into St Louis proper. The river is wide and deep, carrying an immense volume of silt to deposit in the delta. Even now, upon occasion, a stern-wheeler will pass along the river, to recall for a brief moment the glories of the nineteenth century....

The first view of St Louis quickly dispels any illusion about it being a "hick" Middle-West town. It is a truly modern city with public buildings and cathedrals worthy of any great capital.[6]

LEO P. AGGER, in *Chambers's Journal*, Edinburgh

342. Chicago and its Influence

Chicago, the great grey city, interested her at every instant and under every condition. As yet she was not sure that she liked it; she could not forgive its dirty streets, the unspeakable squalor of some of its poorer neighbourhoods that sometimes developed, like cancerous growths, in the very heart of fine residence districts.... But the life was tremendous. All around, on every side, in every direction, the vast machinery of Commonwealth clashed and thundered from dawn to dark, and from dark till dawn.... The blackened waters of the river, seen an instant between stanchions as the car trundled across the State Street bridge, disappeared under fleets of tugs, of lake steamers, of lumber barges from Sheboygan and Mackinac, of grain boats from Duluth ... while on all sides, blocking the horizon, towered the hump-shouldered grain elevators....

Suddenly the meaning and significance of it all dawned upon Laura. The Great Grey City, brooking no rival, imposed its dominion upon a reach of country larger than many a kingdom

[6]In 1960 it had three-quarters of a million people. By 1966 it had grown to over two millions.

of the Old World. For thousands of miles beyond its confines was its influence felt. Out, far out, far away in the snow and shadow of Northern Wisconsin forests, axes and saws bit the bark of century-old trees, stimulated by this city's energy. Just as far to the southward, pick and drill leaped to the assault of veins of anthracite, moved by her central power. Her force turned the wheels of harvester and seeder a thousand miles distant in Iowa and Kansas. Her force spun the screws and propellers of innumerable squadrons of lake steamers crowding the Sault Sainte Marie. For her and because of her all the Central States, all the great North-West roared with traffic and industry; saw mills screamed; factories, their smoke blackening the sky, clashed and flamed; wheels turned, pistons leaped in their cylinders, cog gripped cog, beltings clasped the drums of mammoth wheels, and converters of forges belched into the clouded air their tempest breath of molten steel.

It was Empire, the resistless subjugation of all this central world of the lakes and the prairies. Here, mid-most in the land, beat the Heart of the Nation, whence inevitably must come its immeasurable power, its infinite, inexhaustible vitality. Here, of all her cities, throbbed the true life—the true power and spirit of America.[7]

The Pit, by FRANK NORRIS

343. The Middle West

From Toledo I flew to Chicago.... The Stock Yard is not quite so busy now, but there were still thousands of pens of fat cattle and pigs, and enough noise to convince anyone that it is still an important market....

From Chicago I went by bus to Madison, Wisconsin. Almost all the houses in rural America, and in the smaller towns, are built of wood with attractive sun porches and verandahs. Wisconsin is known as "the Dairyland of America", and I went round several dairy farms....

Naturally, as a farmer, I was anxious to see as many farms as possible, but whereas the farms in Iowa, Ohio and Wisconsin are fairly similar in size and type to our own, the farther West

[7]In 1960 it had 3½ million people. Now the population has almost doubled.

you get the greater the difference, until you reach the ranch country, with vast areas of bare range and desert. Here is the worst problem of land erosion, where land, which was suitable only as range, has in the past been ploughed and cropped with corn, and now blows away in dust storms, or is carried away by seasonal torrential rains. Soil conservation projects of all kinds are being undertaken with State and Federal help, and many new strains of grasses are being developed which will stand intense heat and drought, and anchor the soil. Irrigation is a "must" for all crops, and water rights are jealously guarded.

ELAINE KELLETT, in *Home and Country*

344. The Climate of Illinois

The weather in Illinois reigns with violence for the greater part of the year, a violence created by the vast homogeneity of the space between Eastern and Western mountain ranges, the enormous sweep of the flat prairie country, the immense and treeless plain. The summer of desperate heat follows the bitter winter with only a brief wet interval between them to mark the place of spring. The winds have a long way to go and nothing to stop them; the summer's heat is uniform and deadening when the winds have gone; the winter's ice and snow are the same for many hundreds of miles in every direction. This immense simplicity, this black-and-white climate, all heat or all cold for millions of square miles and for months at a time, resolves the year into two important seasons with a transitional episode at either end, a sort of doorway from the tropics to the North Pole, through which the passage is brief and is melancholy with the certainty of what lies ahead.

Spring does not amount to much : it rains, and there are roses, but with unwanted haste the blazing summer descends and installs itself for almost five months, far beyond its legal allowance. Of the two, the better doorway is autumn—better because it lingers awhile, and because in that lingering altercation between summer and winter the flat, weary country has its precious hour of beauty. The leaves burn brighter than they do in more civil climates. The warmth returns to the air by day and deserts it by night, so that the most insensitive vegetation, blighted and revived in turn, must show some sign of the struggle before it succumbs and dies.

Bird of the Wilderness, by VINCENT SHEEAN

345. The Good Farmers of Iowa

And now ... across the wide Dakotas and down to the middle of Iowa, which is the heart of the Corn Belt. Rich black soil, stretching mile upon mile, the country so long settled that nearly all the pioneers—native-born Americans, Swedes, Danes, Scots, Germans and men of many other races—are all dead. There are farm orchards, gardens and plantations. The little patches of salty marshland that formerly lay interspersed with the cultivated fields have disappeared. Going westwards along the full width of the State in July, there was an endless succession of tall, sturdy maize; straight, clean rows of soya beans; rich swards of lucerne and clover; herds of Friesian and Jersey cows; more herds of white-faced Herefords and Black Angus cattle from Scotland; and pigs and pigs and pigs. ... They said last summer that you could hardly step on Iowa without making a pig squeal. ...

It is not surprising that the farmers of Iowa ... look to the future with some anxiety. They are constantly building up their capacity to produce food, and they cannot help wondering whether food will continue to be saleable. At times they wonder whether the Big Slump will come again. And yet they seem to feel remarkably little suspicion or jealousy towards farmers in other parts of the world. They look upon these not so much as competitors in world markets but as fellow labourers in the great common task of feeding the world's people. ... There have been mistakes: some have gambled and lost; some have wasted good earth in an attempt to carry off its riches and have been duly punished. But the great bulk of the people have learnt how to live. They want to be good farmers for, like most Americans, they despise inefficiency.

J. A. SCOTT WATSON, in *The Listener*

346. In America's Far West

This is the real America. Here in the great prairie and mountain States of Colorado, Wyoming and Montana, America begins. That is what the large-hearted people of these immense areas say. Wherever America begins, it hardly ever ends. This train started at eleven o'clock last night to cross half the State of Montana, and to mount the Continental Divide in the Rocky Mountains. It is now eleven o'clock in the morning, with a brilliant sun shining on the snow peaks. But we are still in Montana, and it was astonishing to wake up and find the Northern Pacific Express running alongside the headwaters of the Missouri River which I had left days before at Omaha in Nebraska over a thousand miles away. . . .

Here in the prairie and mountain areas the car is essential to life. The thirty or fifty miles drive to church is an ordinary occurrence, and some people come further. . . . In Montana the largest town is no bigger than 25,000 people,[8] and the isolated ranches and homesteads are the places where the people really live. . . .

As I write, the train is rolling on by the side of the Clark Fork River to Missoula. The flat valley, with its immense peaks in snow, is reminiscent of Switzerland. There are little fields of corn and fresh Spring grass, with lonely shacks in the shelter of the pines.

REV. CECIL NORTHCOTT, in the *British Weekly*

347. Developments in the Missouri Basin

The Missouri River Basin, 1,300 miles long and 700 miles wide, includes approximately one-sixth of the continental area of the country. It covers all or part of ten States—all North and South Dakota and Nebraska, nearly all Montana, more than half Wyoming, one-fourth of North-West Colorado, the northern half of Kansas and parts of Missouri, Iowa and Minnesota.

Approximately seven million people live in these 530,000 square miles. They produce half the bread supplies of America, a fifth of the butter, a sixth of the pork, a fifth of the beef, a fourth of the mutton and nearly a third of the wool. Previous irrigation-reclamation schemes have enabled 550,000 acres to yield some of this food and clothing without fear of natural disaster year by year. But where there are no scientific defences

[8]Helena, the capital, had 20,227 in 1960.

against the elements it is a hazardous enterprise, and there has been no stable economy. In drought the thin topsoil of great stretches of plain has crumbled to dust. The winds have swept it away, leaving a desert in their wake. . . .

Work has begun on a government project to control the vast Missouri River so that the dry earth which has been bleeding to death will be given transfusions of water by the turning of taps whenever needed. The millions of tons of rain, which have caused millions of pounds of flood damage every year, will be harnessed and mobilized to produce electric power. . . . The scheme will bring benefits in irrigation, power, flood control, navigation and water supply worth nearly £45,000,000 a year.

STUART GELDER, in the *News Chronicle*

348. Yellowstone Falls and Gorge

The great falls of the Yellowstone are indeed a noble sight. The water, like that of Niagara, is perfectly clear and free from sediment, issuing as it does from a great lake in which all suspended matter has been retained. It has a delicate sea-green hue which contrasts delightfully with the warm tints of the surrounding precipices, while the great height of the fall appears magnified and ennobled by the dense volumes of spray which wrap round and quite conceal the base of the watery column.

The Grand Canyon of the Yellowstone, however, surpasses in beauty anything else in the Park, and indeed few more striking and fascinating specimens of rock-colouring and sculpture have ever been described by travellers in the New World or the Old. At the falls the depth of the gorge is about 700 feet, but the depths increase to 1,000 feet five miles lower down; the mouth of the chasm varies from a quarter to three-quarters of a mile in width. It is not however, the dimensions, which are in no way remarkable, but the wonderful colours and sculpturing that give to the canyon its peculiar interest. It has been gouged by the river out of a thick mass of pale yellow or pinkish rhyolite of the plateau, which has become softened and disintegrated by the action of the hot springs and fumaroles, many of which are still to be seen steaming along its walls. . . . The whole gorge is moreover painted in the most brilliant hues,

from sulphur-yellow, which predominates, to deep orange
streaked with warm vermilion, crimson and purple.

H. M. CADELL, in the *Scottish Geographical Magazine,*
Edinburgh

349. Yellowstone National Park

With its two million acres Yellowstone, the oldest national park
in the world, is easily the biggest and most impressive area set
aside in the U.S.A. for the protection of wildlife and natural
resources. At the height of the tourist season more than 28,000
visitors enter the park gates daily to enjoy a landscape different
from any other because of the volcanic activity smouldering just
under the surface of the ground and throwing up spectacular
hot springs and geysers, and to see superb examples of wildlife in a magnificent setting.

There are the deer, the large wapiti, and the even larger
moose, measuring up to six feet at the shoulder. Another
animal at Yellowstone owes its survival to rigorous protection.
This is the pronghorn, or American antelope, which was almost
exterminated by hunters. But the bears are the main attraction
for tourists—and the main danger. There are two kinds of bears
in the park, the huge grizzlies, which luckily keep themselves
to themselves, and the American black bear, which tends to
haunt the roadside and has become almost a professional
beggar.

Radio Times

350. The "Big Inch"

A pipeline two feet in diameter, popularly known as the "Big
Inch", has been laid across the United States from Texas, in
the south-west, to Pennsylvania, in the east, and it has been
done in about eleven months. The line runs for 1,388 miles.
It would reach from London to beyond Leningrad.

It starts in Long View, Texas, where black crude oil oozes
up from one of the vast subterranean lakes which are part of
the wealth of America. It heads away across the States of
Arkansas, Missouri, Illinois, Ohio, West Virginia and Pennsylvania to Phoenixville, where it splits into two branches—a short

one which leads to refineries in the Philadelphia area and a longer one which crosses New Jersey to the Bayonne refineries, on the doorstep of New York city.

The pipe—the biggest ever laid on this scale—was in forty foot lengths, each weighing two tons. It was laid in a ditch four to eight feet deep which was dug mainly by heavy machines with vicious steel teeth, but in some places was blasted out of rock. The ditch made its way over plains, hills, valleys and swamps, across 200 rivers and streams, under railway lines, over the Alleghany Mountains, dipping and climbing sometimes at a 45 degrees angle. It went across farm, field and orchard, and the farmers were paid half a crown a rod, plus compensation for damage. It cut through forests where heavy timber had to be felled and tree roots torn from the earth with dynamite. . . .

The oil will travel through the pipe at three miles an hour . . . helped along by twenty-five pumping stations "en route". It will take every gallon of oil twenty days to make the long trip from Texas.

ROBERT WAITHMAN, in the *News Chronicle*

Note. It is now found to be cheaper and more convenient to send the oil by tanker from ports like Houston and Galveston.

351. The Erratic Mississippi

(*a*) On issuing from Lake Itasca the Mississippi is only twelve feet wide, but before leaving the State of Minnesota it is already a noble and beautiful river. It runs through many lakes, many more that are but broad reaches of the river, and again many others that were once sections of the Mississippi, though now parted from it.

First Impressions in America, by JOHN AYSCOUGH

(*b*) The Mississippi river is probably the most utterly unreliable thing within the North American continent. He has shifted his course so many times within the brief century that white-skinned men have known him, that the oldest of them have lost all trace of his original course. And so to steer a vessel up and down the stream is a doubly difficult art. The pilot does not merely have to know his steering marks, he has to learn the entire thing anew each time he brings a craft up or down the river.

The Personality of American Cities, by EDWARD HUNGERFORD

352. The Mississippi in Relation to the Plantations

In the south and east of the United States are the plantations —world-renowned in song and story, and worked largely by Negroes.

Tobacco plantations are commonest in Virginia, Kentucky, Tennessee, and the Carolinas, though most of the states east of the Mississippi raise fair quantities.

The Mississippi forms a natural link between the other plantation "belts". The chief cotton states lie in a belt fringing the northern shores of the Gulf of Mexico and extending from Texas, the chief cotton state, to Georgia. The long, warm summers and light soils of this belt favour the growth of the cotton plant.

The Mississippi flood plain is bounded for many miles by high bluffs; in the flat silt-burdened valley between them the river curves in wide swinging meanders. When this bends near the bluffs, towns have sprung up—towns that owed their early prosperity to the river traffic, e.g. Baton Rouge, Vicksburg and Memphis. Lower down, the river banks are artificially reinforced to prevent floods; these levées serve also as convenient wharves for riverside cotton plantations.

Sugar needs a moist, hot climate, such as is found on the Gulf shorelands. Rice grows best in the irrigated lands of Eastern Texas and Louisiana.

At the mouth of the Mississippi is the "Delta City" of New Orleans, built on the shores of Lake Pontchartrain, more than ninety miles above the delta exits. It is the chief cotton port, and gathers up the products of the lower Mississippi basin.

The World We Live In, ed. GRAEME WILLIAMS

353. The Tennessee Valley Authority

The area of the Tennessee Valley is some 42,000 square miles

—about four-fifths of England and Wales. Proper control of the 900-miles-long Tennessee River, which flows through this area, had become crucial for the prevention of disastrous floods on the lower Mississippi. . . .

Thousands of square miles of bare hills, which first confronted the engineers entrusted with the Tennessee Valley campaign, were, within the memory of living man, rich virgin forests. Then the lumbermen had stripped the trees from the hills, and when the timber was gone they had to turn to agriculture for a living. This increased the pressure on the land, and as the years passed, the settlers, hard-driven by poverty, were forced to clear fresh acreage from the remaining wooded mountain-sides. With its natural cover removed, and the failure to apply fertilizers, the land rapidly lost its fertility, and, due also to the heavy rainfall, the top-soil was steadily washed away. . . . Outcrops of bare rock stood out where three generations earlier rich soil had lain over a yard in depth.

What the T.V.A. achieved in this impoverished area in little more than ten years reads like a first-class fantasy. Within eighteen months reafforestation was beginning to reclaim the gullied, eroded hillsides. In the next ten years, along the river and its tributaries, twelve vast dams up to 300 feet in height achieved an engineering feat greater than that of the Panama Canal. A number of these regulate the flow of water, while all serve for power generation, supplying electricity to every resident in the Valley at about a penny per unit. . . . With a new fertilizer, developed by T.V.A.-powered chemical plants, the area's 800,000 farmers[9] (more than twice as many as in the whole of England) grew forage crops, forestalling erosion and enriching the land.

MAURICE BENSLEY, in *Chambers's Journal*, Edinburgh

354. Florida and its "Everglades"

(a) A single track led to the dead-end station of Lake Witterwittee. Three trains a day came in and out, connecting with the main line. To the south of the lake, one of some 200 in the same county, lay Florida's greatest inland stretch of water, Lake Okeechobee, surrounded by its flat plains, home of

[9]i.e., farm-workers.

T

the cattle-raising industry. The small town of Witterwittee, taking its name from the lake, sixty miles in diameter, consisted of one Main Street, in detail exactly like 10,000 Main Streets throughout the United States.... Down the centre of the wide street, in such shade as a dozen languid palm trees offered from the sub-tropical January afternoon, the local automobiles stood parked, with a blue-jeaned Negro sprawled on a bench in optimistic make-believe that he was guardian of them....

Presently, from a rise, they had a view of the orange groves. The trees, with their bright metallic-looking green leaves, were almost geometrically spaced, and seemed to stretch for miles. The oranges hung like golden globes among the thick branches, which also bore the blossoms to become in turn next year's crop.... As if to emphasize the nearness of untamed Nature, there was a sudden screeching and chattering of monkeys in the branches of a great magnolia tree.

One Small Candle, by CECIL ROBERTS

(b) From Naples, on the west coast of Florida, the Tamiami Trail cuts right across the primitive Everglades jungle country, where you drive for miles without seeing a soul except an occasional Seminole Indian.

The Everglades teem with wild life. White-plumed egrets roost in thousands by the road and the rivers teem with fish. It was when I pulled off the road to get a close-up of a colony of egrets that I nearly ran over the alligator. He was only a little fellow, not more than a couple of feet long, but I'm quite sure I was more scared than he was. When I sounded the horn right in his ear he stirred himself leisurely and slithered quietly into the swamp.

Then, as I got out of the car, I heard a rustling in the rank grass, and an enormous black snake, moving amazingly fast, passed almost over my feet. That was quite enough. I got hurriedly back into the car, wound up all the windows and abandoned all further investigations into the habits of American flora and fauna!

ARTHUR HELLIWELL, in *The People*

355. Mexico — Past and Present

The first man to ask what Mexico was like was probably the

Emperor Charles V who questioned the explorer Cortez when he returned to Europe. Cortez crumpled a sheet of parchment and cast it upon the table. "It is like that, your Majesty," he said.

And "like that" it is: great ridges of mountains, active volcanoes, high plateaux, enormous cultivated valleys, tropical forests. We were fascinated by the many contrasts that the country provided. ANCIENT MEXICO—in deserted Aztec cities and temples throughout the country and the modern anthropological museum in Mexico City. MUSICAL MEXICO —when the Aztec civilization came into collision with the Spanish conquistadores and then remained under direct Spanish rule for three hundred years, a rich store of folk and dance music resulted. REVOLUTIONARY MEXICO— Spanish rule ended at the beginning of the nineteenth century and more than a hundred years of revolution was to follow. HOLIDAY MEXICO—sunshine, tequila, blue skies, warm seas. And MODERN MEXICO—no longer a place where the peasant tilts his sombrero over his eyes and sleeps under the cactus tree, but a country sitting squarely upon a launching pad of enormous industrial potential.

ALAN BURGESS, in *Radio Times*

356. Seen in Mexico

Mexico City, nearly 8,000 feet above sea-level, is not only the capital of a great empire, but also the social and business centre of a great area. Here patient "burros" (donkeys) and Indian pack-carriers share the thoroughfares with Rolls-Royces. Mexico City is one of the best planned and most colourful capitals of the world. It is located on a fertile plain beneath snow-capped mountains of impressive beauty....

Orizaba is one of the manufacturing centres of Mexico, having large textile mills, a cigar factory, and a brewery. It is a pleasant old city, and the trails run out in every direction along cool, tumbling streams, down to coffee and sugar plantations, and up along the foothills of the Pico do Orizaba (the mountain).... This perpetually snow-capped peak is a sort of sentinel over the gateway to Mexico; for centuries those who entered Mexico stopped at Orizaba (the town) to rest before making the final climb to the plateau.

Time Out for Adventure, by LEONIDAS RAMSEY

357.   Another Glimpse of Mexican Life

As is the case with the largest city in any country, Mexico City is not nearly so representative of Mexico as any of the smaller cities, or as the countryside, which change so slowly. Let us pass, therefore, to the unique and charming city of Guadalajara, the second in Mexico, where foreigners are comparatively few and where old Mexican ways and customs still have the flavour of the past. Situated about 300 miles west of Mexico City, it lies at a much lower altitude (5,500 feet) and, being on the Pacific slope, the climate is almost completely perfect. Here it is soft, quiet, sun-lit, luscious, restful. The sun has a way of shining that strokes you gently. Here is the Indian with his many-coloured blanket shawl, his wide sombrero, and his flat leather sandals, a living touch of colour against his woman in her softly-toned grey-blue "rebozo" and black skirt. Spread on the sun-baked earth are the little mats bearing their small pyramids of fruit, vegetables, or sweetmeats. . . .

Penetrating through the long streets of old-fashioned houses, you arrive at last into the wider spaces of the "Colonias", intersected by tree-lined avenues bordered by flower-laden gardens. The houses here are those of the well-to-do and wealthy, immaculately kept, pink, white and cream, imitating every known style of architecture. . . . You begin to wonder whence comes all the wealth to support such luxury. It comes from the broad acres of Indian corn, growing as high as a man standing on his horse's back, from wheat, sugar, coffee, fruit of many kinds, fat cattle, herds of horses and mules, factories and shops, and to a dwindling extent from gold, silver and copper mines. This is a rich and gracious countryside, overflowing with milk and honey.

CAPT. GRENVILLE HOLMS, in the *Latin-American World*

358.   Henequen in Northern Yucatan

(*a*) In the south-east corner of Mexico, Yucatan projects

northwards like a tongue, dividing for a space of some 200 miles the Gulf of Mexico from the Caribbean. It is flatter than any other part of Mexico and in the north is only sparsely scattered with trees and shrubs, though farther south, where the plateau rises to merge later into the Central American sierras, a dense jungle is spread like a carpet over the landscape. The region is only lightly populated, and was until comparatively recently considered of little interest. But two crops, henequen or sisal in the north, and the "zapote chico" tree—whose sap, chicle, forms the basis of chewing-gum—in the south, have brought it unexpected wealth.

ELAINE BICKERSTAFFE, in *Chambers's Journal*, Edinburgh

(b) On every side were vast fields of henequen (a species of cactus) from which is derived the sisal fibre. These aloes consist of a central core, attached to which are great, thick, tough, dark-green leaves, three to four feet long, five to six inches broad, each tipped at the point with a huge black thorn. The outer leaves are cut from each plant at frequent intervals and carried to the mill, where they are beaten and scraped till all the pulp is removed, and only the beautifully white silky fibre remains. This is hung on wires in the sun to dry. Lastly the hanks of fibre are compressed in hydraulic presses into great bundles bound with hoop iron, in which form they are exported to the United States where, converted into thin, loosely-woven rope, they bind the sheaves of corn cut by the reapers from Canada to Mexico.

In an Unknown Land, by THOMAS GANN

359. Some Aspects of Central American Life

Central America is a section of the continental backbone pushing up out of the sea, and a little more. It is a tent on a tropical beach; a roof, with eaves in the warm, blue waters of the Pacific and the Caribbean, and a gable of volcanoes. . . .

On the central tableland has grown up a homogeneous little nation—there are only about half a million people in all of Costa Rica,[10] which is about twice the size of Holland—of industrious, prosperous, and literate citizens, white or nearly

[10]In 1965 there were estimated to be 1,430,000.

T*

so, with few large landowners and many peasant proprietors. Except for bananas, which are exported almost exclusively by an American corporation, coffee is the only considerable thing with which Costa Rica can bargain with the rest of the world. It is good coffee and commands a high price....

Honduras is almost twice as large as Costa Rica. It has minerals, probably the best cattle country in Central America, and more bananas are exported from its east-coast plantations than from any of the other Caribbean banana neighbourhoods with the exception of Jamaica....

Salvador is a rich, beautiful, and industrially cultivated country through which the train climbs to the capital. There is sugar-cane and corn on the lower levels, and far up the mountain sides one can see, every now and then, the roof of some coffee estate....

Corinto (Nicaragua) is in the classical Central American style —heat that sends the sweat streaming down the languid flesh; negro women squatting beside baskets of tropical fruit; palm and sand; a long unpaved street or two; in the distance a string of sharp volcanoes fading off into the heat of summer.

The Central Americans, by A. J. RUHL

360. The Charm of Central America

The charm of Central America is not a thing to be put into cold print. Here is the mystery of ancient stone cities, buried in tropic jungle; here is the grace of the Spanish colonial centuries; and here are scenes of beauty that enchain the heart—forest, volcanoes, blue lakes and tempestuous rivers, bright birds and flowers....

Guatemala City will always have charm. It has a delightful situation in an enclosed valley 5,000 feet high, with a climate that is bright and cool all the year round; the woods and hills and ravines near by are of a sweet luxuriance; and then there are the ravishing contours and colours of the watching volcanoes....

To me the jungle of British Honduras is the most beautiful tropic jungle, the rivers the loveliest tropic streams. They are the very realization of romance—the great, green, deep-flowing waters, overhung with fiercely struggling creepers, huge buttressed trees draped with orchids, bordered with tree ferns and lilies, alive with the gay colours of parrot and toucan. . . .

The front-door of British Honduras is the reef-sheltered Belize. From the sea Belize is extremely pretty. All the houses, built of wood, painted in white, airily balconied, are raised on piles above gardens flaming with scarlet hibiscus. All about and beyond the town are grassy savannahs and woodland that sweeps away into the deep, surrounding forest.

Central America, by L. E. ELLIOTT

361. British Honduras

Alexander Pope reminds us in "Windsor Forest" that "seas but join the regions they divide". The westernmost waves of the Caribbean Sea wash the shore of Britain's only Colony in Central America: British Honduras. North of it is Mexico and the great waters of the Gulf of Mexico. On its western borders is Guatemala Republic, and to cross Guatemala westwards is to arrive at the easternmost waters of the Pacific Ocean.

Far away then is British Honduras, an undeveloped country about the size of Wales, with a sparse population of less than 80,000 people,[11] 26,500 of whom live in the capital city of Belize,[12] straddling both banks of the Belize River. An aeroplane brought me from Kingston and Montego Bay in Jamaica across to the Cayman Islands and farther westwards above the Caribbean Sea until we looked down at the second largest coral reef in the world, which together with many small islands (or cays) makes the harbours and roadsteads safe for ships. The 'plane now dipped and was soon at rest at Stanley Field aerodrome on the low swampy land near the coast. Inland the country rises and near the border of Guatemala the Maya Mountains look down imposingly from several thousand feet above sea-level. . . .

The export of mahogany has been the Colony's main industry for nearly two centuries, and in an age of three-ply and hardboard it is stimulating to see scores of mahogany trees lying in the open, side by side, some already sawn through, or lying in the river that has brought them down from the forests farther

---

[11]The population was estimated in 1965 to be 103,000.
[12]In 1960 Belize had 32,824 people.

inland. This undeveloped Colony has only 280 miles of main roads, including the Humming Bird Highway of thirty-two and a half miles, completed in 1954 and built across virgin country to connect Stann Creek with Belize and the Western District.

REV. J. H. WILLIAMS, in The Bible in the World

362.   The Panama Canal

Briefly described, the Panama Canal is a water stairway. The passage from the Atlantic to the Pacific consists of three stages; first, climbing the stairway of the locks; next, passing through a lake high above sea-level; and then coming down the stairs again on the opposite side.

And now our ship is going to climb the flight of stairs known as the Gatun Locks. These locks are constructed one above the other in three double flights, so that two ships can ascend at the same time. The speed with which the locks are worked is nothing short of miraculous.... The level of the water rises swirling in the closed quadrangular pockets, and both ships are lifted above the level in which, a few moments ago, they were still floating; and still they rise, from the second trap door and the third, until finally they are some twenty-five yards above sea-level. From the bank electric motors tow the great ships and guide them through the locks. From the third of the Gatun Locks, our ship passes on to the lake of that name.... The lake stretches out at a varying width for about thirty-eight miles until it reaches Gamboa.... But it is at Gamboa that the most difficult and impressive part of the work begins; it is here that the mountain range forming the spinal column of the isthmus is pierced; here is the famous and terrible Culebra Cut where so many men have perished.

The narrow water trail extends to the locks known as the Pedro Miguel Locks—the name of a town nearby—and here the plateau ends and the stairs down the other side begin. Our ship descends the flight from the Pedro Miguel Locks to Lake Miraflores, sixteen yards above the sea. The locks at the end of this lake bring us down to the level of the Pacific. Continuing on our way for thirteen unbroken miles we pass the modern city of Balboa, and the ancient city of Panama, and at last our prow dips into the waters of the largest ocean. The crossing has taken us exactly eight hours.

A Novelist's Tour of the World, by VINCENTE BLASCO IBAÑEZ

363. The Peoples of the West Indies

Christopher Columbus, trying to discover a new route to India, landed in 1492 on an island in the Bahamas, which he called San Salvador ("Holy Saviour") but which we know today by the pedestrian name of Watling. New civilizations faced older civilizations, and of course the older civilizations went under. Carib and Maya and Arawak gave way before the civilization of western Christendom, before the explorers and traders and buccaneers of Spain and Portugal, of France, Holland and England. Greater infiltrations lay ahead. Thousands of African slaves were brought over to the West Indies to labour in the agricultural activities of these islands : in the sugar and banana and other fruit industries. The East, too, was destined to infiltrate and add her coloured children to the already colourful scene for, when the international conscience condemned the slave trade as an evil thing, agricultural labourers had to be brought over from India, and with them came the Hindu and Muslim religions. And even here the story does not end, for the Far East is represented by the many Chinese who voyaged to a new home in these beautiful and interesting islands of the Caribbean Sea.... Peoples of different colours stemming from different civilizations and continents are living, working, studying, playing happily together.... "East is East and West is West", but, Mr Kipling, the twain have already met in the islands of the West Indies.

REV. J. H. WILLIAMS, in *The Bible in the World*

364. West Indian Problems

The West Indians of today are doing what their fathers did before them; they are emigrating to a country where workers are wanted. Earlier in the twentieth century, Jamaicans and Barbadians went in their thousands to work on the Panama Canal. Some proceeded into Costa Rica to build the Northern

Railway and to work on the fruit farms. People from the Leeward Islands found work in the Dutch islands of Aruba and Curaçao, when the Esso Petrol and the Dutch-Shell Companies opened their enormous refineries there. During the Second World War the United States employed thousands of West Indians on her farms. Only Trinidad with its rich oil industry can claim full employment for all her people. The other colonies set a poor island economy alongside the growing population, and the alternative before many of their people is starvation at home or work in the United Kingdom. . . .

In a few hours a hurricane will rip roofs off buildings and transport masonry, crush wooden homes as a match box is crushed in the hand, sweep away hillsides of long and rich cultivation, dislocate transport and threaten whole populations with typhoid epidemics because the water supply has become fouled. Hurricane "Janet" in 1955 destroyed the nutmeg industry in Grenada, and fifteen years of economic difficulty must pass before the industry can flourish again; so long does it take to produce the nutmeg.

REV. J. H. WILLIAMS, in *The Bible in the World*

365. Glimpses of Some Caribbean Islands

Most of the Caribbean islands are of volcanic origin, and craters of extinct or dormant volcanoes are found in nearly all of them. . . .

Hispaniola has three chains of mountains running east to west, between which are great fertile plains and savannahs. The mountains are covered with vast forests and the country is one of the most fertile spots in the west. . . .

There are wide savannahs in the interior and extensive areas of fertile land on the coast of Puerto Rico. Of minerals, iron, copper, lead and manganese-ores and traces of gold have been found. San Juan, the capital, is built on a small island joined to the mainland by a bridge. A quaint old Spanish city, yet the American influence is very evident. The narrow streets hum with motor-cars, lorries, and electric tramways—presenting a striking contrast to the scenes in the country, where ploughing by ox-teams, and pack-horses climbing the mountain paths, may be seen. The houses, painted in vivid colours, are built of stone or brick, and are mostly of two storeys. . . .

Hidden treasures found from time to time show that the Caymans were at one time the rendezvous of buccaneers. . . .

Unlike other neighbouring islands, Barbados has now no snakes or wild animals—due to the fact that practically the whole island is under cultivation.

The West Indies, by GEORGE MANINGTON

366. Jamaica Today

Although Jamaica has, after 300 years as a British colony, achieved independence and changed in many more immediately obvious ways, it retains much of the charm of a tropical paradise. . . .

The erstwhile "kings" of the island's economy—the banana and the sugar cane—have been ousted by a newcomer, and the modern industries, in order of importance, are bauxite, sugar, tourism, bananas, rum, coffee, pimento (all-spice, produced nowhere else in the world), cocoa and tobacco. Very rich deposits of bauxite are mined and exported, mainly to Canada and the United States (last year[13] about half the total ore consumed by the United States aluminium industry was provided by Jamaica).[14] Some of it is converted into alumina in the island, but the comparatively high cost of electricity makes the electrolytic process by which aluminium is won from the ore cheaper in North America. . . .

The West Coast of Jamaica is, as yet, largely undeveloped. But on the westerly tip of the island lies Jamaica's resort of the future, Negril. It is at present a green finger of woodland fringed by an unbroken seven-mile stretch of white sand beach, laced offshore by coral reefs of every shade of blue and green. . . .

There has been tremendous urban expansion in the capital. Kingston is a sprawling, bustling city in a broad plain under the Blue Mountains and built round one of the largest harbours in the world. Yet, especially in the dim regions of West Kingston slums, there still remains financial poverty among

[13]1964.

[14]In 1968, Jamaica, with over 8 million tons, was the largest producer of bauxite in the world.

sections of the population, together with a high unemployment rate.

THOMAS HARRISON, in the *Yorkshire Post*, Leeds

367. Trinidad's "Pitch Lake"

Some sixty miles from Port of Spain we come to La Brea, where is one of the largest asphalt supplies in the world.... "Pitch Lake" is half a mile across and covers 114 acres, depth unknown. It is a carboniferous deposit of vegetable origin, like coal or peat, formed from the petroleum escaping from the oil sand beneath. To us it looked like no more than a large black patch of asphalt pavement, edged with palm trees. Sir Walter Raleigh in 1595 had used this pitch to close the seams of his ships. He declared the supply was inexhaustible, and modern geologists agree with him, for as fast as the bitumen is dug out, the holes are refilled by pressure from within and show no mark after twenty-four hours. We saw labourers chopping out chunks of the asphalt with picks, and loading it into swinging buckets which move by cable to the port of La Brea, a mile away. Our guide explained that the pitch solidifies again during transport and has to be chopped out of the hold of the ship when it is unloaded. It was a sizzling-hot spot, with the sun beating down into this humid bitumen, but we ventured to walk out on the surface of the "lake". A little way out the pitch was so soft that our lightest footmark left an impression, and we began to sink a little.

South American Adventures, by ALICE C. DESMOND

South America

368. Caracas is Going Underground

(NOTE: Caracas is reached from its seaport La Guaira, six miles away as the crow flies, by a railway and a modern concrete road, which wind through twenty-three miles of hill country, climbing 2,984 feet in the process.)

Caracas, the capital of Venezuela, has resolved to end its traffic problems by going underground. Plans to build between thirty and forty miles of underground railway are almost complete after years of study of the acute traffic situation in the continually-expanding capital.... The first line to be built will extend for eleven miles in an east-west direction along the valley beneath the Avila mountain range overshadowing the city. It will not be underground all the way; there will be stretches of open track.

The growth of Caracas has followed the pattern of all Latin American capitals with a population increase of about one million in sixteen years. A small city of about 250,000 inhabitants before the Second World War, Caracas has grown from a population of 694,000 in 1950 to an estimated 1,700,000, or about one-fifth of Venezuela's total population, in 1966[1]....

It is estimated that there is one car to every seven people.... Nearly 1,400,000 people travel in Caracas each day, using almost 450,000 vehicles.... A unique feature of the transport system in Caracas and other major cities in Venezuela is the "por puesto", or shared taxi, which carries passengers from point to point along fixed routes.... The Government is confident that once the Metro is constructed, "por puesto taxis", one source of traffic congestion, will virtually disappear.

PETER SMITH, in the *Yorkshire Post*, Leeds

[1] In 1968 the total population of Venezuela was 9,859,174, and that of Caracas 2,064,000—which is still about 20 per cent.

369. Venezuela and Oil

Oil is king in Venezuela, which today is the world's second greatest producer. Probably no other country has ever put so many eggs into one basket! After the discovery of petroleum in the Lake Maracaibo district at the end of the First Great War, Venezuela's many other natural resources were (until recently) most unwisely neglected; and the national fortune rose or fell with the vicissitudes of the petroleum wells, whose output formed ninety per cent of the total exports.... The vast agricultural resources of the country were largely neglected by governments which could think only in terms of oil.... Lack of internal communications has proved a vicious circle. It has not appeared to be an economic proposition to build roads to serve the sparse population beyond the coastal belt; conversely, settlers have been discouraged by the absence of such roads....

The years which have passed since the death of Gomez have seen the steady transformation of Venezuela from a medieval to a modern state. Using the huge fortune which the dictator had amassed, a good beginning has been made in the colossal task of highway construction, drainage, sanitation.... His vast estates have been cut up into two and a half acre holdings for married men; and his pedigree stock used to build up the country's cattle industry....

Raleigh sailed up Venezuela's great waterway, the Orinoco, in search of El Dorado ... but the expedition was a failure.... Oil, cattle, timber, coffee, rubber and asbestos may appear less romantic than legendary cities of gold. Yet in her vast natural resources Venezuela has more wealth than Raleigh ever dreamed of.

A. E. BALLARD, in *World Review*

370. Curaçao: New Treasure Island

The Dutch West Indies comprise Surinam, better known as Dutch Guiana, and six islands in the Caribbean Sea. These islands are divided into two groups, the lesser of which occupies only twenty-nine square miles, being made up of three islands —St Martin, St Eustatius and Saba. (Only the southern part of St Martin belongs to the Netherlands, the remainder being French. The main group consists of Aruba, Bonaire, and

Curaçao, from which the islands take their territorial name.[2] The total area of all the islands is 436 square miles, 210 of which are taken up by Curaçao.

Curaçao lies within four hours' sea journey of the mainland of Venezuela, northernmost country in South America. A non-stop service of fast tankers, known as Jitney boats, brings crude petroleum from the vast oilfields of the Latin-American republic to the spacious refineries of the Dutch-owned islands. Their chief port of call is Maracaibo, Venezuelan oil port.... Fully equipped with refineries which figure among the largest and most up-to-date in the world, Curaçao handles almost the entire output of Venezuela....

There are two harbours on the island of Curaçao. The principal one is the land-locked Schottegat, approached by a deep canal which bisects the town of Willemstad. Ancient fortresses overlook this only entrance to the inland bay where in days gone by pirates came to careen their ships and to rest their crews. The two parts of the town are connected by a pontoon bridge, which is swung open when required.... Products of the islands include salt, phosphate, lime and the well-known liqueur.

PABLO SALKELD, in *The Trident*

371. Cali: Dream City of Colombia

Cali looks more like the European conception of South America than almost any other town except Rio de Janeiro. The first time I came here, by a winding, back-breaking mountain railway from Buenaventura, I was informed by an enthusiastic Colombian fellow-traveller that Cali was "Heaven's branch office on earth". Another passenger added that Caleno women were like walking statues.

Both statements seemed improbable, as one looked out at the straggling negro villages bordering the track, where malnutrition and inherited disease were in universal evidence. But, as the train topped the heights of the first of the three mountain ranges which split Colombia, there came in sight the smiling green valley of Cauca, surrounded by purple hills with the white city of Cali set like a jewel in the middle.

[2] I.e., in common parlance. Officially they are called the Netherlands Antilles.

Colombia is one of the few South American countries not dominated by a single overgrown capital. Owing to the difficulty of transport, its many cities are as foreign to each other, as different, as if they were in separate countries—steamy Barranquilla, colonial Popayan, bustling industrial Medellin, and the sprawling mountain capital of Bogota.

But to the Caleno there is only one city worth considering in Colombia. Through the centre of Cali, bordered by gardens and crossed by picturesque bridges, flows the River Cauca, whose soft murmur pervades the warm nights. To the music of the water is added the music of humanity, quiet voices, and sudden laughter, and the almost tropical beat of local music. . . .

But the picture is not all so light-hearted. The proximity of the tropics has brought not only gaiety but violence. . . . This gives a nightmare quality to life in what might be an earthly paradise.

J. HALCRO FERGUSON, in the *Belfast Telegraph*

372. The New Railway and Port in Northern Ecuador

Potential agricultural development in Ecuador lies in the lowlands, rather than in the Sierra, where there is considerable population pressure on suitable land. Although the development of the lowlands east of the Andes is hindered by their isolation and inadequate transport, the western lowlands, with only ten per cent cultivated, are accessible to export markets by sea, and much of the underpopulated forest country has been proved suitable for commercial agriculture. In the late 1940s the banana became the boom crop in these coastal lowlands, and since 1952 Ecuador has led the world in banana exports. The main areas of banana production have been in the central and southern lowlands where adequate transport is available. Bananas are grown near the ports of Esmeraldas and Puerto Bolivar and inland around Quevedo and Santo Domingo, which are linked by road to the ports of Guayaquil and Esmeraldas respectively. With the completion of the Ibarra-San Lorenzo railway and the opening of port facilities at San Lorenzo, larger-scale banana production in northern Ecuador is now possible. Previously limited banana production close to San Lorenzo was marketed by canoe at Limones.

As early as 1926 the Guayaquil-Quito railway had been extended to Ibarra and it was planned to build a line west to Esmeraldas. Later, however, San Lorenzo, sixty miles northeast of Esmeraldas, proved to be a more suitable railhead port. . . .

San Lorenzo, once a fishing village, is now a boom town. . . . With its thatched houses, coconut palms and negro population, it is African in character. . . . Its site has considerable natural advantages. Connected by rail to Quito, it could form an important port for Sierran exports and imports.

A. M. S. GRAHAM and D. A. PRESTON, in *Geography*,
(Vol. 46, 1961, pp.245-247)

373. Panama Hats in Peru and Ecuador

(*a*)   I visited Catacaos (Peru), a small village on the very edge of the desert, where the best quality panama hats are made. These hats are made exclusively in the north of Peru and southern Ecuador, and their quality entirely depends on the selection and preparation of the fibre that is grown in the low swamp land along the coast of Ecuador. Workers can be seen sitting outside their huts, patiently twisting the long, fine fibres into the desired shape and design, and in the market place stacks of them are bought by merchants who come to buy them up wholesale.

Tschiffely's Ride: Southern Cross to Pole Star,
by A. F. TSCHIFFELY

(*b*)   Nearly everyone in and around Montecristi (Ecuador) makes headwear. . . . The hats are woven over blocks according to the size of the crown. The block is placed on a support on the knee and on top of it is a pad. The weaver then leans over and rests his chest on the pad. He holds one lot of straws in each hand and plaits them together, working always on the side farthest from him. He does not continue round and round the hat, but from a central line weaves his way once round and then back again. The start is made in the middle of the crown, and more and more straws are added as the work proceeds.

Amazon and Andes, by K. G.[3] GRUBB

[3]Now Sir Kenneth.

374. Arrival in Peru

I had been flying over a familiar region. And now here was Peru, never before seen.... From the narrow strip of coast, ranges of mountains rise, each higher than the other, until they mount to the grand Cordillera of the eastern Andes far away in the interior.

There is Peru, unrolled before you: with a cold mountain wall, far and dim on the east, which draws every last drop of moisture from the saturated south-east trade-winds of the Atlantic blowing across the forests of Brazil. From the air it is easy to realize that by the time the winds reach the coast they have had all the rain squeezed out of them. As your eyes travel from the Andean ranges to the desert plains and promontories of the coast, and to the Pacific washing blue about the fluted barren line of the shore, Peru seems to you, physically, one of the most extraordinary countries in the world....

A stir in the 'plane broke into the thoughts which followed down the coast. We were approaching Lima. Below was the Bay of Ancon, set among barren, sand-covered hills; its houses dazzling white, its trees dusty. Beyond Ancon the lower Andes had advanced farther towards the sea; and bare black foothills, mottled with pale sand, bordered the valley of the Rimac, with, back of them, the Andes, blue and high.

And then there was Lima—its plazas—its bull ring—its churches—its boulevards. Four days and a half from New York by air, and I was looking down upon Lima!

Peruvian Pageant, by BLAIR NILES

375. Peru — Past and Present

The native flora of Peru, owing to the great differences of elevation of Inca Land, and its consequent wide variations of climate, is one of outstanding richness and interest, although the first reaction of a traveller arriving at Lima (only some six miles away from the Pacific Ocean and a bare five hundred feet above sea-level) is likely to be one of disappointment. With the exception of the nitrate region of the Chilean coastal desert, and the grim country of Southern Peru, it would be difficult to find a more arid zone than the barren wastes of rock and sand where that amazing Spanish adventurer, Francisco

Pizarro, decreed in 1535 that the new capital of the country he had conquered should be built to replace the Imperial capital of Cuzco.

Although a small country compared with Brazil, which covers an area greater than the whole of the United States, Peru (the third largest Republic of the Southern Continent since the treaty for the definition of frontiers with Ecuador) is nearly five times the size of Spain.... Travel off the beaten track in Inca Land, although many places can now be reached by car in a long day's run, which twenty years ago necessitated an arduous week's ride on mule-back, still offers the charm of adventure ... (there are) the magnificent scenery; the splendid ruins, pottery and textiles of the pre-Columbus civilization; and the monuments of Spanish Colonial days.

CHRISTOPHER SANDEMAN, in *Homes and Gardens*

376. Peru's Guano Islands

(*a*) All along the west coast of Peru runs the cold current from the Antarctic known as the Humboldt Current. Such is its chilling effect that the average temperature of the water is twenty degrees Fahrenheit below its theoretical value for these latitudes. This has its corresponding reaction upon the atmosphere, and the days are consistently cool and frequently sunless. At the same time there is little or no rain, only a damp and persistent mist. The low temperature of the Humboldt Current allows the presence of thousands of small fish, chiefly anchovies, along the coast. Frequently the water is discoloured by them. The result is that several species of sea-birds in enormous numbers thrive there.

Amazon and Andes, by K. G.[4] GRUBB

(*b*) Along the extensive Pacific coast of Peru lie innumerable small islands, desert islands in the truest sense—rocky, arid, almost inaccessible, and completely lacking vegetation....

For untold centuries the only inhabitants were gulls, cormorants, pelicans and other sea-birds. Infrequent visits by parties of Indians from the mainland hardly disturbed what were perfect bird-sanctuaries—perfect because the waters in

[4]Now Sir Kenneth.

that part of the Pacific are, as a result of currents, heavily stocked with fish. Ample food and safe resting-places being assured, sea-birds throng there in millions—literally millions.

When Indians crossed the few miles of sea to the islands, it was for one specific purpose. They went to fetch bird-droppings, which in their own language they called "huanu" (dung) —whence "guano", the Spanish rendering. It was known that soil to which guano was added produced superior crops.

CHARLES E. HOWARD, in *Chambers's Journal*, Edinburgh

377.   The Llama and its Kindred

(*a*)   The rolling uplands (of Peru) were alive with llamas, alpacas and sheep grazing together as one family. The llama is the aristocrat among animals. Ever silent—if he has a bleat or cry, I have never heard it—he gazes upon the world about him with an expression of timorous disdain and the indifference of convinced superiority. The guanaco and the vicuna, found chiefly in the wilder regions further south, are never domesticated. The latter, graceful and delicate as a fawn, produces the most valuable wool to be found in the Western Hemisphere.[5]

Vagabonding Down the Andes, by HARRY A. FRANCK

(*b*)   Its gentleness, sure-footedness, ability to go long distances without water, and to live on surprisingly little food, make the llama peculiarly suited to the lofty and rocky Andes where it lives. These animals will carry about one hundred pounds; but if overloaded, they lie down and decline to move till their burden is lightened. They travel slowly, grazing as they go, and will not be hurried.

South America, by A. J. WHITBECK

(*c*)   His bones are made into musical instruments. His wool provides every form of garment which the Indians wear, and his hide gives them leather. He is the only means of transport in the mountains. The Indian never beats his llama. When he wants to remove the animal from the path of a motor, he seizes him in his arms and pushes.

Eight Republics in Search of a Future, by ROSITA FORBES

[5]Owing to the resulting lucrative trade, there is a danger of the vicuna becoming extinct.

378. Lake Titicaca

(*a*) Lake Titicaca has no counterpart in all the world. As large as the Straits of Dover, it is both the highest and the most beautiful of inland seas. At the little Bolivian port of Guaqui, some two and a half miles above the sea, the great blue expanse of Titicaca bursts suddenly into view; a sunlit ocean in a cradle of distant, shadowy, snow-covered mountains. No more curious sensation can well be imagined than that created by the waves and the thousand-ton passenger liner awaiting to embark passengers at the top of the Andes.

Modern South America, by CHARLES DOMVILLE-FIFE

(*b*) One of the most remarkable incidental features of the range is Lake Titicaca. The volume of water composing this is in itself sufficiently surprising, since the lake measures about 130 miles in length and a little over 44 miles in breadth. It is thus infinitely the largest stretch of inland water in the continent. The main feature of interest about Lake Titicaca, however, is its altitude, which slightly exceeds 12,000 feet. When it is considered that large steamers run on this roof of the world— and, in the ordinary nature of things, are tossed about from time to time by the gales that rage over the wide expanse—the strangeness of this phenomenon becomes still more apparent.

The World We Live In, in a chapter by W. H. KOEBEL

379. La Paz — Capital of Bolivia

(*a*) La Paz is one of the picture cities of the world. As the traveller gets his first glimpse of it lying in a valley more than 1,000 feet deep, with vertical walls ten miles long and three wide, surrounded by snow-capped mountains, it makes an unforgettable scene. . . . One sees llamas loaded with ice from the north (the Bolivian plateau) coming into the market place to meet there mules loaded with oranges and tropical fruits from the eastern borders (the lowlands).

Understanding South America, by CLAYTON S. COOPER

(*b*) Some of the streets in the town are reasonably level, but most of them are extremely steep. The newcomer, unaccustomed to such rarefied atmosphere, will find himself obliged, by lack of breath, to ascend by short stages, his heart pounding and his lungs feeling as though they would burst. The houses, as of all the other towns on the Bolivian plateau, are built of sun-dried brick—adobe—nevertheless many of them are of quite respectable size. The walls are necessarily very thick, owing to the friable nature of the building materials.

Six Years in Bolivia, by A. V. L. GUISE

380. Chile in Brief

(*a*) The great length of territory makes Chile a series of separate regions with different climates, vegetation and industries. In the north there is the mining area, with the copper deposits of the Andes as yet only partially exploited, and the vast deserts with their almost inexhaustible supplies of nitrate of soda, the finest fertilizer known. Central Chile is commercial and industrial with the two great cities of Santiago, the capital, and Valparaiso. The country surrounding the capital is one of the principal agricultural areas. Further south comes the agricultural and pastoral section of the country. Here also are great coal mines. Still further south is the Pacific slope with its marvellous lakes, and its snow-capped volcanoes surrounded by vast forests.

Modern South America, by CHARLES DOMVILLE-FIFE

(*b*) There is no doubt that in the course of time the frontiers of these three zones will not be so rigidly defined as is the case at present. Even now agriculture is eating downwards into the forests of the south, and with the clearing of the masses of timber the superabundance of rain is becoming lessened. To the north the irrigation and the sinking of wells are beginning to paint the edges of the desert green.

South America, by W. H. KOEBEL

381. An Hacienda in the Aconcagua Valley[6]

He drove us ... along a country road lined with Lombardy
[6]About forty miles north of Santiago.

poplars, now bright yellow in the late May days of autumn. Then, entering the farm through a gate in a high mud wall, we followed through avenues of eucalyptus, poplar and weeping willow a couple of miles by a round-about road to the house. Most of the land we saw was in alfalfa, with cattle and horses grazing its short-cropped growth. We passed a few fields of grain and saw well-kept vineyards rising row on row along the foot of the hills as far up the slope as canals could supply them with water. Each individual field was enclosed by rows of tall poplars, the red roots of the trees exposed along the half-filled irrigation ditches. Long lines of weeping willows too bordered some of the plots. The house was a one-storey structure of some twenty rooms. It had thick adobe walls and a tile roof.... It stood in the midst of gardens, occupying several acres and filled with flowers and fruit and ornamental trees. It was built around several "patios", or enclosed courts, as are most of the older houses in Chile, each of these open to the sky and paved with tile or cobblestones. Potted plants stood about these spaces, while a small fountain and pool occupied the centre of the principal court. The rooms opened on long covered porches which surrounded these patios on all four sides.

Chile: Land and Society (American Geographical Society, Research Series, No. 19—by A. MACBRIDE)

382. The Peoples of South America

There are three main groups of people to be considered. First, the original inhabitants still persist in the jungles of the Amazon and the great pampas. They have been there in much the same primitive stage of cultural development for literally thousands of years. They are thought to have migrated to their present homes from North America, having come from Asia across the Bering Straits. Some, like the Incas, created high civilizations, but most of them remained as simple nomadic jungle tribes as they are today.

This basic Indian population was profoundly affected about the year A.D. 1500 by the impact of European civilization in the persons of the Spanish and Portuguese conquerors who, though few in number, imposed a new pattern of life on the aborigines, intermarried freely with them and produced the common South American type known today as the "Mestizo"— the people of mixed blood. Both Spaniards and Portuguese also brought the Roman Catholic religion which has become dominant throughout the continent.

Thirdly, from about 1800 onwards, there was a steady inflow of immigrants of Anglo-Saxon stock from Europe, and increasingly of people from the Far East and especially Japanese. All these different types are scattered over the Republics of South America and the Guianas.

REV. N. J. COCKBURN, in *The Bible in the World*

383.   The Indians of Tropical South America

The men wear moderately civilized clothes. Their peaked and coloured caps have flaps to fold over the ears. Over their shoulders hang the folds of their ponchos. Another blanket will perhaps be around their necks. They split their trousers for a short distance up the back seam to facilitate turning them up when crossing streams. The women indulge in a multitude of skirts. A coloured blanket is worn round the neck and shoulders and their black hair tucked inside it. Babies, as usual, are borne on the back. Ear-rings form a common adornment, and hats, made of local wool and resembling a soft felt, perch on top of the head. . . .

Sometimes they make for themselves small shelters of the most rude and elementary type, and during the dry season they will come down and camp on the beaches. At other times they wander carelessly through the forest, throwing themselves down at night, naked and unprotected, among the leaves and ants, sleeping even through the showers of rain.

Amazon and Andes, by K. G.[7] GRUBB

384.   Guyana in Brief

British Guiana was[8] . . . the only British possession in the

[7]Now Sir Kenneth.
[8]Until it became independent under the name of "Guyana".

South American Continent. It occupies a land area of 83,000 square miles, is roughly triangular in shape and is bordered on the north by the rolling Atlantic and in the south penetrates deep into the Amazon hinterland. Most of the population is to be found in the low coastal belt, and access to the interior has been, in the past, mainly by great rivers of which there are several. The coastal belt is bounded in the south by the Guiana Highlands which run down into the deep jungle of the Brazilian rain belt.

The records state that the low coast-line was sighted by Columbus in 1498, but that he did not land. Later Sir Walter Raleigh travelled through the country seeking to locate the fabled city of "El Dorado", but without success.... The original inhabitants of the country were called "Amerindians", of which there are six distinct tribes which have almost entirely disappeared. During the cruel period of slavery, Africans were brought in to work on the sugar estates and, at a later date, indentured labourers were brought over from India. Today the East Indian population is the largest in the Colony, with the Negroes a close second....

The Colony has rich agricultural interests in sugar, rice and cattle. There is a wonderful variety of hardwoods, and minerals such as gold, bauxite and diamonds are to be found in considerable quantities. Much of the country's natural wealth remains untouched so far.

REV. JAMES INNES, in *The Bible in the World*

385. The Casiquiare "Canal"

Shortly before we sailed an interesting newcomer pulled into port: a small launch flying the Venezuelan flag that had come to Manaos not by way of the Amazon, but through the Casiquiare Canal and down the Rio Negro. This natural canal, the only one of its kind in the world, connects one of the tributaries of the Negro with the Upper Orinoco in southernmost Venezuela, thus providing a continuous inland waterway from the Caribbean Sea to Manaos and the heart of Amazonia. More than 200 miles in length, it is broad and deep enough during the rainy season to accommodate ships of considerable draught, but the region it serves is so remote and commercially

U

undeveloped that only a handful of boats traverse it in a year.

The Other Side of the Mountain, by J. R. ULLMAN

Note. The watershed in this region is so low that sometimes the Casiquiare River or "Canal" flows N. to the Orinoco and sometimes S. to the Amazon.

386. The Amazon

The Amazon, the second largest river in the world, rises in Peru, and, after a course of some 4,000 miles, flows into the Atlantic in North Brazil. In the source region the snow-crowned peaks over 20,000 feet in height look down in disdain upon the infant stream, which flows through profound valleys often some 10,000 feet in depth. At certain altitudes and over certain stretches the vegetation is dry and thorny. As the rain forests are approached the smaller trees obtain a footing, and beautiful tree-ferns may be seen in abundance. Over these stretches the current is swift, the river forces its way through successive ranges, and the hills close round, forming dangerous gorges. Finally, the mass of water breaks through triumphantly on to the level plains, where the forest assumes a characteristic appearance. The land is uniformly low, and behind the immediate banks a low lagoon or swamp is often encountered. The channel is interrupted by numerous islands and maintains a width of several miles.

Amazon and Andes, by K. G.[9] GRUBB

387. Impressions of the Amazon Forest

(a) I have been wandering by myself in a Brazilian forest: among the multitude it is hard to say what set of objects is most striking; the general luxuriance of the vegetation bears the victory—the elegance of the grasses, the novelty of the parasitical plants, the beauty of the flowers, the glossy green of the foliage, all tend to this end. A most paradoxical mixture of sound and silence pervades the shady parts of the wood; the noise from the insects is so loud that in the evening it can be heard even in a vessel anchored several hundred yards from

[9]Now Sir Kenneth.

the shore, yet within the recesses of the forest a universal stillness appears to reign.

Diary of the Voyage of H.M.S. Beagle, by CHARLES DARWIN,
ed. N. BARLOW

(b) The forest consisted of a most bewildering diversity of grand and beautiful trees, draped, festooned, corded, matted and ribboned with climbing plants in endless variety. There was not much green underwood, except in places where bamboo grew; these formed impenetrable thickets of plumy foliage and thorny jointed stems, which always compelled us to make a circuit to avoid them. The earth elsewhere was encumbered with rotten fruits, gigantic bean pods, leaves, limbs and trunks of trees.

A Naturalist in the River Amazon, by HENRY W. BATES

Note. A highway is now being built through 2,000 miles of steaming jungle and barren mountains, across Brazil and Peru, from the Atlantic to the Pacific.

388. Across the "Bulge" of Brazil

The Amazon is the lifeblood of Brazil. It drains nearly half South America. After rising only a hundred miles from the Pacific, it courses 4,000 miles to enter the Atlantic on the Equator. Over the 200-mile-wide mouth of the river, so painfully explored by generations of Europe's adventurers, huge commercial aircraft now fly daily schedules.... The plane for Rio bumps over the reedy runway. Again the Amazon maps itself out and the forest can be seen rapping like doom on the doors of Para (Belem).

Here the forest is implacably, evilly purposeful. As you pass south over the great bulge of Brazil, thin cloud starts to form as though the forest were intent on hiding itself from prying eyes. Every now and then, through a rent in this garment, you can see far below the awful tangle, a motionless death-grapple, nature at war with herself with all the still horror of serpentine statuary. After a while this gives itself up, in a hard, grudging sort of way, to a less intricate patchy scrub. When five hours have gone by, the wheels of the plane are flattening the fresh weeds on the table-top of Barreiras, a Conan Doyle-like airport on a 1,000-foot cliff.

It exists in a sea of vegetation like a lifeboat in the Atlantic. . . .
When ten hours have gone by, during which you have not seen
a single house except for the huts at Barreiras, the plane is
circling over the harbour at Rio, loveliest, most exotic city of
the world.

PETER GRIEVE, in the *News Chronicle*

389. Rio de Janeiro

Rio de Janeiro is a city of incredible beauty. How could one
forget that first breath-taking view of the harbour entrance, the
rugged sky-line dominated by the gigantic figure of Christ on
Corcovado, the endless chain of golden beaches and behind
them the countless inverted match-boxes which prove to be
skyscraper hotels and business-houses? Then the charm of the
island-studded bay with its white-sailed yachts and yellow
launches and ocean-going vessels from all parts of the world.

Or how describe the teeming life of the city with its complicated racial admixtures of Portuguese, Italian, Negro, Dutch,
Mulatto and Indian? They say there is no colour-bar in Brazil,
and that is almost true for, theoretically at least, there are equal
rights for all—though one notices that the menial tasks, scaven-
ging, etc., fall to the lot of the negro.

What shall we say of the striking contrasts of wealth and
poverty, civic pride and neglect, bustle and leisure, all very
much in evidence to the most superficial viewer of life in Rio?

Wealth? Never have I seen such magnificent buildings in
course of construction, many privately owned, more belonging
to the State or large business concerns. Rio is an architect's
paradise indeed, and behind this façade of marble and cement
is all the wealth of the coffee plantations, the diamond mines,
the rubber plantations and the new industrialization which is
spreading through the country. . . .

Poverty? Perhaps one lifts up one's eyes to the hills which
girdle the bay, only to discover, behind all the architectural
magnificence of the city centre, a series of squalid slums known
as the "favellas".

REV. W. J. BRADNOCK, in *The Bible in the World*

390. Coffee in Brazil

The development of the Brazilian coffee industry has been one of the industrial romances of the nineteenth century. The first plants were brought from Southern Arabia in 1727 and planted at Para; from there they spread, especially in the State of Sao Paulo. Its tableland of from 2,000 to 4,000 feet above sea-level has an ample rainfall, and the plant flourishes in the "red earth" found here in such abundance. . . .

Santos, begun by the Jesuits with a chapel and a hospital, is today the world's greatest coffee port. The river was lined for miles with long rows of wharves, and ships were anchored two or three deep. As we went on shore the hot breath of the tropics was fragrant with the familiar odour of coffee. Behind the wharves we saw the warehouses, and from their doorways an endless double string of stevedores—Portuguese, Italians and Negroes—jogged from train to warehouse, from dock to ship ceaselessly. Each man carried a bulky sack on his back. Coffee was everywhere in Santos. In the warehouses in the wharf district, women and children were picking over the beans; all along the street in bewildering abundance were cafés. Soon we too learned the habit of stopping several times to sip a cup of this thick strong Brazilian coffee.

South American Adventures, by ALICE C. DESMOND

391. Brasilia: The New Capital

Brasilia still lacks most of the amenities usually considered essential to the capital of a country the size of Brazil. Theatres, a plentiful supply of cinemas, shopping centres, sports stadia, even street corners—all are missing from this brand new capital city. Yet even its most severe critics agree that there is no chance of a future Brazilian Government abandoning the city to the wilderness out of which it was carved and moving the capital to Rio de Janeiro. . . . It is inconceivable that any future Government would stop the process started by Brasilia— namely, opening up the country's vast interior to civilization and development. . . .

While the Diplomatic Corps wait in Rio with mixed feelings for the mass exodus to what they regard as the wilds of Brasilia, local tradesmen are eagerly awaiting their arrival. . . .

But that is still in the future. At present, the sites of over sixty Embassies-to-be are marked by plain wooden signposts stuck in the scrub on the shores of Brasilia's lake. . . .

Whatever may or may not have happened to the rest of Brasilia since President Kubitschek left office, he had time to ensure the completion of the main Federal public buildings, each one a masterpiece. The Congress, with its two saucer roofs—one inverted—marking, respectively, the Senate and Chamber of Deputies, the elegant presidential "Palace of the Dawn", and the Palace of Justice flanking the spacious "Square of the Three Powers", have long been accomplished facts.

LIONEL WALSH, in the *Yorkshire Post*, Leeds

Note. Brasilia is designed for a population of 500,000. In 1968 it had 300,000 people. Skyscrapers are now numerous.

392. Brazil's Mineral Wealth

(*a*) In the field of mineral resources, Brazil has been making great strides. In all Brazil's twenty states iron ore is to be found, most of it of high content. Experts estimate that there are 15,000 million tons of iron ore in the country. With Anglo-American assistance, financial and technical, Brazil will soon be able to export some two to three million tons of ore per year. Simultaneously, large-scale production of steel is being developed.

Yorkshire Post, Leeds

(*b*) Brazil's iron is found chiefly in Minas Geraes, where there are seventeen plants. At Itabira, and at Cauepeak not far away, the Government is opening up what are believed to be the richest iron ore deposits in the world. . . . An existing railway running from Itabira to the port of Victoria, on the Atlantic coast, is being largely rebuilt to handle ore trains. . . .

The country is the second largest western producer of chrome ore; it is fifth in output of mica, third in zirconium. Manganese ores of high content are important; coal production is increasing.

News Chronicle

Note. It is believed that there are large reserves of oil, but the only important wells are at Bahia.

393. Bahia — A Touch of Old Brazil

It was with Bahia[10] that Brazil—and one can legitimately say
South America itself—began. Here was erected the first pillar
of the great cultural bridge spanning the ocean. It was here—
from European, African and American substance—that the new
still-fermenting mixture came into existence. Among all the
towns of the South American continent it is the one city blessed
with the privilege of age. With its nearly four hundred years
of life, its churches, cathedrals, and its forts, Bahia is a cultural
sanctuary, the city of old Portuguese Brazil, and it is only here
that one feels Brazil's origin and its ancient tradition.

One senses this tradition everywhere. Bahia, as opposed
to all other Brazilian towns, has its own costumes, its own
cooking, its own colour. Though automobiles honk their way
through the main streets, in the old town mules still carry
fruit and wood in their swing panniers, and donkeys can be
hired by the hour. In the harbour, as in Roman and
Phoenician times, freight is hauled on to the ships not by
cranes, but on the backs of men. The street vendors in their
broad-brimmed hats carry across their shoulders a stick, from
both ends of which their wares are hung. In the night market
the traders do their business sitting on the ground by the
light of candles or acetylene lamps, surrounded by mountains
of oranges, bananas, coconuts and pumpkins. While huge ocean
liners lie off the stone quays, sailing ships rock to and fro on
the shore, waiting to go out to the islands. And even the unique
"jangadas", the canoes of the old Brazilians, are still to be seen.

Brazil: Land of the Future, by STEPHAN ZWEIG

394. Uruguay — The Small Republic

Uruguay is situated on the Atlantic coast of South America,
south of Brazil. The Uruguayan coastline at its southern
extremity curves inland—that is to say, westwards—to become
the northern shore of the estuary of the River Plate. Out of
sight, on the opposite—southern—side of the estuary, is
Argentina. . . . Montevideo, the Uruguayan capital— known to
the British as "Monte"— is situated overlooking the area where
the river and the ocean mingle.

[10]Also called Baia, and nowadays Salvador.

Uruguay is the smallest of the South American republics, and, unlike the others, is populated throughout the full extent of its territory. It has no big territorial gaps to fill, and so it has already attained a sort of equilibrium, a balanced and moderate way of life. The climate, too, is temperate, lacking the extremes of heat and cold which occur in the other South American republics. The people—who number about 2,000,000[11]—are mostly white, and therefore the Indian "inferiority complex" which often produces aggressiveness elsewhere, is absent here. So Uruguay really is a nation, having no need to keep up her courage by behaving nationalistically. Furthermore, as a buffer state between those great powers, Brazil and Argentina, and having an extensive coastline of sandy beaches which are a playground for holiday-makers from the neighbouring countries, Uruguay has a vocation for moderation. It suffers neither from revolutions nor earthquakes; and the national sport is football, not bullfighting.

GEORGE PENDLE, in *The Listener*

395. The Pampas

(a) Flying from Buenos Aires to Mendoza in an aeroplane is an admirable way to see the Argentine pampas. Hour after hour the passenger looks down on what is doubtless one of the largest level plains on the globe; looks down on the great grazing lands where cattle scatter like electric toys under the roar of the aeroplane engines. In appearance the pampas of the Argentine, the prairies of the United States and the downs of Australia are quite alike.

Sky Gipsy, by CLAUDIA CRANSTON

(b) Between Buenos Aires and Rosario (180 miles), and indeed right on to the Andes, the country is dead flat. As far as the eye can reach there is nothing visible but large herds of cattle grazing in the paddocks or vast expanses of crops, chiefly wheat and corn.

Tschiffely's Ride : Southern Cross to Pole Star,
by A. F. TSCHIFFELY

[11]Just over $2\frac{1}{2}$ millions in 1965.

396. The Gaucho of the Pampas

It needed imagination, and the instinct of the agriculturalist ...
to see that the Pampa held treasures surpassing all the mines of
precious metals in the world. On the Pampa, nature offered a
vast field for agriculture and a vaster field for grazing. In the
earliest Spanish days escaped cattle and horses found abundant
grasses to satisfy their hunger all the year round, for no winter
snow covered the ground.... Presently creole and Spaniard
discovered the new opportunity that nature thrust upon them,
and took advantage of it. In the good old days on the Pampa,
in the days before the immigrant came, the "gaucho" was developed almost wholly by his environment. He was not a herds-
man who cared for cattle, not a breeder who improved the race,
not a careful owner who counted his herds and saw to their
sustenance, but a hunter of horses and cows who lived on an
abundance that nature came very near thrusting into his hands.
The animals cared for themselves. His occupation was the chase;
his prey, the half-wild cattle. He reacted to the environment
truly. When they tell you today that the gaucho is extinct, they
are thinking of him ... as a master of horse-and-cattle-hunting,
the man who needed only a knife and a rope and the Pampa
to provide himself with horses, cattle, clothing and food. There
is no need for such prowess now, nor has there been since
steamers and railroads brought labouring men to the Pampa.
In his quintessence the gaucho has long disappeared.

Peopling the Argentine Pampa (American Geographical Society,
Research Series, No. 16—by MARK JEFFERSON)

397. The Land of Roast Beef

It was noon when I went down the narrow Calle Reconquista.
The four cable-layers had knocked off. They were waiting for
lunch in their tarpaulin hut. The table was a box. There was a
clean cloth over it, and on the cloth were plates of crisp lettuce
and sliced tomatoes, fresh rolls and butter, a bottle of red wine.
But lunch wasn't quite ready. It was being cooked by a man
outside the hut.

Over a low brazier of charcoal he had spread a length of
thick wire netting. On the netting, sizzling and hissing, shoot-
ing blue plumes of savoury smoke over the street, was the main

dish—an Argentine mixed grill. It looked to me, as I went by, as if the best part of an ox lay on that netting.

The staple food of the people of Buenos Aires—of Argentina generally—is meat and bread. In one month, says a Government report, the 3,000,000 people of Buenos Aires[12] ate 145,932 head of cattle, 40,634 sheep and 32,534 hogs. And, of course, they occasionally eat turkeys, geese, ducks, chickens, and mountains of "fideos"—noodles (sometimes made with eggs), spaghetti and ravioli (stuffed with chicken, ham, olives or eggs, or the lot).

But meat from the ox they like best of all. . . .

When meat-freezing was perfected the wealth of Argentina was assured. . . . Money in meat rapidly became concentrated in the "frigorificos" and other processing establishments. There are now ten main packing-plants in Argentina—Swift, Liebig, Smithfield and Argentine, Anglo, Wilson, Sansinena, Armour, La Blanca, Bovril, and the Corporacion Argentina de Productores de Carnes.

PETER GRIEVE, in the *News Chronicle*

398. Buenos Aires — Capital of Argentina

(*a*) One of the peculiarities of Buenos Aires is that you can see no end to it. Since on the side of the pampas there is no obstacle to building operations, small colonial houses make a fringe on the edge of the city, that extends ever farther and farther into the plain as building plots in the city rise in value. Some of brick, some of plaster or cement, these villas make comfortable quarters in a land where no chimney stacks are needed. The big grain elevators are no whit inferior to the best of the gigantic structures of North America. . . . We wandered pleasantly amongst the millstones which transform the small grey wheat of the pampas into fine white flour. We were told that it is the richest in gluten of all known species.

South America Today, by GEORGES CLEMENCEAU

(*b*) The newcomer finds the Argentine capital the largest Spanish-speaking city on the globe, second only to Paris among the Latin cities of the world, equal to Philadelphia in popula-

[12]In 1966 the population of Buenos Aires was estimated at 3,876,000.

tion, resembling Chicago in extent as well as in situation, rivalling New York in many of its metropolitan features.

Working North from Patagonia, by HARRY A. FRANCK

399. Is Buenos Aires a Dying Port?

(*a*) A desolate waste of choppy, muddy waves, flowing between dark mud-banks, with here and there little floating islands of lilies and trees drifting seawards from the great rivers of the interior—such is the mouth of La Plata. At Montevideo the river is sixty-four miles wide. At Buenos Aires it is thirty-four miles wide. All this gigantic estuary is obstructed by shoals and sandbanks.

The Cruise of the Falcon, by E. F. KNIGHT

(*b*) Unless some drastic action is taken, Buenos Aires could suffer a fate similar to those ancient cities which died because the sea receded from their harbours as they became silted up....

Barely a generation ago, 8,000-ton tramp steamers used to sail up river to the ports of Rosario and Sante Fé, returning loaded to capacity. Today, they load part of the grain in the Parana river ports and sail down to complete loading at Buenos Aires. The reason is that the channel dredged in the River Plate to permit ocean-going vessels to move 200 miles upstream has become too shallow. Shippers grumble that this means a big loss of time and money.

Now, the invasion of mud, which is isolating upriver ports, is also blocking the port of Buenos Aires. The Presidential Palace in Buenos Aires was last century a gun-protected fort battered by the waters of the River Plate. Today, it is 500 yards from the river.... Experts agree that the only permanent, comprehensive solution would be to build dykes and locks—at great cost.

"A.M.", in the *Yorkshire Post,* Leeds

400. Patagonia and its Sheep

"Well ventilated and plenty of it" was an American's description of Patagonia, and it still remains as good as any other.

His subsequent remark: "All you have to do is to settle down with a few sheep and get rich—in spite of yourself", no longer holds good. . . .

Patagonia can be roughly divided into four zones—Rio Negro Territory and northern Chubut . . . southern Chubut territory . . . northern Santa Cruz territory . . . and lastly southern Santa Cruz and Tierra del Fuego, which is probably the best sheep-farming country in the world, but suffers from its long and somewhat grisly winter.

Each zone has its widely varying conditions and problems, but sheep are the prop and mainstay of them all, and cover the country in all directions, except in the oil district immediately around Comodoro Rivadavia. Not that one would see many sheep in a day's travel; on the contrary, a handful of sheep amid miles of coarse grass and scanty bush are inevitable where from one to five hectares are necessary for the support of each.

Therein lies one of the secrets of Patagonian prosperity, however, because although poor in pasture it is healthy for stock; sheep contract few of the internal diseases common to richer pasture and can consequently be managed cheaply in large numbers. . . .

The Patagonian climate is very variable . . . but dry and healthy, and has been much maligned on the subject of wind. . . . That story about every Patagonian being bent in the middle from leaning against the wind is quite untrue.

"A Farmer", in *Britannica*, Buenos Aires

Index to Principal References

The numbers refer to pages, not extracts